In His care
with much LOVE

www.InHisCareMinistry.com

They Called Me A

Me A

Dirty Jew!

They Called Me A Dirty Jew!

For copyright information:
Usama Dakdok Publishing, LLC
P.O. BOX 244
Venice, FL 34284-0244

ISBN 978-0-9824137-5-3

Dewey decimal system number: 920, Autobiography

Published in the United States of America

I was like a garbage dog that wiggled its tail to everyone

and for no reason at all.

| Yona visiting pregnant Pnina | Yona's fire-eating act. |

Happier Times! Yona with husband Kent at their wedding

Dedication

First, I would like to apologize to my three children; Aussy, Miriam and Ahmad, for the pain and confusion I cost you because of my mistakes. I love you with all I have and I thank God daily for your compassionate hearts toward others.

Only evil can comprehend evil, therefore, I dedicate this book to my parents who outlived the horrors of the concentration camp, but barely survived afterwards. I also dedicate this book to all the victims of hate and ignorance.

I would like to thank my husband for not giving up on me. Also, I would like to thank Ed Mogford and his family for their constant encouragement and love. I also thank Bonnie K. McNeal, Ed.D, for all the help and time spent editing to put this book together.

For the wonderful graphics of the cover I would like to thank Randy McWilson and, for final tweaking and publication setup, Lee Hutcheson. And a big thanks to Usama Dakdok for his courage in publishing this book.

Thank you all.

As for me, I wrote this book for the Glory of His name, but mostly to reflect the shining truth from my heart to yours.

FOREWORD

We are in the prison of this world, not recognizing the lies of the enemy. We struggle for one more dollar, for one more pleasant amusement, or just one more of something that will bring us happiness and joyful peace, but most of all—acceptance. As I slid through life's patterns in agony, I ceased to recognize that struggle in myself.

The truth and the lie in my mind were as brothers, and in my confused state, I did not recognize either. Therefore, even if we garnish the words with gold and precious stones and with a thousand promises, without God, there is no understanding, and without Jesus Christ, there is no redemption.

There were times that I disregarded anything concerning God or the Bible, which I considered as a nice fairytale belonging to the weak and the ignorant. I was above that holy nonsense!

However, there were moments when I allowed myself to gaze closely at the reflection of my soul, and there in the midst of dark shadows, the grace of God shone, inviting me peacefully to come back home.

I was lost and painfully lonely. I thirsted just for one drop of love in the empty recesses of my heart. I desperately missed something valuable that left me restless, along with the uncomfortable knowledge of the simple truth that there is a struggle in this world between good and the evil.

Moreover, there came a day in the midst of dark emptiness that I placed myself on the scale of this life to choose God or the devil's playground, and I chose to be born again. Touched by divine understanding and forgiveness, I felt great relief and tremendous peace. When I placed myself in God's embrace, my soul cried with joy, realizing at that moment I was honored with the Master's degree and was chosen to be His ambassador! Therefore, I do have it all, and I have it on the Highest Authority!

This truth of salvation, I wish, with all of my heart, to share with you. I pray that my story will bring peace and understanding, but most of all glory to God. I pray you will see and understand how God holds the heart of one such as I, in His Hand, and is restoring my soul every second of every day.

Introduction

He is always with me in His presence Divine,
As in blood He wrote His Name on my heart.

Nothing is certain in this world of mine
But the comprehension of the living God.
Lost would be any ignorant heart
That lives and believes in this world of lies,
Yet I was told:
The will of God will never take me
Where the grace of God will not protect me.

I faced the ugliness of the human race,
A contagious disease that spread everywhere.
My heart yearned for the comfort of a loving hand,
A touch of some sort
That would wipe my pain.

Often I ask myself if the agony of pain led me to the right path of compassion and understanding, or if it just stopped my overall development and helped me to stumble all over myself. At times, a smell or visual stimulus will bring a tear to my eyes, but soon my heart blocks any concern or feelings, transferring my whole being onto the stage of a different reality, so I ask myself, *Who am I, and why am I here?*

My past and my heritage were a crown of mockery, of which I was ignorantly ashamed. Some called me *a dirty Jew* and some called me simply a *Jew* which was equally painful. If I had had a Christmas list, I would have put on it just one request: not to be a Jew...not to be JEWISH. I knew painful moments that often laughed in my face, as darkness was my path and persecutions were my life.

I was cold and beaten, ridiculed and scarred. I belonged to no one and was rejected by everyone, until one day my spirit did not cry anymore.

Today my childhood memories are still shadows of desperation; my nights are sleepless and restless as foggy memories morph into horrifying events, and I never know whether I slept, or if I just managed to escape to a fortress of temporary sanity. I do believe that I well deserved what I endured, but in spite of everything, I was given heavenly keys to unlock the chains of guilt. I call upon my Lord and Savior because His Name is powerful, and His Light is eternal.

When I face my past, I am aware that I was definitely in the category of people who refuse to check the reality of God, out of concern that it may hit the core of truth. Nevertheless, the enemy worked his power by efficiently spreading lies through the New Age movement with its appealing sophistication, always hidden under modern educational studies, and sadly, these lies were and still are acceptable against the simplicity of truth.

A few years back, my husband and I visited a historical museum in Denver, Colorado, and an older woman walked along with young children, explaining to them that "millions and millions of years ago we came into existence from the gorillas; therefore, they are our ancestors."

I could not believe what I heard! Immediately and without hesitation, armed just with my poor English and a thick accent, I confronted the woman for an explanation: "How do you know all of that?"

"This is a scientific fact," she replied.

"Oh?" I said in a surprised voice, "and why did the gorillas stop reproducing little children and instead they are reproducing little gorillas?" She looked at me in disbelief, as I smilingly pointed at the gorillas, saying loudly: "I am sorry, but no one in my family ever looked like that!"

I do hope that the children will remember me in the future, maybe as a crazy person and maybe not, but the bottom line is that they heard something else to consider. I know how the educational system can pollute the innocent mind.

When my firstborn daughter told me that she learned in college that we evolved from a fish, I wasn't surprised anymore because at that point I'd heard all the nonsense possible. I simply said, "WOW!?"

"That's it, Mom," she said in confrontation. "Are you not impressed?"

"I need to think about it," I said, "and then we will talk."

A few days later, I bought three beta fish for my two daughters and my son. I called my oldest child, telling her about the beautiful fish and asking her to pick them up. "Mom, when I have time, I will come and pick them up. And Mom? Thanks! You are so cool."

Oh yeah, we will see...

I smiled in satisfaction, enjoying my little mischief. Two days later, I called again, and then again and again, asking her to pick up the fish. By that time my daughter was quite irritated, asking me, "What is the hurry?"

"Just pick them up today," I insisted.

"What is the matter with you?" she asked.

"Frankly," I said, "I am afraid that they will humanize and look like you!"

"Really, Mom, do not try to be smart with me! You know better!"

Do I know better? Yes, indeed I do! I refuse to accept the fish theory, or any other like it! Thank God, for His Spirit allows me clear discernment. God has no mystical secrets; everything is clear and everything is in His time, if we just heed His Word with our hearts and souls. Unfortunately for many, the acceptance of the unexplained phenomena becomes the ultimate truth and a victory of the enemy.

I love my children and I acknowledge them as a precious gift from God. Still, I cannot help but worry about my firstborn daughter. She is very intelligent and she grasps things very quickly, but sadly enough, the wrong things, which are shadowed by educational lies. My sense of humor can easily be translated into a personal attack, so I constantly watch my choice of words to avoid hurting her. At times, even though we love each other very much, we are both on heavy-duty guard, and amusingly, in extreme defense mode.

I cannot talk to my children about God, or about His love or His sacrifice. They have good reason for avoiding this subject with me. Being Jewish and later becoming a born again Christian and their father a radical Arab Muslim, we did not contribute at all to the reflection of God. We were very bad examples as parents, and our afflictions polluted their little hearts.

Today I give what is left of my life to my Savior and God because the damage that was done can be restored only by God's supernatural power.

I face some difficulties and insecurities around educated people because I do not possess any formal education and that has always forced me to accumulate more knowledge. Knowing four languages has opened doors to many different relationships and social circumstances.

One day when my daughter and I talked by phone, the subject of Jesus Christ came up, and my daughter sarcastically said, "Mom, what if you are wrong about this Savior of yours?"

I knew that my daughter craved a fight, so I politely asked her to repeat her question, as I hoped to establish the significance of the subject, as well as my awareness of her sarcasm. When she repeated it, I said, "If I am wrong, I don't lose anything, but if you are wrong, you lose everything."

The reaction was a deep silence on the other end of the phone, and then without saying goodbye my daughter hung up on me. Naturally, I hope and pray that these confrontational times will be resolved one day with the truth because, strangely enough, she is seeking my counsel in everything she does, with one exception, and that is God.

I remember long ago, when my daughter was much younger. We had a casual disagreement, but somehow it made her furious! With her little hands on her waist, she announced victoriously: "I did not ask to be born!"

I stared at her as seriously as I could as I said, "So what in the world are you doing here? Hurry back to where you came from."

My daughter opened her mouth in disbelief at what I had just said. She asked, "And where would that be?"

"You mean, you do not know?" I said, acting surprised. "You just accused me of kidnapping you, so where is the evidence?" She looked at me for a second and left the room.

At this time, I thank God constantly, for He indeed is at work, healing the wounds of my children, and choosing me once again to be a willing participant. How gracious and supreme is our God in His everlasting wisdom. No matter how much education we possess, it would be unsatisfactory to us without the Holy Spirit which lights the truth in our hearts with endless comprehension and wisdom that leads us to great satisfaction by our recognition of His power.

Chapter 1

Poland, 1950

I was born in Poland, on October 22, 1950, in a small town called Tarnuv. My parents were concentration camp survivors. I have a brother who is one year younger than I, a beautiful, peaceful angel, very delicate and cherished by God Himself. His name is Shimon; mine is Yona. Those are not the names that we were given at birth, but are the names of our grandparents who found their death in the gas chambers.

I'm still trying to understand how human ignorance can build up such intense hate. Many people died in the most horrifying ways when Adolph Hitler wished to create a superior race and failed. Nevertheless, hate is still celebrated in vacant hearts which are chained and imprisoned to the will of evil. If we do not know God and His Word, we are facing invisible danger. Therefore, it is necessary to be armed with a heavenly shield against Satan's supernatural existence.

Our Redeemer Jesus Christ is such a shield; we must accept the fact that without God there is no way to understand and calculate the difference, because Satan with his lies looks very appealing and exciting, but most of all, irresistible!

My first memory is when I was about six or seven years old. My brother and I were playing on the street which was populated only by Jewish people, so we couldn't hide our identity from the children that lived close by. For them and their parents, we were Hitler's forgotten waste; therefore, persecuting us was dignified.

At the corner of the street sat a big truck, and our curiosity led us to investigate more closely. My brother climbed into it, reporting the items he discovered. I encouraged him to take some of the stuff and to hurry up before someone saw us.

On the way home, we checked the items in our possession: there were a few bars of soap and some arm bands with a twisted cross. We didn't know the meaning of the items, but it was exciting to find all this stuff. As soon as we arrived home, we faced our mom.

We explained about the truck, and my brother hurried to show her the treasures. When he put them in her hands, my mom's eyes instantly came to life with a most distinctive realization, followed by a painful cry. The bars of soap dropped to the ground, and my mom's voice broke into horrifying whisper, as she repeatedly whispered that the soap was made from Jewish flesh. Tears ran swiftly down her face, as she silently picked up each bar from the floor.

One by one, she placed them close to her heart, cleaning them from unseen dust and embracing them gently. Suddenly she stood up, raising her face to the sky, as she cried with all her might: "Oy, my God... Oy, my God." We felt like we were nailed to the ground and we could not move, yet we were puzzled, trying to understand her pain, as it also touched us so deeply and profoundly. When Mom spoke again, it was her broken voice that captivated us.

"Your father and I, we lost most of our family in Auschwitz. We barely survived..." she spoke in a distant voice, and the look in her eyes painfully enhanced the news we were hearing for the first time.

My brother was in tears. "Why? Why?" he asked her, "What did you do?"

Touching his face gently, she replied, "You do not want to know why." Then ignoring us intentionally so there'd be no further discussion, she left the house.

Today I understand her pain, and I know what I thought in the past: that the bizarre behavior was simply a protective wall for her sanity, or what was left of it.

Our dad was invisible most of the time, and there were many times we didn't see Mom for days. We were hungry and cold, but she'd always come back cheerful, with sweets for us. When Mom came back from her trips, with a cheerful spirit, she would treat us like babies, putting bread in a bowl of milk and feeding us. As much as I remember, we loved her and her bizarre love for us.

She was tall and beautiful, with blond hair and hazel eyes. She had a pleasant personality, even with few bottles of vodka in her system. It wouldn't be so bad, I thought, if she drank by herself, but her drinking was a ritual which involved another woman, and they drank until they froze into oblivion. We as children hated all these annoying episodes of memories and pain, which left us emotionally vulnerable.

I remember a picture on the wall, which had a very important role for this suffering group of women. After a few empty bottles, with drunkenness approaching, they used to bring visual testimonies out of this picture. It was always disturbing, but most of all, I hated the constant smell of alcohol. Even to this day, it sickens my spirit.

We spent most of our time on the streets being chased by the Polish kids. We were beaten, insulted and accused, and there was no place to hide. "Dirty Jews, dirty Jews," we heard them laughing and screaming. "Where are you hiding, Jews, rats…? Doggie, doggie, Jewish doggie, we have a bone for you. Come out."

We held each other in fear, holding our breath for long periods; as a result, we did not cry, but the impact of their contempt began to take root in the depths of our young souls. Repeatedly, I was ruptured by senseless confusion; I felt deep pain that wouldn't stop. There was no place to hide, there was no one to explain, and there was no one who cared. Nevertheless, I was my worst enemy, as my senses viciously whispered that I was nothing. Privileges belonged to everyone else, so my world gradually lost its colors, as I searched for a glimpse of hope for just a speck of light in the darkness.

As a child, I was stronger than my brother; he was very delicate, like fine china, so I always protected him. He was like an angel, and when he cried, I cried with him. I remember that my brother used to disappear for hours and I desperately searched for him, but he always returned and to this day, he has never revealed his secrets.

In contrast to myself, my little brother simply killed his life in Poland, including the Polish language. He doesn't remember much; nevertheless, memories that are shaped by abuse and pain have a language of their own.

I do thank God for my guilt and His discipline. Today I know that the Lord was with me always, in my fears and in my tears, and in spite of my rebellious spirit against Him. Now I do understand the core of salvation; as a child, I did not understand much, but I knew without a doubt that He is, and indeed He was, everything to me. He was my salvation and my comfort; He was my Father and my Teacher and my Judge. Now, if I experience doubts, I remember my young heart, and I know that He is, and He was, and He will be...always.

As I am writing my life away, I face a recurring dilemma: Should I write everything that I remember? Am I going to glorify the people I am writing about? If I do, will that glorify my Savior? Is mine really a testimony that will encourage others? I believe it is, but most importantly, the Lord has been with me all the way, and He was there to pull me out of that life into this one.

Most of my life, I lived in very toxic environments, and I could easily blame them for my destructive behavior. I would not dare do that, because surely I have always known the difference between right and wrong, in spite of any age or any circumstances.

I thought that I loved my parents, but as I looked in the reflection of my character, I really did not understand love. I remember my painful cravings for my mom's love, but her rejection left an ugly scar in my character. I used to have different imaginary dreams about a better life, which could happen only if my parents died. Of course, I felt heavy and painful guilt to the point that I allowed the kids on the street to hit me and ridicule me, without seeking refuge.

My brother and I cared for each other because in the slough of this life, there was no one left to care for us. My mom, in her own way, loved my brother, and I assumed that she hated me. "You are like your father," she used to throw at me. "You look like him, you talk like him, and this will bring hell into your life!!!"

At times, she fixed my hair to look like the French actress Bridget Bardot. I knew that she liked to change my appearance and it sure didn't contribute to my self esteem. Even though I was older and stronger than my brother, I still needed his presence in my life because it meant I belonged to someone. My parents, in their afflictions, could not provide shelter or security for us.

I remember the day when fury was born in my heart, out of desperation, pain, and abuse. It was deep and dark and strangely evil. I remember the hate and the darkness that engulfed me with a strange power, as I went to the street to take my life back by confronting my abusers.

"Come on!" I shouted, "Come on, little cowards!" They just ignored me, and that made me more furious, so I picked up a stone. In seconds, they were all over me, kicking, beating, pulling my hair, not to mention all the names they called me. When they were done, I was left alone, and strangely enough, I realized that the loneliness was more painful than the physical hurts. Bruised and bleeding, I could hardly stand on my feet, but yet, I discovered something about myself, I was willing to be beaten and insulted, only not to be alone, and that added to self-disrespect and hatred.

I was always ready for some sort of attack, jumping to any sound, and fear was my constant companion. However, in order to complete the map of my personality, I would like to say that I tried very hard to overcome my fears and doubts, but I didn't have the recipe for that, at least not yet. I had never been exposed to positive emotions; therefore, my world was tragic and unstable. Nevertheless, my heart yearned for some sort of expression of love, which I did not understand, and as vulnerable as I had been, I shut my feelings to reason and to compassion, exposing myself to the pit of evil.

Thankfully, I don't remember many things before the age of six or seven, but cloudy memories are still imprisonment of an evil embrace. The next thing I remember is that I am seven years old and Mom is taking me to school and holding my hand in a forceful grasp and I cannot keep up with her. She is dragging me behind her, and I feel like a lost feather in stormy weather.

I recall at times longing for a bit of affection or for a little smile, or a little word or something, but instead I got a blank gaze in my mom's eyes and to see her happy become a rare event. It was like she was closing all the doors to her heart.

Mom took me to the gates of the school and let me go with a big uniformed woman who took me to the classroom where everything was big and gray in my eyes. In this great event, I saw that the kids wore the same blue uniform as I did. Lost in my emotional confusion, I hardly understood a word when the teacher spoke, and in this big crowd of kids, I felt overwhelmed with fear and I just wished to disappear.

Furthermore, the kids in the school found out my Jewish heritage and there wasn't a place for me to hide as they reveled in the game of chasing me, pulling my hair, spitting on me, and hurting me. The most painful of all, though, was to be called a Jew, *a dirty Jew...*

It took a long journey into the depth of my soul to overcome what was forced on me and it took a tremendous amount of supernatural love that only the pure Spirit of God could and would lavish on my wounded heart and confused mind.

Today I know that cruelty is born in the establishment of families who have a history of arrogance. Unfortunately, people who live in this darkness have sleeping consciences; therefore, they do not realize that they are cursed, and they cannot see beyond their own lie.

They exude pure hate, and their tactics easily influence all those who seek relief, but instead, they get a glass of poison wine. I knew these people as I drank from the same glass and from the same poison.

Our home was one long room with a big straw bed that we all shared. There was also a closet with a foggy mirror and a round table with a few chairs. The toilet proudly stood in one corner of the room. It was built from ugly wood, but was a privilege in those days because it was indoors. There were windows on both sides of the room. The left window was facing the street, and the right was facing the back yard, which was constantly in motion with all the rats searching for food and multiplying themselves. I empathized with those rats for the mutual hunger we shared.

We lived on the first floor of the building. At night I was terrified to go up the stairs because of all the cockroaches. Shivers would go through my whole body at the sound of the crunch as I smashed them under my feet. Still today in the calm of the night when the memories break through, I can hear once again the intense sound of the crunch.

In school I did not understand a thing, so I stopped listening. I believed that my abilities to learn were very slim. I do not remember everything, but somehow my mom found out about my difficulties, and sure enough, it woke her up from her apathy and with final determination, she took matters into her own hands. My mom, with a live hen under her arm, and her hand grasping mine, went across the street to the apartment of a well-known Jewish teacher who guided me to be the best student in the class.

For about three years, my mom gave a live chicken to the teacher, although my preference would be not to mention the source that provided the teacher with such a luxury. Nevertheless, the truth is, I never forgot embarrassing times sneaking into people's farms and catching those chickens which the teacher enjoyed eating much more often than we dared dream about. However, when we had chicken soup it was a feast! It was my mom's chicken soup.

I loved to go to the teacher to study, but not because I liked her. I just liked the fact that she somehow uncovered my abilities to learn and to understand. Her help gave me self-worth. Finally, when things started to work for me, I became sick with a kidney infection.

In the hospital I was forbidden to eat anything with salt, but regardless, the hospital food was fabulous and returning home to nothing at all was always sad. One time my dad picked me up from the hospital and we came home and he tried to fix something to eat, but we had nothing except a jar of leftover fat and some dry bread. He combined them with water and warmed it on a fire and it was good. Dad used to tell me that he loved me, and I was very desperate for love.

Unfortunately, my trust crumbled because of my dysfunctional family and my twisted understanding. Therefore, the results of my actions appeared to be wrong. As I realized the consequences, I showered myself with guilt and contempt. I was ashamed and vulnerable to the point that I was not able to meet people's eyes. In moments like these, I wished to become someone else; indeed, the lie became reality as I hid from my identity. I appeared always as someone else until the day I called out desperately to God.

Embraced by God's love I was led to my roots and to my identity. As the Lord opened my eyes, I found deep compassion and understanding for my parents, and I wish I could tell them just once that I love them, and that I'm not angry or confused anymore. In my heart there is a vision of my Lord wiping their tears, the same tears that never dried upon this earth.

Chapter 2

Most of my time was spent in a local park sitting on the bench with concentration camp survivors, who shared with me everything I didn't need to know. Nevertheless, I listened with great curiosity, learning their pain and their dreams. One of these dreams was to go one day to the state of Israel created just for Jewish people.

Absurd, I thought to myself, *how desperate they must be to come up with such a story!* Nevertheless, I went along with their dream, imagining a great and beautiful place, colorful and friendly to all, the kind of place that did not exist but is always great to dream about. Dreams are available in any time and any place!

In my world of imagination, I could not identify myself with other hated individuals. When I asked my older friends for an explanation as to what precipitated the hate for them, they all had this strange expression on their faces when they told me: "People must have been afraid of us," or "People are afraid of things they don't understand, and we are probably one of those things."

Yeah, sure! Go ahead and try to understand this kind of answer.

Today, when I look back to my childhood, I know the privilege I was given to listen to my friends' stories. I learned their wisdom and their hopes, and as I shared my heart with their agonies, the world stopped spinning around me, and I began to mature.

Still, their horrifying experiences affected me deeply, as I knew the probabilities of persecutions and my fears were inescapable; therefore, every shower I took brought the gas chambers to life.

I didn't cry or complain in my childhood because I wasn't privileged to do so, and I sure disliked all those that could. When things were overwhelming, I welcomed those tears, and if I had just one reason to cry about, I always ended with a hundred more! I still do this today and thank God for these tears that comforted my soul with an invisible string of hope and relief.

Everything was sad and dreary back then. Even my dreams became hazy but one special morning, I woke up to the world's enchanting embrace and a happiness I never knew existed.

In the midst of hunger and pain and persecutions, I witnessed the pure manifestation of love. The sun shone brightly in the warmth of my unknown soul unraveling the passion for life as the golden beams of light danced all around the blue spread blanket of fluffy clouds, and the beauty I beheld was out of this world!

The birds were dressed in their magnificent suits exchanging colors between themselves. They were incredibly soothing to the eye and desirable to the touch. As they spread their wings, I was surprised with a rush of love, as their tunes carried the assurance of existing hope. Indeed, it was a presentation of a soft and most divine sound, aimed precisely to the depth of my heart, marking a new and promised reality when the birds sang just for me. The multiple variations of green moved swiftly as the waves of the sea, gently brushing the leaves upon the proud trees to discover the dew upon them, which sparkled in the feast of a million precious jewels and my heart rejoiced at the internal beauty and peace.

Today I realize that God Himself addressed me with this incredible vision encouraging me to live and not give up so I can share His love language with other desperate hearts.

I know I fall short in my description of this vision, but I will always remember the incredible touch of love and security to which I was so divinely introduced. If all the words in the world would be available to me, I would still fall short of the description. But life did go on, and it seems that everyone else had charge over my life but me. I was so lonely and sad after that incredible one-time experience, it was like I took a peek into the heart of an incredible happiness, and I thank God for a new hope which was conceived in my heart at that time.

One day, Mom encouraged my brother and me to visit the local Catholic church. She gave us some money to put in the basket for the charity and we were excited to do so. We knew that we did not belong in the church, but we craved so badly to be like everyone else.

The first time I saw the statue of Jesus Christ, it shook all my soul, but somehow I knew that behind this statue there is a living God. Finally I felt like I found what I searched for. So from that day on, I went to the church to pray like everyone else, finding comfort and a pure hope. I knew nothing about Jesus Christ, only what was in my heart. I knew that He was God, and no one had to tell me otherwise. At times, I even suspected that God was hiding behind the statues and watching me pray, so at these times my prayers intensified, as did my guilt. I closed just one eye while the other was wide open, hoping to catch God peeking from behind the statue.

Nevertheless, I found my shelter and my comfort and I was home, but not for long, because I was caught by older children who screamed at me with hateful remarks and accusations: "You Jews killed our God." They screamed time and time again, and though I was beaten and hurting on the ground, I knew that no one could kill my God! But someone killed theirs, and I was confused and I didn't know if they were talking about the same God. Between kicks and beatings, I heard them say: "You Jews crucified our God!" I was more confused than ever, because in my heart I prayed to a living God not a dead god.

After the dispute with the kids, I was very careful coming back to the church. I also was deeply disturbed at the new knowledge about God and what I had been told regarding my own people. I knelt in front of Jesus' statue, confused and overwhelmed with a load of unjustified guilt. I could not understand the perplexity of God.

If the Jewish people killed their God, where is my God? Where is the Jewish God? If we kill their God, maybe they'll kill ours, but honestly, I didn't believe that we have our private God; no God would want us.

Somehow, deep in my heart I knew that my God could not die, and I assured myself with this knowledge. Well, I was happy with my conclusion, even though I had this urge to fall on my face and cry forever, asking His forgiveness. While I was still in deep thought, trying to unravel the mystery, I felt a touch on my shoulder. Jumping in fear, I faced the priest and on the spot I informed him that I was leaving. "It would be nice if you would stay," the priest said pleasantly.

"I can't stay," I said, whispering.

"And why not?" The priest whispered back.

I eyed the church surroundings as I whispered secretively, "I'm Jewish."

The priest smiled as he raised my chin with one hand and with the other he pointed to the statue of Jesus Christ. "He is Jewish," he said.

Wow! Now I was confused for real!

"Do you want to know about Him?" the priest asked.

"Oh, yes, I do," I said, and I knew that there was nothing in the world I would like more.

If we would comprehend the love of God, we could have it all, because when your heart beseeches you, your mind will follow, but when your mind beseeches you? You will look for directions. As for me, my mind took over and then the things that really mattered faded along with the knowledge of God. I began to feel the tremendous loss of precious moments that have been given only by existing facts and which are living testimony of my heart.

Often people wonder if there is a God, but I would challenge anyone who is wondering, or angry, or lost, or just has no will to live anymore: Look into your own heart, and if it is dark and empty, ask Him to come in.

I didn't know anything about God except the knowledge of my heart. It was like God was waiting for me, and I for Him, and for the first time in my life, I knew the sense of belonging and these feelings were indescribable but it wasn't a need I searched for; it was a need that only God could fill.

The priest became my friend, the first friend I ever had. Unfortunately, as a result of the treatments I received, I don't remember his name, along with some other names and events. Life on the streets became much easier to handle, especially because I had something to run to. I didn't have much knowledge about Jesus Christ, but the light which dwelt in my soul completely over took every corner of my heart.

In school, everything progressed very well; I jumped one year ahead and at the age of nine I was ready to go to the fourth level. The persecutions did not vanish; to the contrary, they become more and more intense, especially with this one girl that used to chase me, spitting in my face and calling me names. She was everywhere I was, and there was not a place to hide from her.

One day on my way to school I was in deep thought. All of a sudden this girl popped from nowhere, spitting in my face. I didn't move as I had been instructed by my Jewish teacher when I confided in her about the abuse. "You need your education," she used to say. "Ignore the pain and conquer the universe."

I always did as she told me but not this day, when this girl started to scream at my face: "Dirty Jew! Dirty Jew!"

All of a sudden, the taste of evil overwhelmed me and I took her by the hair, smashing her face in the dirt beneath her feet and whispering viciously into her ear: "Who is dirty now???"

The school found out about this episode and of course, I wasn't allowed to defend myself, and to add to it, I got my final report card, indicating my violent nature, in addition to a strong suggestion not to accept me to any other institute whatsoever.

Then things become complicated as my mom's illness got progressive and in her condition, I chose not to tell her about the school judgment. I was very sad thinking about the recent days. I remember how my heart rejoiced with anticipation to tell my mom about her success in my accomplishments. I needed to believe that the good news would make her better, but she never found out, drifting in and out of consciousness. She held on about a year until her final rest, and my father cried himself to death until he rested at last.

Chapter 3

Many things took place when I was with my parents, some painful, and some disturbing, but out of respect, I will not bring any of the events to light now. Today I understand that my parents loved us as much as they could, and after the horrible sufferings they endured, I understand that they gave us all they had, in every bit of their hearts, and when nothing else remained, they gave us the last breath. At times, when I remember all of it, there is no one with whom to be angry, and there is no one to forgive, because today, with divine understanding, I can see my own wrongs.

It was 1960 when my parents found their final rest. I was ten years old, my brother was nine. In the first week, the police found us wandering on the streets, and we were taken to separate orphanages. However, I would like to come back to the events of my parents' funerals.

Mom was buried with a gray dress color that I didn't care for. A week or so before my mom died, she asked friends and some extended family to come for final goodbyes. I remember my mom was mostly sleeping, and when she was not, she was hallucinating from the morphine, I overheard my father say.

The events of family and friends gathering will stay in my memory forever. Mom was not drugged or confused that day; she was very clear-minded and I was as astonished as everyone else when Mom just gave a piece of her mind to every visitor in the room. She told them how hypocritical they had been. She told them that they lied and deceived. She told all these things to their faces, and it looked to me like she emptied a basketful of garbage. Shortly after and without any confrontation, she dismissed them by saying, "Now I can go in peace. Goodbye!"

At times, I wonder if she felt any satisfaction, and I still don't know why she waited so long to say all these things which must have plagued her so deeply, how she knew that her time was short, and that she was going to die. As for me in my complex character, I wished to form some courage, in addition to other possibilities that my mom unknowingly addressed. However, I did not see any cruelty in my mom's statements, but simple, courageous honesty.

At this present time, my comprehension is final realization of God's tremendous love and His gentle approach expending every day to a meaningful wisdom and supernatural guide, because indeed, there is a peace and comfort in His presence.

Mom died at home, as my father wished. She lay in a beautiful casket dressed in that horrible gray dress, but she looked peaceful and beautiful. Only thirty-nine years old, she worked hard, drank hard, and suffered much more. I knew in my child's heart that, after all, she must be fine. I held my brother's hand as he was sobbing endlessly. I was feeling cold and in great apathy. *Do I not care?* I thought to myself trying to justify my lack of concern. *After all, I did wish her death more than once, and now I got my wish. What kind of monster am I?!*

But she never liked me, I tried to excuse myself. Then I remembered the day when she took me to the teacher. She was very animated: "Don't worry, you'll be just fine," she said, "and you will have an education, in spite of everything!" Then, when we visited her in the hospital, she took us from room to room, proudly introducing us, "These are my children, and they are such good kids." *How can I forget this?*

Mom's body lay in the house three days. On the day of the funeral, four men came and carried her out. As they were leaving, a sudden fear sneaked into my whole being. *They are taking my mom away.* Like a lightning bolt, it hit my heart and my soul. Holding the casket with all my strength, I cried aloud, "Don't take my mom! Please don't take her!"

My brother approached me, crying and choking on his own tears. "Let go," he cried, "Let go," and gently he released me from my grasp.

We marched after the casket like everybody else. Still, something strange was taking place in this scenario. There was a priest wearing a long black dress with a big cross in his hands. He said many words in a different language, and it sounded stupid and even funny. I hoped he didn't give Mom directions to her final destination! I almost laughed at that thought, but shame and guilt overwhelmed me.

Again, I did not like myself, because even in my child's heart, I knew that something must be wrong with me to think and to feel the way I did. They proceeded to conclude the ceremony by putting my mom into the big hole in the ground.

My apathy returned when they told us to drop dirt from the ground onto the casket. Even in her death, I thought, they called her a *dirty* Jew, so I refused to dump dirt on the casket. At that time, however, I did not care to understand why my Jewish mother was being buried in a Christian cemetery. Completely disconnected, I amused myself by traveling to different dimensions of my private world. Today, embraced by the King of justice, I know that all my distractive behavior was the only tool of survival that I knew.

I knew that most of the people in the funeral expected from us some sort of hysterical entertainment which I, by my own means, didn't intend to provide. I was done with crying, and I hoped my brother was too exhausted to honor anyone's morbid curiosity with his tears of sorrow. Exactly as I thought, people started approaching us, making deep emotional statements that didn't mean anything to me or to them, but they needed to say something so they did. In the corner of my eye, I saw my father on his knees, moaning and crying and his whole image was small and vulnerable in his sorrow.

Unfortunately, he cried himself to death. He built a beautiful headstone for Mom's grave with a beautiful poem that he wrote. This seemed very strange to me but deep in my heart I knew that, in spite of everything else, my parents shared deep love indeed. For three months my father did not stop crying, by night and by day. He bled internally and died in the hospital.

Just before my father's death, the police found us wondering on the streets and we were sent to separate orphanages. I was in an orphanage for sick children because of the constant kidney infections. A few weeks later my father died, so they gave me a black dress and I was sent to the funeral with an escort, an employee of the orphanage.

I was happy to see my brother. We exchanged a few words and we promised each other that we would escape and meet by Mom's grave. Suddenly, strange things started to happen. First, we realized that this cemetery was different. I looked around to see something familiar, but as I tried to figure out this new mystery, the lovely escort pulled my sleeve and through her clenched teeth she dropped two words: "STAY PUT!" And I did!

People started to come to the funeral. They all wore black, and there weren't any women with them. They all had beards and two strange curls rolling down on each side of their faces. I knew that this scary picture would freeze in my memory forever! My poor dead father was in the most horrible wooden box, wrapped in a white sheet, and thrown into the deep ground, followed by some foreign language and moaning.

This was a moment that I was sure that my father must have done some bad things in his life to deserve a funeral like that, but suddenly from nowhere, the space was filled with the most beautiful melody that pierced my heart at once. I heard the song of all songs!

A man began singing with a strong and authoritative voice. I did not understand the words, but it touched my whole soul. When the singer raised his eyes to the heavens, all my doubts vanished, because it was like God Himself with this amazing song was receiving my father into His arms. At that moment, I remembered the beautiful voice of my father. He always told me that he was singing for God.

Many years later I found out that my father was a Hazan in a Jewish temple, and it is very honorable to be a Hazan and to sing for God. *Ha* is a name for God and *Zan* means nourished, so Hazan means nourishment from God. After this funeral, I was shaken and confused, and with the death of my parents, the hope for a better future died as well.

Shortly after that, my brother and I met in the cemetery by our mom's grave. He told me the manager of the orphanage took him under his wing, and he was having the time of his life. He was happy and excited to share with me his new learning experiences about some environmental and scientific developments. I didn't understand any of it but I pretended I did. We spent some time together and then my brother needed to get back to the orphanage, so we said our goodbyes until the next time.

I spent one year in the orphanage hospital because of my recurring kidney infections. Then I was transferred to a different orphanage in a different city, about two hours by train from my hometown which was where my brother was.

Chapter 4

Krakow was a big city, and the orphanage was big as well and very beautiful. There were girls everywhere. As I looked at the surroundings, I felt a familiar sense of fear. A woman approached, inviting me to a large office. There I was checked for lice and perhaps other crawling things. Another woman entered the room with some papers, which I assumed concerned me. After some time in complete silence, the women raised her eyes from the papers asking, "Are you a Jew?"

I didn't respond. "I asked you if you are a Jew," she repeated with a higher voice.

I'm not going to answer, I thought to myself with stubbornness. Enough is enough!!!

"Are you a Jew!?" She almost screamed her question this time.

If she only knew that I really don't want to be Jewish, but no one cares. I learned quickly enough that there is no hiding place from this kind of hate and I wished just for one day not to recognize it.

After a long silence in my annoying resistance, the woman said, "We know who you *are*! We would just like to hear it from you, so say it!" She screamed into my face, spitting all over me.

"Yes, I am Jewish," I said, choking on my tears. My heart rushed like a thousand horses as I said quietly to them, "My Mom used to send us to church and she told us that we are good as Catholics."

"Oh, one of these Jews tried to fool us," the woman said. "Remember your heritage." Then she added, "A Jew is a Jew, no matter what you say or do!"

At that point I lowered my eyes to the ground not to intimidate anyone. I knew that the three women were staring at me; my neck was in painful turmoil as I measured the ground around my feet.

"Before we take you to the place where you belong," one of the women said, "we want you to be familiar with the rules which apply to you and your kind. First," she proceeded, "you are not allowed ever to come to this level of stairs! At all times you must stay in the basement with your own kind. We do have a few of your kind," she added with a twisted smirk.

As she continued with her list, I stopped paying any attention to what she said, and when she was done with her wonderful speech (that was addressed mostly to herself, I thought, in self-satisfaction), she asked, "Do you understand?"

I nodded my head with agreement.

"Take her away!" she ordered.

The basement was dark and cold. There were some mattresses on the ground and a few girls were peeling potatoes. The woman in charge pushed me inside and in a rude voice she added, "One of these mattresses is for you!" She gave me a bag and said, "And these are all the things you will need." All the eyes in the room were fixed upon me. Embarrassed and flushing, I wished to hide, but the room was not quite outfitted for an idea like that, so instead I sat on one of the mattresses, staring into the ground.

"Hey, my name is Adel," I heard a whisper. I raised my head to look at a tall beautiful girl. She had long black hair and wide black eyes; her skin looked like porcelain, and her smile would warm any heart. She looked more like a painting than a real person and I couldn't take my eyes off of her.

"You are the most beautiful girl I have ever seen," I told her.

"You're not serious," she replied. "In here they all call me ugly, and when I ask why they do that, they say it's because I'm Jewish and everyone says that the Jews are ugly."

"I'm not surprised," I said, "but it is our choice to believe them or not."

Adel just smiled when I started to talk with raising confidence: "Let's just say we are ugly for them that hate us without reason, so how could they see us with a reason?"

"That is a smart remark for a young girl like you," Adel said.

I felt proud at this remark but I also needed to add and explain. "You see, I have learned a lot from the people that were in the camps and, through their testimonies, I know very well the painful meaning of our heritage."

Adel was older than the other girls and she had a very warm personality. "To dim the pain," Adel said, "we have learned to laugh in the face of hate and we all have a very healthy sense of humor that protects us from harm."

Unfortunately, I didn't understand at that time that only the divine power of God protected us. In no time we all sat on the floor sharing stories from our short lives, and we all agreed that we wouldn't want to be like our persecutors who were hateful, empty, and dull. We shared a lot and these things brought us closer.

I found out that I was the only one that knew how to read which made me sad. I promised that I would share all I knew and we would take it from there and continue to study. I shared with them the story about the ugly duckling and we all ended up crying. We laughed when I introduced myself with my whole name: "Urshula Martha Leviniowska and (Hofiud)." Adel mentioned that Jewish people have just one name and asked why I had two.

"I know," a very soft voice said. I looked around, facing the cutest smiling face with freckles and fire red hair. "My name is Ruzha [Rosa], but my real name is Sarah. I think I have my grandmother's name. I never did use it, but one day I will, for her memory, because the Nazis killed her as they did the rest of our families."

"Yes," Adel said sadly, "we all lost most of our families and they hate the fact that some of us survived. Our parents and relatives tried to give us Christian names with hope that those names would protect us, but the Polish people have ways to recognize us. And they always will!"

We heard a strong, commanding voice from behind us. "Why aren't you working, you stupid miserable Jews?!" She approached me, and for a second, she stared at me intensely. Then in a cold voice she said, "I can smash you like a rat, Miss Levi----niowska," and grabbing me by my hair, she dragged me after her.

I understood that I was not allowed to go upstairs, and a great fear started to sneak into my heart. I knew that, whatever was going to take place, no one could prevent it, and no one could help. I promised myself whatever was going to happen, I wasn't going to cry or beg. I wasn't going to give anyone that satisfaction, but my heart cried out to God with great confusion and despair, and I was so terrified.

When we were upstairs, she loosened the grasp on my hair, and then she opened a door and pushed me in. The room was beautiful and looked very comfortable. There were pictures on the wall and a lot of books, and there was carpet on the floor with many variation of red and brown and gold. The room looked like it was not from this world; it looked more like something from the stories I had read.

"Are you hungry?" she asked me surprisingly.

Oh, boy I was hungry! But just to be on the safe side, I said, "Not much, Ma'am."

"You can call me Miss Maria," she said, "but only when you are in here, or if we are in complete solitude, understood?" (I must say that I can't recall her true name)

"Yes," I answered, puzzled.

She looked at me softly now, "I'm sorry," she said, "but some things must be hidden. One day you will understand."

Then she handed me something; it looked like a half moon. "This is a banana. It's growing in your country," she said.

My country? I was perplexed. This woman must be crazy! I thought to myself, *a country? Now I have a country, wow! That is the reason she is so nice to me! She thinks I have a country! O dear God, I am in trouble!*

"Your hands are shaking," she said, waking me up from my desperate thoughts. "You don't know what a banana is," she concluded. "Give it to me. I will show you how to peel it."

After she peeled the green cover of this so-called banana with its white insides, she handed it to me and encouraged me to eat it. It was gummy and slimy and I didn't like it at all, but I ate it! After all, who needs trouble?

"Do you like the banana?" she asked.

"Yes, Ma'am. Thank you."

"When you go to your country, you will eat them as much as you like," she said.

I hope not! I thought to myself, and at the same time, trying to give this woman a wide smile of appreciation.

"You know of course about Israel, do you?" she commented.

"No, Ma'am! I do not!" I knew that I answered too fast and she knew I lied.

She took my hand and said, "There is no reason whatsoever for you to be concerned when you are in my company, understood?"

I shook my head up and down, up and down.

"I don't know how much you know about Israel," she continued, "but there is no place like it in the whole world, and anyone would be considered blessed to be there."

Blessed Israel, indeed...I remembered sitting on the bench in the local park in my hometown. It seemed like I listened forever to the painful memories of the older Jewish people who experienced the horrors of the concentration camps. Their dreams were to get to Israel one day. I understand the privilege that I was given as a child to be a part of their lives, but their disturbing stories haunted me even in my dreams. I was forced to gaze into the face of my own Jewish heritage, inviting self-inflicted torture. In all those horrible events, I did realize that there was a hope in spite of the fear residing in my heart.

Jacob's story was exceptionally painful. He had three beautiful children and a beautiful wife. They were hiding in a house of a good Polish family, but not for long, because most of the Polish people hated Jews, so in no time they were found and taken to the camp.

It was wintertime, and the snow was deep and it was freezing cold. The German officers ordered them to take off all their clothes and when they stood naked in the snow, shivering and frightened, one of the officers approached Jacob with a gun. "Take it," the German said, "kill your family and you will live."

Jacob wouldn't reply, as he said to me, "They stripped me from my clothes and my dignity. I couldn't do a thing for my family, I cried to God but He was silent, I raised my hands to the heavens and I begged God for mercy but He was silent. So I took the gun and tried to shoot myself but the gun was empty. I heard the sound of their laughter and they shot me in both of my legs. While I was still conscious, they killed my family in front of my eyes and my heart froze forever. They left hoping that, in no time, I would find my death. I just wanted to die and to join my family, but God was silent. 'Take me, God, please take me,' I cried and I screamed till I couldn't hear my own voice anymore, and God was silent."

Jacob looked at me and said, "You are still a child, but you must always remember: when God is silent, it's not because He can't do anything. It is because He is doing everything for the right reason and for us all at the same time! Remember," Jacob said, "God always knows, always...always...always..."

I was a child indeed, and very much infuriated with God, because as a child I saw God more as a person's private magician. I still ponder the meanings of Jacob's words, and most of all, I will never come to forget his lack of anger or hate.

Yes, he was sad, very sad, but the peace that surrounded him was comforting. He was very wise because he knew the meaning of forgiveness, which I as a child could not comprehend. He never raised his voice to anyone, but he often told me that God spared his life for a reason and those reasons he witnessed every day and until the blessed day comes when the Lord would take him home to be with his family again. Somehow I believed that.

I heard many stories like this one from the survivors of the concentration camps. I listened and I cried because I knew that most of my family was executed there and now from the ashes of these painful memories they reappeared vividly as a reminder that we the Jewish people are still the hated link to everything and anything. All of my older friends had the same dream, to go to the promised land of Israel, so I knew about Israel as I tried to understand this impossible dream. I was in the orphanage and well informed as to my disgraceful identity and all the limitations that came with it.

We all were very hungry. They never gave us enough food. We were eight girls and we received food hardly enough for three. We worked very hard; we peeled potatoes for so long that our hands were hurting and bruised from holding the knife for so long. We cleaned and scrubbed and we were screamed at. As we worked, we smelled the baked goods and the fresh bread and our hunger intensified to a point of sickness, and by night we fell asleep, exhausted from work and hunger.

In my deep thoughts, I believed not to belong to anyone, or anything, even as friendly as I had been to the other Jewish girls. My resistance against my race grew sharply as my yearning for hope stopped to be reachable in the face of this new situation. I began to escape, walking the streets, stealing food and sleeping mostly in the train station or on the train.

When I was on the train, I knew that I must pay attention to the conductor who checked the tickets, so every time that the train stopped, I jumped from it and went into the section that I assumed was checked already. However, I was not very wise; therefore, I was always caught and brought back to the orphanage to face my punishment.

To make a statement to all of us, I was punished publicly. I was beaten mostly on my face. Then they put me in the kitchen corner, instructing the cook not to give me any food. He always disregarded their orders.

Nevertheless, in no time I was on the streets once again, hoping that I would find a church like the one in my hometown. I needed to talk to God. At that time, I believed that God listened to people only in church. I needed to tell Him what was happening, in case He did not know. Deep in my heart, I was convinced that God was very unhappy in all the happenings. I just didn't understand why He didn't strike the bad people with some sort of a horrible event, or some great sickness from which they would never recover.

Still deeply involved in my vindictive thoughts, I realized that I was standing in front of a church. What a surprise! As I entered, I could not believe it! Wow, it was more beautiful than the one in my hometown! There were many candles burning and the flames were moving swiftly as I entered the church; everything was festive and colorful and the familiar smells welcomed me with the security I missed so much.

I knew that this was Christmas time, and I stood there, thankful and overwhelmed with all the surroundings. Then I heard a voice calling me. "Urshula?" My heart skipped a beat. *Was God Himself calling my name?* "Urshula?" I heard the voice again. I looked around, and there standing before me was no other than my dear friend the priest, the same one that taught me about my Lord Jesus Christ.

"It is you…" I managed to whisper, choking on tears.

"What are you doing in here?" he asked me.

"I escaped from the orphanage," I said simply.

"And why would you do that?" he asked, so in one breath I told him everything and when I finished, I realized his concern, so indeed at that moment I stood tall, protected, and secure.

He ordered me to wait while he left the room in a hurry, and I could hear my own heart pounding against my chest. When he returned he was holding a big box in his arms, "It's for you girls," he said with a wide smile. "Gifts from the Lord Jesus," he added softly.

This time I'd believe him, and I hoped that there in the box would be a lot of food, because every time that any kind of emotion overwhelmed me, I felt myself starving for food.

The priest had his own car which impressed me a lot, and especially when he allowed me so graciously to sit beside him. My heart was very disturbed at our arrival and the building of the orphanage suddenly took an ugly shape. Even though I dared to see it with less fear, the internal beauty could not erase its true ugliness.

I had already learned that the true beauty has depth, and it was up to me to seek it because the surface is only what my eye beholds, but the depth of all things reserves its own wisdom. As I recognized the truth beneath the surface, I recognized the hope conceived in me.

"Stay beside me," the priest said, and I did. *O boy, I did!* The door opened wide, and then in the most respected way that I ever beheld, the manager welcomed the priest, bowing and praising the Lord Jesus Christ. *Wow, this was a sight to my eyes!!!!*

Then she saw me, and the humble expression changed to an evil rage: "YOU!" she said, pointing a long finger at me, "You're going to get it!"

She took me by my hair to show me the way to the punishment, when the priest spoke: "Leave the child be!"

"But, Your Excellency," the manager insisted, "this Jewish rat has been creating constant problems, and this is maybe the fifth time that she escaped."

"Does this child have a name?" the priest asked.

"Well, yes," the manager replied.

"So call her by her name!"

"But, Your Excellency," the manager insisted, "this is not a child; this is dirt, and we just take them in because the government demands it!" She stood tall and proud and almost victorious as she clarified her point, but the priest wasn't impressed and I couldn't wait to see the next segment of this debate, but the priest turned to me and softly he sent me away to stay with the girls. I left with a deep disappointment as the evil fire in my heart screamed for revenge.

After what seemed like forever, I was called back to the room, and to my relief, the priest was still in the room with the box. "I will take the box to the girls, Your Excellency," the manager suggested.

"No, thank you," the priest replied. "I would like to see where the Jewish girls lodge."

"Very well then," the manager replied humbly, "this way," and she pointed to the basement.

I ran in front of them, jumping two and three stairs, because I was hurrying up to inform the other girls of the *falling empire*.

It was warm in the basement at that time of the day because we were near the kitchen, but by night, it was very cold because there were no active heaters in the basement. By night, we used to put all the straw mattresses together, and this way we all warmed each other. The priest saw and understood everything without a word being said.

First, he ordered the manager to relocate us with other girls, and he expressed this request vocally in front of all of us. He said, "You interfered with God's authority against these Jewish orphans and you must remember not to offend our Lord who was from the line of Jewish descendants."

Wow, that was big!!! Bigger than I could comprehend and I got my satisfaction as I stood taller. However, in my ignorance, I did not recognize the power of God. Nevertheless, I sensed a supernatural Spirit that overwhelmed my heart with inexplicable gratitude, in spite of my confusion.

We got a room upstairs, all of us Jewish girls, and we knew how great it would be to lie down in beds and on clean sheets. We also knew, that even after priest's unusual speech, we were still hated and now more than ever! It was obvious to us that we were never going to get tickets to more privileges. However, we already got much more than we anticipated and we were grateful.

We were united, and we did not desire to interact with the Christian girls who showered us with insults. On the other hand we were very jealous of them because, somehow, we had learned to believe that everyone was better than us. And yes, we were all very much surprised as the priest stepped up to defend us. Furthermore, I witnessed the power of the priesthood, and I knew that it does not matter which category we were put in, the poison of our Jewish identity was still active and inciting vindictive behavior in others.

We were all overwhelmed with joy at the fresh start. The priest came upstairs with the box, as all of us surrounded him with anticipation. First, there was a long fat sausage, and then bread and lemons and oranges. Wow, I often dreamed about oranges; I knew how hard it was to get them and if you could, you needed to have a lot of money! After that came the most delightful: chocolate, clothes and shoes. I got a beautiful pair of shoes that were my constant companion, even in bed!

Many things took place in this orphanage that would have a tremendous influence on my developing personality, but today I don't need to remember much to form painful nightmares. There is no measure of how much pain can be inflicted on a child to pollute the sense of reality.

My late night teacher became my secret friend. Every night she used to wake me up to teach me different things. One night, she woke me up to teach me how to walk properly. With my nature, I obviously thought she was crazy. Other times, she taught me how to dance the twist, waltz, tango and more. She used to say, "Urshula, you must walk like a queen, and talk as if you swallowed the whole encyclopedia, and you must dress like no one else! When the time comes and you start to paint yourself, do it in the most delicate way. Never too much, because it would be vulgar and vulgar is no good, but a little bit will present itself wisely and mysteriously. As you take care of those things, you must be fast and efficient.

"Do it every day, not spending more than ten minutes on your face, and remember, more than ten minutes means that something is wrong with you! And no more than ten minutes on your hair! Gain practice with that! Understood? And now about the perfume: Remember Urshula, there are many perfumes out there, but yours must be unique! So what do you do? I will tell you! You take two good French perfumes that you like and mix them together and never reveal your secret!

"And the last one for you to remember is this, Urshula: When you are in a room in the company of five or more people, and you would like to address something, first you raise your voice enough to get their attention, and then you proceed to talk in a much lower voice to attract their complete attention. Most importantly, remember to address everyone in an individual manner so they would be complimented and with that, they will remember you."

I must say that I wish I could remember her name because everything she taught me helped me in the years to come. Nevertheless, I must mention one other thing she taught me. On one of those special nights we shared, she called me to her room, screaming obscenities against Jews as she always did so no one would suspect her good attributes. She sat in front of me, holding a beautiful scarf in her hands. Before I complimented her on the beauty of the scarf, she tore it in half.

As my mouth opened with surprise, she said, "You can close your mouth now because I going to teach you how to put it together without a trace. This kind of sewing requires a lot of talent and patience, and this will be my art gift from me to you."

"I can't fix that," I said desperately.

She just looked at me and said, "If you really can't, it means just one thing: I'm the one that failed in judgment by being a bad teacher!" So I learned and I fixed the scarf, but most of all, I got a gift for life.

I never learned the English language traditionally. However, when I am praying or writing, the Holy Spirit is in charge, and the words I am able to say or write are not my own, as I cannot even pronounce them. At moments like these, my heart rejoices as I can see through the veil of eternity, and I am thankful in my definite security because indeed, *if God is with me, who can be against me?*

One night my personal teacher woke me up whispering, "I have news for you, not from this world," and as I woke up completely she looked at me with a gaze of victory! What now, I thought to myself, did she discover a new America or something? "Urshula," she said, "you are going to Israel!"

"I am?" I was in state of shock.

"Do you know a woman by the name Maria Dirdal Kiewibasova?"

"Yes, I know her," I said, "she was my father's friend, and I don't like her at all!!! She used to sell vodka illegally, and involved my father in this business among other things!"

"Well, I am very sorry," my teacher said, "but she is the one that is going to take you and your brother to Israel. Apparently, your father had some savings for a black hour, which he gave to her to buy your freedom and to take you to your own country, to be protected and secured. Regardless what you are thinking, Urshula, this woman must have at least some integrity to keep her promise and to followed through, so at least grant her some respect."

I thought about it for a second and I agreed, she must have some integrity or something.

At that time, I was informed well enough about Israel, although with great disbelief. Oh my God, I sighed, I really do not wish to go to the country that sheltered the world's Jewish misery in its holy desert!

I almost cried when my friend the teacher handed me a book. "This is a romantic book. It will be the first romantic story for you to read and I hope not the last, and Urshula," she said, "I know that you are afraid, but after you read the book, you will see many things in a different perspective."

I did, oh boy, I did! The story was about an American girl visiting an Arab country when she was suddenly snatched by a Bedouin Arab and taken on a long journey through the Sahara desert. The story also included an incredible tale of love. I personally didn't know anything about Arabs before reading this book, but as I gazed at the book cover showing an Arab in traditional clothes, my heart was deeply troubled. As I read the whole story, I determined that I would never agree to be a part of this women-demeaning culture. It is hard to believe and sad to say, but later I did just that.

I often wonder why I remember the names of people that hurt me but not the names of the most precious people that blessed me with their love, generosity, and hope. Their influential actions gave me the courage to fight and to conquer this life, so why I cannot remember their names is strange indeed. I just hope that through this venture of writing and revealing myself in such great detail, I may find the answer to this riddle.

Before I speak about my journey to Israel I'd like to honor the memory of my dear and beautiful Jewish friend Adel. She died before the age of eighteen, *and I am responsible for her death.* I will live with this guilt until my last day on this earth. Adel had confided in me about her fear of leaving the orphanage because, as she would reach the age of eighteen soon, she would have to leave the orphanage.

Adel did not have anyone to turn to, and sadly, she had never learned to read very well, only what I taught her and it was not much. Often she cried at night and when I asked her what was wrong, she would say, "They want me to be a prostitute, but I am not giving them that satisfaction. I will die first! It is in my power to shut their mouth, and no one would ever say, 'There is a Jewish prostitute on the street!'"

One day Adel told me that she was feeling very bad and she was in pain. "You know, Urshula," she said, "we will need some aspirin for all of us, you know, just in case, so just go to the nurse's office, take a prescription form, and write an order for 40 aspirins for the orphanage. Then go to the pharmacy and pick it up; they will charge the orphanage for the purchase."

I did as Adel asked me; it was very exciting and adventurous to outsmart the management of the orphanage. I sneaked into the nurse's office, and I did as instructed and gave the purchase to Adel.

By nighttime, she was in horrible pain; she was crying loudly and we did not know what to do. With fear and a bit of courage, finally, we woke up the manager asking for help. At first she refused, but after our constant begging, she called a doctor. When he arrived, Adel was given something for pain and it seemed like she went to sleep, but she just stopped breathing. The doctor's final diagnosis was suicide by a huge dose of aspirin. At this moment, I felt like Adel took my life as well, and I did not know if I could ever be healed from the guilt of my responsibility. If only I were smarter.

Chapter 5

Maria Dirdal Kiewibasova took me and my brother to the airport in the middle of the night. We flew in a big Boeing airplane to Italy. There, we were arrested for leaving Poland illegally, and without any relatives in Israel, there was no one to claim us, so we were brought back to Poland and put in prison for two days, next to the cell of a drunken woman who managed to entertain us.

The moment she saw us with the police she screamed with sympathy, "Oh, you poor babies, how can they do this to you?" Then in one breath, she screamed with all her might: "Murderers!! Hitler!! Nazis!! Go, go borrow a heart from someone, because no one can live without it, except you swine!!! Go and find you a conscience. Hey! You want some of mine???"

She sang and laughed and screamed almost all night. We slept the next day, and the day after that, we were taken to the orphanage. A few weeks later, Miss Maria informed us that everything was in control because apparently Israeli officials intervened, and the door for our final destination opened.

I hoped that the light I was searching for would fill my lonely soul. I hoped that the shattered hopes would take the shape of wisdom and strength. However, most of all, I knew that I would praise the Most High, even with my wounded heart....I did not know yet, that this life would finish faster than lightning and before I would realize the mystery of the heart, I could lose my soul.

Israel, 1963

The big airplane landed in Israel. My ears were hurting very badly, and as usual, I was complaining to myself. My God, I thought in fear, here we are in the dark Jewish desert that exists after all. It was the month of May, and I expected an attack of wind and cold, as in Poland; instead surprisingly, waves of warmth welcomed us. My brother didn't stop expressing his educational knowledge which irritated me quite a bit. Deep in my heart I believed that God blessed my little brother with many gifts, and I was forgotten. I acknowledged my brother's gifts with admiration yet jealously, and once again without comprehending the simple truth.

A group of people approached us, explaining to our escort, Miss Maria, something quite important because, in one second, Miss Maria became taller and a big smile of importance spread all over her face. "Come on, children," she said to us in determination, "you are going to meet your destiny!"

I didn't like her, and I didn't like her motives, and as well as I knew her in my child's heart, I knew her motives were never pure. It was then with anger, shame, and confusion, I tried very hard to ignore her rusty voice which said that honesty belonged to fools. The moment we entered the terminal, flashing lights welcomed us from every direction. I was in a state of shock. I heard voices all around me, people talking, asking, touching; *it was horrible, what did they want?*

After a while, we were taken to a room with a few people. They invited us to sit down in nice comfortable chairs, which swallowed us completely and as tense as we were, our legs pointed straight toward their faces. In front of us on the table, I discovered chocolate candies! In one single moment, this Jewish desert transformed into a promised land, as my eyes froze on those candies!

"Take some," I heard someone say in Polish and I did. It was my first positive taste of the Holy Land. A short man explained to us that all the flashing lights were newspaper cameras and that they would like to know about our life in Poland and our experience in the orphanage.

Strange... why would anyone want to hear about that? But today I do understand: people have need for tragedy but as long as it's not theirs. I finally learned by my own interpretation, that to be an orphan is to be a second-class citizen. People will always look down on me, and yet, without me, there is not superiority, and without them, there is no little me. I also came to the conclusion that, if I had no parents, people would think that I lack other things as well.

The reporters asked us many questions, all of them at once, and it left us in deep confusion; therefore, we said nothing, but amazingly, in the newspaper reports, they wrote all of their stories without a bit of truth. I did understand from people talking that our arrival to Israel was apparently not kosher at all. That is why, in our first journey, we were forced to return to Poland. Nevertheless, this time, arranged by a smart individual from the Israeli government, promised a much better future.

At times, miracles happen in the least expected ways, and we don't recognize the strength that comes from weakness. Yet after the storm and pain, there is relief and peace. Because of the wisdom of our Father in heaven, His love is complete for us all, by His perfect plan.

From the airport, we drove into the empty spaces of the Israeli desert. It was night and not many lights were visible, but what I saw I didn't like. Fear started to overwhelm me: the same fear that found me to be a suitable companion in the future to come.

I did not trust Miss Maria, and in my heart, I respected her even less. Knowing her power, I watched my mouth and my steps. I am still ashamed, remembering her pick-pocketing. I hoped she would stop when in Israel, but she didn't. It somehow killed the sliver of hope that still shone like a tiny light in my broken heart because, in a strange way, I related to her because there was no one else.

However, I must say more about Miss Maria, who was not as bad as I chose to see. Miss Maria was a German officer in a concentration camp. Her duties were to control the work done on time in the camp. She used to stand on a rock, with a whip in her hand, encouraging the prisoners to work. Somehow, she befriended a Jewish woman who got pregnant by a Nazi officer.

This woman begged Miss Maria to save her child. When children were born in the concentration camps, they were immediately murdered in most horrible ways. Miss Maria saved the Jewish child, and for the rest of the war, she was chased by the Nazis and marked as a traitor. Because of that heroic act, she was highly rewarded by the Israeli government. A tree was planted in her name, beside other great and courageous people who helped or saved Jewish people at tremendous risk to their own lives. Her name is engraved in stone in the Israeli museum: YAD VA SHEM [hand and name].

At times in my sorrow and at times in my joy, my whole soul is yearning for Thy presence, my Lord, and my gratitude is beyond fleshly sight, because You, my Lord, gave me a new heart.

Some things I do not remember and some I wish I could forget. For example, I disregarded Miss Maria, and when I was around her, I always had a heavy feeling of dismay and fear. I knew when I was a child that Miss Maria helped my dad sell vodka. She was the supplier, and I knew what they did was wrong because of the frequent visits from the police. My dad hid the bottles in the hole that he dug in the wall behind a closet, and he marveled at how easily he outsmarted the police.

I knew that with that much talking, the police would be on his tail in no time. And indeed, the day came when the police came to the house, and without hesitation, approached the hiding place. Nevertheless, before they put the handcuffs on my dad's hands, Miss Maria appeared from nowhere, greeting the police officers with a smile and money, which obviously released Dad from the chains of prison.

It was at that time that the good and evil took a turn on the scale of my life. The evil was more appealing, more inviting and more promising, and in my ignorance I sincerely believed, at the age of thirteen, I knew it all and in my mind, no one was good! Indeed, it was an easy conclusion as I gazed honestly into my own character.

Unfortunately, I was already convinced as to the negativity of my roots. I knew in my small world of confusion how bad I was, so I lived accordingly, gradually killing the distinguished privilege that God by His grace wrote upon my heart: His love for me. In all the pain, and persecutions, His love became an echo of a distant hope and my Jesus was framed by me and blamed by me. Worst of all, Jesus Christ was imprisoned and forgotten in the dark corners of my heart. Now, ugly shadows of fear and contempt started to take occupancy in my soul. In the midst of all that, a flash of a memory embraced me at once, with the strong voice of a woman saying to me, "You must always pray, Urshula, and if you're not allowed to pray, find a bathroom and pray there!"

Woe to me, the little insignificant person, that in my ignorance I set aside the beautiful truth of my Lord and exchanged it for an ugly lie of this world!

Was I really so ignorant? Certainly not! Ignorance was just one item from a long list of my convenient excuses! But every time I was in the bathroom, I heard again this voice of a woman saying:

"Pray, Urshula, pray," and in time the voice became louder and louder, forcing me to stare into the face of my dying mother which so often whispered into my soul. "Pray, Urshula, pray." Her whisper became like thunder and a mark upon my heart.

Indeed, God never abandoned me; there was always a way--a better way! And it was God's way that I refused to accept. Time and time again, God talked to me in many ways. I did not hear His voice, as you may hear the sound of a voice, but it was always clear. He talked through people, through circumstances, through joy and tragedies. Today He talks to me through His Word which is the Bible. His truth never put me down, His Word is my ultimate assurance, and His love is my security forever.

As we drove through the empty spaces of the Israeli desert, the fear was choking me, remembering bad things that took place in the darkness of many horrifying nights which I desperately tried to brush away and the more I tried, the more vividly they reappeared.

Our first stop was Miss Maria's daughter Luna, the one that she saved from the death camp. She was married and a mother to four very handsome boys. She had a very comfortable home, and it seemed that she possessed all she wanted, and even more. My conclusion was based on the big basket of oranges that lay in the corner of the kitchen! I picked one up hesitantly, when Miss Maria asked me, "Did you see all the orange trees on the way here?"

"Oh yeah," I said, "Were those the orange trees?"

Sadly, I did not see a thing, just the empty spaces of the Israeli desert that matched the vacant space of my disturbed personality. So Miss Maria gave me permission to eat the oranges until I wanted no more which, of course, was very suspicious to me. To be on the safe side, I ate just one orange, and making sure no one saw, I hid three more in my private bag, just as a precaution for the future.

We spent the first night at Luna's house. Her boys were very nice, trying to give us cookies and different foods, which we accepted happily, and that made them happy as well. We did not understand a word they said, and it was not encouraging at all. Then we saw the Hebrew writings and we could not figure it out. First, it looked like upside down writing, so we turned it over, and it still looked wrong! Oh, great, I thought to myself, I will never learn to write like that; I am too stupid to learn that!

I truly believed that there were two kinds of children in this world, the normal ones (according to my understanding, of course) and those such as us. The normal children have normal parents that hug them and kiss them when they fall. They let them know how precious they are by buying nice clothes and candies for them. They don't have to hide their identity because they are not Jewish.

Compare that image to my parents who were vulnerable and hurting and distant, worked day and night to feed us, and in their silence they taught us the meaning of sacrifice. In their silent pain, we learned that hate and anger belongs to fools, but most of all, in their ways they paved our way to Christ.

Today I would give my life if I could spend even one moment with them. As a child, I loved them because something was very special about them. It was the title of Parent that they carried with significant pride. For my brother and me they gave their last breath. Perhaps they weren't the parents I would ask for, but today I do understand: they were the parents that God honored me with.

Anyone can be a parent, but not everyone deserves the title of such, and my parents earned it, because in the midst of a hateful environment, nothing was about *them*, but everything was about *us*. Their pain lived in the midst of horrifying memories against the Jews, and even alcohol couldn't take it or burn it because their eyes beheld hell on earth.

Supernatural beings surrounding us all,
Hell's fire ignited in my desperate soul.....
My heart is torn out and gone, my spirit doesn't cry anymore...
There is no light and no peace but the dark cloud of the beast.

We woke the next morning to a lot of noise; the boys were running all around, with horrible vocal improvisations. All the windows were open and the beauty I beheld took my breath away. It was my first positive glimpse at my new home and I loved everything about it: the sun and the trees, the gentle breeze and the smell of the oranges in the air, but most of all, I loved all the festive colors of the Israeli nature that danced blissfully, promising tranquility and smiles for a great future to come.

Miss Maria, along with her daughter Luna and her son-in-law, sat by the table reading articles to each other from a big pile of different newspapers. As I approached, I understood that the stories were about me and my brother. One of them read in Polish, and I overheard the gruesome report about our lives in Poland. Standing there and listening, I felt nauseated and very much ashamed; all my hopes crushed at once and all my dreams to be respected in our new environment vanished. I did not wish to be a focal point of weakness and sorrow. I needed to be a new person in the new place, and it was taken from me.

After we were exposed to the media, many letters with money and packages arrived at the house, expressing generous sympathy for us, and Miss Maria took care of it all, some she gave to her daughter and some she took for herself. "This is the Israeli reward for bringing you here," she said.

Who cares? After two weeks at Luna's house, we were going to the destination that eventually would become our home. "Great people will adopt you," we were told, "but you need to be on your best behavior."

Sure! As if I did not pretend enough... but I was excited to have new parents, and maybe I would get normal parents... I knew that I would be so good that they would have no choice but to love me! I will do anything for them, I will listen to them, I will clean their house, I will fix their torn clothes, and I will clean all their windows! I could clean windows very well, as it was one of the chores we did in the orphanage.

We had been told that the place we were going to was called a kibbutz and it existed only in Israel. It was communal living. I stopped to listen because I did not understand this kind of living and I felt very stupid. I just wished to be like other normal kids, hoping to stop the crazy mind search and finding out why my Jewish heritage is so painful.

Nevertheless, I did conclude that as a hated nation, indeed we needed a hiding state.

I was confused and fear started to sneak into my heart, so defensively, once again, I opened the door to my imagination, establishing my adoptive parents with a perfect resemblance to a royal family. I was the princess, and their house resembled a palace, of course! Oh, boy! This was some palace!!

I thank my Father in Heaven who blessed me with a colorful imagination that became my shield. He gave me hope and understanding that most of the time I refused to recognize. However, and most of all, my Father made sure that I would have some sense of belonging and self-respect. Today I have learned to cherish His Love as the greatest gift of all, wrapped with the plan of salvation. When the shadows of the past are haunting me, I know that my eyes must have gazed upon this world, forsaking my God and my Lord.

Presently, my deepest need is to please my Lord. However, I do fall and sin every day, and when in deep sorrow I repent and I ask my God for His strength to be obedient and full of faith. In the presence of His Spirit, I accepted myself once more, because it is me that I learned to hate so vigorously and in God's love I was born again and in God's victory I put my spirit at His feet to worship Him forever.

I woke up from my daydream, dreamily facing fields of green valleys and flowers spread proudly all around white, identical houses. It was like a real dream! Even in my wild imagination, I never beheld beauty as such.

We were welcomed by two people that introduced themselves as Shiki and Fani Borovich. Fani was a small woman with dark curly hair and dark cold eyes which totally ignored me but stared intensively at my brother. I desperately tried to catch her attention by composing wide smiles until the muscles of my face ached. Shiki was a short person with white hair and blue eyes and without expression; he approached me speaking in Polish and as I looked at him, all my composed smiles froze, and I realized at once that I did not want a father!

He was very nice, which scared me even more. "My name is Shiki," he said. "I am a teacher." I gave him a glance with mixed respect, trying to back off from his presence, but then in a friendly manner, his arm closed on my wrist and I became terrified! I released myself from his grasp and I ran as fast as I could. I heard only the sound of my own heart beating in fear, with an incredible strength, faster and stronger, until a sharp pain pierced my head. Then suddenly, to my surprise, I collapsed on the ground, waving my hands in desperation. Looking up, I was deeply embarrassed, as I faced the people that were supposed to adopt us.

"What is the matter with her?" the woman asked.

"Nothing," Miss Maria said. "She is just tired and a little confused."

"Well, I hope so," Miss Fani said with her cold voice. "We do not need more disturbed individuals in our environment."

My brother stood beside me and whispered in rage: "You're going to ruin this for me." I felt like a thousand stones were blocking my airway, which was good, because otherwise, I would have burst into tears, embarrassing my brother even more. I couldn't lose him; he was my only family.

I was highly concerned about what had just taken place. Honestly, and in true reality, I am not sure if these episodes actually took place or if they had just played out in my sick mind. Yet, I refused to understand what was happening to me, and why a touch would scare me so much, whether reality or not, it still happened to me.

When I stood on my feet, I couldn't ignore Miss Fani's contemptuous stare, and I just knew she didn't want me around, so I lost the chance to be adopted. Now even one smile couldn't sustain my face, but along with that, I was losing my identity by losing my brother.

After this puzzling episode, we went for a tour around the kibbutz, and it was indeed surprise after surprise: the Olympic pool with the blue water, the small zoo with exotic animals, the playgrounds for different ages, and the big cultural building that held lots of rooms, each providing different intellectual interests. There was a great library with many books and comfortable chairs, with the addition of a carpet that provided a very soft and relaxing atmosphere. There were music rooms with pianos and other instruments to practice; there was a place with record players, and along the wall, there were many records. There was even a movie theater! Other rooms had newspapers in different languages. I was so overwhelmed that I overlooked many things.

The next stop was a huge restaurant where everybody ate three times a day, but if they wished to eat in their homes, they could, if they didn't mind being bothered with preparation. Of course, everything they needed was provided in the local store.

Shiki explained to us about the wide selection of food always available. Proudly he mentioned that professional chefs that were also members of the kibbutz prepared all of the food. If we choose in the future, any desired profession, the kibbutz will provide for us basically all our hearts' desires! For example, if I choose to be a doctor, after I graduate, I have to come back to fulfill my duties in the kibbutz, as a doctor if needed, but also to perform other chores and jobs, including work in the fields, the kitchen, or with children and so forth. "This is our home," he said. "We do all tasks equally, and we all serve in the military."

Presently, as I'm writing my story I feel lonely and vulnerable in my human flesh, but in the strength of my Lord I'm learning compassion, which is guided by divine wisdom, and it is indeed gratifying for me. And when I do fall into weakness, facing unjust rejection or persecution, I do realize that I must have visited the dark corners of my past. So when the dusky feelings overwhelm me I just have to remember to say, "do not cry anymore, my soul, because indeed I am loved and I have it all and on the Highest Authority."

My memories often bring me back to Poland to the Gypsies and to our first introduction, as they visited us in our home. I observed them as they sat on the ground, rolling cigarettes and sipping from a bottle of vodka. They were darker than the Polish people but very appealing in their appearance. I liked them because there was some mystery about them that opened a window to my curiosity, especially when one of them pulled a comb and a clear paper out of his pocket and started to play on that. It was very enchanting as I listened with great amazement, and that same evening, I became an addition to the Gypsy family with the circus named Moreno. In no time, I was trained in acrobatics and trapeze, and for the first time in my life, I learned the meaning of self-worth.

Twelve years after the war, the hate against the Jewish people only grew stronger and my parents were in constant struggle for income that was not available to the Jewish people, but my performance in the circus brought some relief into the family kitchen. I loved the time with the Gypsies because I was happy, and it did not matter that I worked hard every day for six hours, practicing the trapeze and acrobatics. I had always had a fear of heights but I felt loved and secure with the Gypsies, so nothing scared me anymore. *Today I know that the Lord introduced me to everything possible and by His grace He allowed me to see, and to feel, to understand, and finally to choose.*

I could write a thousand pages of positive memories with the Gypsies, and only few words about an accident that crashed all my hopes. I fell from a trapeze and only an iron fence blocked my fall and one of the iron studs entered into my left leg. I was rushed to the hospital, and when they sewed my leg, I screamed so loud that people standing around covered their ears with their hands. Nevertheless, I screamed away the pain!

I forgot to mention one thing: in those days, they did not put you to sleep or give you something for relief. The good Gypsies gave me vodka to drink. They put vodka on my wound and vodka in my mouth, and by the time we arrived at the hospital, everyone resembled blurred 8s—88888888888—and my head was moving up and down and side to side. I really enjoyed the echoing sound of my voice, as I screamed with all my might.

It was the end of a happy chapter in my life, I came back home to my invisible parents, and to my brother that was always better than me. And indeed he was.

I was molested and I knew it was wrong, but in spite of that, I tried to do to my brother what was done to me, and thank God, my brother got mad with me and stopped me. I was so ashamed that I could not forgive myself until the day when the Lord found me and picked me up from the ashes of guilt and confusion.

My Savior released me from the chains of this life by giving me new breath... He will do the same for you, if you just let Him, He will love you and protect you, and He will show you how precious and special you are, because in His eyes, each and every one is one of a kind.

As for me, I'd rather write good things about myself and enjoy the cloak of hypocrisy, but I choose to reveal my heart in truth and honesty to encourage all who seek freedom in the light of God. Some of us may have secrets locked deep inside and it makes us sick and unhappy and completely vulnerable to the whispers of the enemy. The enemy knows how to enforce our guilt; he will keep us imprisoned as long as we let him, but God is like a pure rushing waters that will cleanse us and release us to His embrace to be free at last.

Sadly, my life took me through paths of unbelievable hate and tremendous pain and destruction. My nights still reflect horrifying memories, but at the first light of the morning, I remember I am redeemed and no one can take possession of my soul because it does not belong to me anymore.

The kibbutz became a home, promising each day something new which my little brother embraced with all his strength, ignoring me in the process. Shiki and Fani did not hide their intent to adopt my brother and it was fine with me, but my brother did not want me around.

At first, I didn't want to believe it, so I started to follow him. I realized fast enough, that he was ashamed of me and partly because I was a painful picture from the past. I was a part of a hateful Poland. I was not his sister anymore, but a burden of unpleasant memories. In addition, I overheard Fani and Shiki planning something else for me.

Fine! I am not going to stand in their way! I left the kibbutz not knowing my destination; I walked for a long time, remembering different events from my short life and thinking about a solution to my problem. I hated myself, and I believed that God hated me even more. In desperation, I remembered my friend Adel and the night she took her own life. Oh God, I cried. I do understand her pain now because I am hurting so much that I wish to die, and I am lost, and there is no place for me to go. Suddenly, like the flash of a camera, I came to a new solution: I will die! Yes! I will die like Adel! This thought embraced me victoriously with a new hope. After all, death will not hurt as much as I am hurting right now.

Chapter 6

I awoke from my thoughts, realizing that I was standing in front of a farmhouse. "Are you lost?" I heard a woman's voice asking me in Hebrew.

After three months in the kibbutz, I knew enough Hebrew to understand and to talk. "No, I'm not lost," I said bursting into tears.

"It's okay, it's okay," the woman said. "You don't need to cry. Come in and you can tell me all about it." When I raised my eyes to look at her, I realized that I was talking to an Arab woman.

Oh, great, I thought to myself, I am talking to my enemy! In the kibbutz we were warned over and over about the things our enemy is capable of. Maybe she will shoot me! I thought, No, she wouldn't; she looks harmless. On the other hand, she can use a knife. Oh, no, not a knife!!! I don't want to be scarred all over after I die.

"Are you going to kill me?" I asked.

"Why would I kill you?" she replied.

"Because that's what Arabs do," I said.

"I'm not one of those Arabs you've been told about," she said impatiently. "I am an Israeli citizen like you, but with a different belief system."

I looked at her closely now; she was good-looking with big dark eyes marked all around with a black pencil which enhanced her eyes beautifully. Her skin was smooth and shiny like olive oil. She is too tall for a woman, I thought, as my head was falling back, trying to check her out.

"Did I pass the test?" she asked me, inviting me at the same time to sit on the mattresses that were on the floor. As I sat beside her, I was still checking her out. Her clothes looked different than Arabic traditional clothes; they were colorful and cheerful.

"What's your name?" she asked.

"My name? Why do you need to know my name?" I asked suspiciously.

"Because that is what people do when they meet," she said pleasantly.

"Okay then," I said, "my name is Adel."

"My name is Fatima," she said, "and you probably escaped from one of the kibbutzim around here?"

"No, I didn't! I just left," I said sadly. "They don't want me there anyway. They want to adopt my brother, and I'm standing in their way because I have a problematic personality!"

"Who told you that!?" she asked.

"I overheard them talking and I don't know what this problematic personality means, but it didn't sound good, so before they sent me away, I left."

"Where are your parents?" Fatima asked.

"They died in Poland three years ago," I said bravely, without showing any feelings.

Fatima stood on her feet from the mattress pulling me by the hand and I felt really light. *Wow! She is strong! Maybe it wasn't such a good idea after all to lie about my name.*

"Listen," she said to me, "if you are going to stay here, you need to eat something and I promise you that it's going to be the best food you have ever tasted because I am the cook! After that, I will take you to meet the rest of the family, and then we will make a decision what we are going to do with you!"

"Where is your family?" I asked.

"Here on the farm," Fatima replied. "We all live here on the farm. I have a father and three brothers, two of whom are married and have children. My younger brother Haled is only seventeen and he chose to work in the factory instead of here with us on the farm. We have fields of bananas and avocados and a lot of chickens which supply us with eggs. All that gives us a nice income, thanks be to Allah!"

"Who is Allah?" I asked.

Fatima looked at me for a second and said, "Allah is God, and I hope you believe in God," she concluded clearly.

"You mean God like Yeshua....Jesus Christ?" I said.

"No! There is only one God!" Fatima said furiously. "And who in the world told you about Yeshua?!"

"I know Him and I talk to him every day," I said simply.

She glared at me for a second and then she burst out laughing. Between her laughs, she managed to ask me, "Did Yeshua talk back to you?"

"Not yet, but my friend the priest told me that one day He will pierce my heart with a secret message of love and hope and truth," I concluded in confidence.

"That is absurd,' Fatima said in a loud voice. "And you must stop talking about it!!! We the Arab Muslims believe that he was a good prophet, but that is all. If you say anything about him to a Jewish person, you will be in deep trouble! Don't even mention His name, and promise me you aren't going to say anything like that around my family, you promise?"

"Yes, I promise," I said, surprised and disturbed at the same time. "Fatima," I said cautiously, does your Allah speak to you?"

"Of course not! He is too important and too big to talk to little people! And now let's stop talking about this subject and let me prepare some food."

Many desperate thoughts ran through my head. I wondered if there was a possibility that her Allah was bigger than my God.

The food Fatima prepared was good indeed. We sat on the mattress that was on the floor. Fatima spread a white plastic cloth on the ground and set before us a big bowl of rice and another bowl with a colorful salad and a plate with big chunks of lamb. It was very tasty and I complimented her sincerely, time and time again, until she told me to shut up! And I did.

In a strange way I really felt comfortable and secure with her. She did not hide anything; she was easy and friendly. After supper, we washed the dishes, and I followed Fatima to the house nearby. She knocked on the door and a voice invited us in. The room looked the same as Fatima's room, naked walls and mattresses on the floor, but more people were participating in the supper, including children. Everyone looked at me at once, even the kids, and everyone was smiling. *What a smiling family!*

"This is Adel," Fatima introduced me, and once again, I was sorry I had lied about my name. "She will stay with us," she said and everyone said, "Ahalan usahlan," which means *welcome*. After they were done eating, Fatima introduced me to her father: "His name is Abu Hasan," she said, "and this is Hasan, the firstborn and my brother. That is why my father's name is Abu Hasan which means father of Hasan. (Of course, no man would dare to be called after his firstborn female, but this is a different story to come in the future.)

Somehow it was very natural to be in their house and to help Fatima with her chores. The family accepted me as their own, and I really liked the younger son Haled. Mornings were always full of chores. After breakfast, we would clean the house and the yard, feed the animals, and collect eggs, which we delivered to different customers. Fatima made me a long flowery dress that made me feel special and beautiful, even though my heart sang a different song. I knew that one day I would be recognized, and then the punishment would be more severe that I ever imagined.

Every evening before Fatima put her father to bed, she gave him his medications. "It's supposed to help him," she complained, "but it takes all of his energy instead and he barely can walk or talk. I don't give him these pills every night because they just may kill him one day, if I do as the doctor says! Let us clean out this medicine cabinet," Fatima said, handing to me a few bottles of medications.

"What is this?" I asked.

"Those are the sleeping pills; just put them in the garbage."

Today, as I look back, I see clearly how evil works: just one wrong thought, just one wrong step and evil will provide the rest. As I opened that door and let evil in, I declined the difference between wrong and right out of tremendous fear that I might fight this life and lose.

It was a very dark night as I walked to the garbage. My heart was pounding with fear, even though I knew that there were people all around. Why was I so afraid?

In my hand was the solution to life and death, and I knew what I was going to do in case I got caught. I will not let people punish me anymore! I will finish my life as Adel did with dignity! I will just take the pills and go to sleep and never wake up again. With this encouraging thought, I ran to Fatima's room where my private bag was and when I opened it, a bad odor hit me in the face: Oh my God, I am crazy!!!

I was disgusted; my bag was filled with spoiled food which I had been saving for an emergency. I cleaned the bag as fast as I could and put back all my precious possessions which included the clothes I was wearing the first day I had come here and a few books.

I took the pills out of the bottles and hid them in a bag and now more secure, I went back to help Fatima with her father. "What took you so long?" Fatima asked.

"Well, I remembered that I had some things in my bag that needed to be thrown out, so I took it to the garbage."

"Good girl," Fatima said, "I was wondering when you'd finally understand that there is plenty of food and you don't need to hide it, Urshula."

My heart skipped a beat when I heard my name. "When did you find out about my name?" I asked with surprise.

"Three weeks ago on the radio and on every station," Fatima said, smiling.

"Did they mention my Hebrew name?" I asked.

"Yes, they did," she said. "And what a beautiful name you have!"

"You must be angry with me," I said in a sorrowful manner.

"Not anymore," Fatima said.

The news somewhat made me happy, because it told me that there was someone actually looking for me. For a second I was hopeful: "Who are they?" I asked in anticipation. "Who is looking for me?"

"The police," Fatima said simply.

"Are you going to tell them?" I asked her with concern.

"Of course not! I would be in big trouble if they find out that I was hiding you here; we all can end up behind bars if the police find out, but let's hope not," Fatima said with a wide smile.

Sadly, I knew the reality and I began to understand the heavy weight of Fatima's sacrifice. They would have a lot of trouble because they were Arabs, which meant enemies of the state. In spite of what I would say for their defense, no one would ever consider it as the truth, so at that point I was thinking frantically, realizing at once all the tremendous danger which I had brought on this family! Nevertheless, how could little old me stand up to the authorities and outsmart them?

"Fatima," I said, "would you please call the police while I change my clothes and please tell them that I just arrived in here seeking shelter.

"No, I will not!" Fatima said loudly. "This is your home and we will protect you in any case." She did not have any idea how much her words touched me. "You are only thirteen years old," she said, "and you need to be protected."

I looked at Fatima and I knew that she was sincere. I couldn't be thankful enough for the three weeks I spent in their house. I learned that there are still good people in this world and I definitely wasn't going to hurt them.

"Fine!" I said to Fatima. "I will go to the street and wait until the police find me!" So after a long and persuading argument, we agreed what to say to the police. Then Fatima made the call.

In no time, the peaceful silence of the night was crushed by the loud sound of the sirens, and the little farm was surrounded by police cars and flashing lights.

A policeman approached me, staring deeply into my eyes, he asked: "How long have you been here?"

"Ten minutes or so," I lied, without blinking.

"Where have you been for three weeks?" he asked, getting even closer into my face.

"There." I pointed to the left side of the road.

"Are you sure you didn't spend all this time with these nice people?" the police officer insisted.

Staring back at him I said, as innocently as I could, "I just stopped here to ask for some food and they called you."

The police officer looked at me with a smirk on his face, saying, "You will tell us the truth, one way or another!"

"I will," I said, "but not now and not here. I am hungry and thirsty and I am tired. Just take me away."

"Just a moment," the police officer insisted. "What's your hurry? Just answer me, and we will be on the way out. Did you ever see these people before?"

"No, never," I said wearily.

"So why did you stop in an Arab home to ask for food?" he screamed into my face, which put me in defensive mode. Also, when I'm scared, I smile; this way the fear is not as severe as if I would cry.

"Are you stupid?" I heard him screaming in a distant echo. I just kept on smiling which irritated him even more. "Do you know what the Arabs do to children like you?"

Filled with sudden rage I said viciously, "No, I don't know what Arabs do, but I know what the Jewish people do to Christian children!"

"What?! What did you just say?" He was in shock, no doubt about it!

"Well," I said still smiling, "In Poland I was told time and time again that the Jewish people take Christian children, put them in a barrel full of nails, and let it roll until there is enough blood for the Jewish holidays."

The police officer was staring at me now with his mouth wide open. "I cannot believe what I just heard," the police officer said.

"Hey, come over here," he called to his fellow officers. "You have to hear this one!" He asked me to repeat the story which I refused to do.

"And why not?" he asked. I did not react because I was tired and close to a breaking point; the story that had shocked me so deeply in the past, accomplished a strong effect on the policeman as well. As I thought, they focused on me rather than Fatima and her family.

"Do you really believe that?" the police officer screamed into my ear.

"Believe what?" I asked.

"The barrel story!!" the policeman screamed.

"I don't know," I said. "Do you?" What was the difference between this story and the one he was ready to tell me about what the Arabs do to the children like me?

Without a goodbye, we left the little farm. I was thankful in my heart for the privilege to know these good people, and I knew that I would like to see them again in the future.

We arrived at the police station, and I was afraid that they would search my private bag and find the pills and all my treasures. I was glad that I took the pills from the bottles. This way if they found them, no one would be in danger.

"Sit here," the police officer pointed to a chair in front of him. "What do you have in the bag?" he asked me. Without hesitation, I handed him the bag, hoping that the unpleasant odor was still there and he would change his mind, and it worked! "You just tell me what you have there," he said.

"Just clothes and books," I said simply.

"Any food?" he asked.

"No, no food, it got bad, so I threw it away." He knew that I was telling the truth because of the bad odor that still occupied this precious bag.

"Now tell me, where have you been for the past three weeks?"

"Everywhere, I guess."

"And where is that?" he asked. To avoid further investigation, I asked to go to the bathroom, and I asked him if I could rest somewhere. "I will show you the bathroom and where you will spend the night, and I will talk to you in the morning."

"Am I going to a prison?" I asked.

"No, but a proper place will be found for you."

Who knows what a proper place is? Probably a place where no one wants you, or cares for you... In the bathroom I opened the bag, and without thinking, I started to swallow the pills with the water. I almost threw up a few times, but eventually it was done. Now I will sleep forever... no more pain or sadness... no more me.

Chapter 7

But...I woke up in a very strange place. Everything was white except the gray blanket on the bed. I tried to sit up, but I was very week and dizzy, and when I tried again, I realized that I was tied. My wrists were tied with belts. The little survival instinct that I still owned had completely vanished. A dog has more dignity, I thought with anger! I couldn't understand what had happened. I had all night to die, but apparently I didn't.

"What is her full name?" I heard a woman's voice beside the bed.

"Her full name is Urshula Marta Yona Leviniowska," the voice of a man answered. "Mark her as Yona Levi, and check to see if she is awake!"

"Oh, yes, Doctor," the man said, "She tried to sit up, but she gave up after realizing her condition."

Am I in a hospital? What kind of hospital would tie people to a bed?

"You can open your eyes now," I heard the woman say. "I am Doctor Halperin and I will try to help you." *Help me? Why? What is wrong with me?* Realizing at once a sharp pain in my throat, instinctively I tried to touch my neck, but the doctor said, "You will have a sore throat for a few days. We pumped your stomach for the pills you had taken. *What else did they wash? It seems like everything is hurting right now...*

"Do you need anything?" she asked me.

"Yes, I need my bag."

"No," she said coldly, "you cannot have your bag or anything personal for the next two weeks!"

"Why?" I asked.

"Because you just tried to kill yourself and now, you are under observation in the mental hospital."

"I am in a crazy hospital?"

"If you want to put it that way," she said.

I am in shock! My life is marked and finished! How can I be crazy? I am just 13 and a half. I do not have enough time to be crazy, but on the other hand, as the doctor said, I tried to kill myself. The word "kill" really disturbs me. I just thought that the world would be better without me... or me without the world.

I can't thank my God enough for saving me, time after time after time..... Only my Heavenly Father in His infinite wisdom and never ending love could bring every moment of every day with a new understanding into my heart.

In the mental hospital I wasn't tied to a bed anymore, but now it was even worse. After all the injections I received, I could hardly move or think, but after two weeks I started to wake up for longer periods of time. I got some clothes and I joined the apathy walk, along with other patients, through a long corridor of the hospital. At that point, they stopped the injections and I was given some kind of new medication in pills. Half an hour later, I was in horrifying pain; my tongue forced itself out of my mouth and I felt painful pressure in my ears.

I completely lost control over the muscles of my mouth and my tongue proceeded to force itself out; I felt that eventually it would be ripped off! I ran to the nurse with my tongue hanging out, but I just got brushed off with loud laughter. Not knowing what to do, I started to hit my head on the wall. That brought the doctor to the premises and she ordered an immediate injection which released me from this horrifying ordeal. I swore to myself, that from now on, if it was in my power, I would never take any medications!

As I sobered up, I realized that the youngest person in this hospital was probably around fifty years old, so it left me the only child in that "cozy" environment. Most of these people were still experiencing the horrors of the war and once again, I listened to their stories, realizing that their pain was justified and I had no excuse for mine. The visitation days were the worst of all; I felt anticipation in the air.

I watched through the bars of the window the happy reunions. Loneliness embraced me with all its power and hope stopped being relevant. In all my pain in the hospital, I tried not to shed a tear but instead I aimed my broken spirit against God, not realizing at that time that I wasn't really alone. If I had God to be angry with, I had also God to love, but unfortunately I wasn't gifted with His wisdom yet.

I watched the patients walk the corridors of the hospital with blank stares in their eyes, and as I watched them, great sorrow overwhelmed me because I recognized the imprisonment of medications which were cruelly forced on these vulnerable souls.

With many tricks, I succeeded in outsmarting the personnel of the hospital. All the medications that I was given ended up in the toilet. Some of the patients used to tell a story about a man that used to have unfortunate night accidents. He confided in his doctor who prescribed pills which would stop this inconvenience. A week or so later, the man came back to his doctor, hugging him and thanking him for these wonderful pills.

"Well, well," said the doctor, "apparently the pills stopped your accidents."

"Oh no," said the man, "I still have those, but now with these pills I don't care anymore."

I knew that I needed to escape this very dangerous situation, but in my first attempt, I was caught, and again I was tied to the hospital bed. On the same occasion, I was informed that my condition was worse, and I needed to receive a new treatment: six electroshocks!

The first time I received an electroshock, it was very scary. I was taken to a big room with machines and tied all over to a long table. There was nothing I could do except cry and beg, and I did it in such a loud manner that I ceased to hear my own voice.

Everyone in the room was cold and apathetic. They did their jobs in disturbing silence, like mannequins. A nurse approached me with a stick covered with gauze. "Open your mouth," she said. When I refused, she gave me one squeeze forcing the stick in and holding it there, in case I spit it out. At the same time, someone rubbed something on both sides of my head, while another person approached with two round things in his hands and I was struggling to scream. That was it!

I don't remember anything more, except waking up with a horrible headache and with deep fear mixed with inexplicable confusion. "How are you feeling?" I heard the doctor ask. But I just stared in the space of the room.

If I don't respond, they will leave me alone… At this point strange things appeared in my mind and I was struggling with myself not to face them. Deep in my heart of hearts, the horrifying past reappeared with all its visions, grabbing me treacherously and forcing me to face it.

"We have a nice teacher for you," Doctor Halperin interrupted my thoughts, "And when you complete the electroshock treatments, you will learn more Hebrew."

Yeah, sure, I thought, when you finish with me my ability to think or comprehend would be finished as well.

"Well, Yona," Doctor Halperin's voice interrupted my thoughts again, and I looked straight into her eyes with deep confusion and boiling anger. "Do you understand when I am talking to you?" she asked.

Do I? I smugly realized she had not even the slightest idea about my condition, still staring straight into her eyes. You will never know, Doctor, because my silence will be my shield.

"Yona, do you understand what I said?" She shook my shoulders slightly as I remained frozen in my persistent silence. I surveyed the room with my eyes while Doctor Halperin proceeded with her private interrogation. "I guess not," I heard the doctor say, more to herself than to me. She was puzzled and I understood that they really didn't know the effects of the electroshock, as it apparently varies from person to another.

Today I can see clearly the protection of the Lord. In His wisdom, He gave me enough wit to survive the encounter with evil. I did not comprehend my situation, but something deep in my soul kept on warning me, encouraging me to flee... but where? I have no place to go to and if I sleep on the streets, they will find me!

Currently as I look back, I know how vulnerable my situation was: if I died right there in the hospital, no one would care to ask where I was or even what had happened to me. As such, I was a great candidate for any medical experiment. I knew that I was eccentric and different but certainly not crazy! However, all that was done to me in the hospital, I just considered as another punishment that was overdue.

I received five more electroshocks and as a result, my recent memories were very blurred, compared to my early childhood memories, which were clear and very painful. To this day I have never shared them with anyone and the reasons are simple: *I understood and I forgave, and I let it go.*

I will always hold in my heart that painful discovery that shaped my personality directly by the hand of my Heavenly Father. When I learned to pity myself, I learned to pity others and I understood the generosity of genuine compassion. My heart started to open, and I was able to embrace myself with acceptance, at least for a while.

Silence was my new game for self-entertainment which would last just for a short while because my memories began to clear. I was scared and confused in that new predicament when the vicious memories engulfed me. The medications still found their way into the toilet, and I knew I must be extra cautious. I also observed different possibilities for escape: one of them was a fence in the hospital yard that I previously unraveled few times.
As a result of my carelessness, some of the patients escaped, and I was punished in the solitude of the hospital room. Surprisingly, I was ordered to read books that they so generously put in front of me, so I actually enjoyed those times of punishment, until the day I met Shoshana.

Chapter 8

Shoshana was a new patient and she was young! It seemed like she was very experienced in everything. She was twenty-five years old and very beautiful. She possessed a very attractive personality, and everyone appreciated her company, including the staff of the hospital. I tried to befriend her, but my efforts were rejected, until one day when Shoshana approached me and said, "You must tell your parents to take you home; otherwise, the hospital will destroy you."

"What do you mean?" I asked.

"I overheard your doctor talking about insulin treatment. You have been selected to receive it, and I suspect you are not a diabetic, are you?"

"No!" I said with surprise, "but why do they want to give me this treatment?"

"You are really naïve, aren't you?"

"Not really," I said, elevating my confidence, knowing Shoshana was about to tell me I was going to be a guinea pig.

"They are experimenting on you," she said, "and science has no conscience, so tell your parents what I just told you because no one will believe you or take you seriously. After all, we are in a crazy hospital."

"I have no one to tell," I said.

"Nonsense! Everyone has someone!"

"Yeah, I do have a younger brother, but he can't help me; he's still helping himself."

"Well," Shoshana said, "you must escape!"

"And then what?" I asked. "Where I would go?"

"You can come with me," Shoshana said surprisingly. I unraveled the fence and we were out.

We ran for a while through the streets of Jerusalem, and when we finally felt secure, we were on the Mount of Olives looking down on the old city of Jerusalem. I felt like my heart was bursting with joy and a stream of tears ran down my face.

"Are you going to be a crybaby?" Shoshana said.

"Oh no," I said, as clearly as I could, "can't you see, Shoshana? We are in Jerusalem and we are free!"

"What are you talking about?" Shoshana said. I gazed all around and my heart rejoiced, because at that special moment, I recognized the privilege of being in Jerusalem. "Hey, wake up," I heard Shoshana calling in the distance. "First you are crying, and now you are dreaming! Maybe it wasn't such a good idea to take you with me."

"Don't worry. I'm fine I just remembered what I was told in Poland about Jerusalem."

"So, what did the communists tell you?"

"It was the priest," I said defensively. "He told me about the Son of God walking here in Jerusalem."

"You are out of your mind!" Shoshana said laughing. "How anyone in his or her right mind can believe that God has a son! God is God and He is what is called holy, which means no sex! That is why we are praying to God to forgive us because we have sex and because we are polluting what He created."

Shoshana talked as if she knew what she was talking about and somehow she shook my confidence in God. *If I just shut up about God, life could be bearable…. Therefore, I dried my tears, and I dimmed the fire in my heart and I said goodbye to God and goodbye to Jesus.*

Did I really let it go? Not quite as I never let anything go completely. And the truth spoke for itself… I was selfish! And my selfishness made me ignorant, and in my ignorance, I wanted to taste the forbidden fruits of this life…and I did! And I did! With tears, and vengeance, with sorrow, and pain, and with never ending excuses, which were my biggest lies! Yet, I did not understand that there is no excuse against the truth of God…and there is not true wisdom or understanding without Him…. I was lost, sad, and lonely and I missed my Jesus horribly. I craved the times when my heart gazed upon Him with innocence and acceptance, but I lost this flavor of innocence through the process of the life I chose to live.

Today I forgive myself because He forgave me first. And LOVE, the healing ingredient? I did not find it here on earth until I found Him again.

Shoshana waved to a taxi, and when it stopped, she opened the door and sat beside the driver telling me to sit in the back.

"Tel-Aviv," she said to the driver, and when the driver started to activate the clock, she put her hand on his arm, smiling pleasantly: "There is no need for a clock…"

Oh my, oh my! She was too friendly to this driver and what would happen when he found out that we had no money?

Nevertheless, Shoshana did not worry a bit; she was laughing and talking to the driver, and he enjoyed her company totally. An hour or so later we were by the seashore. We stopped and Shoshana told me to stay in the car. "We are going to the shore," she said, "so don't you worry. I will be back."

But I was worried, and scared! She returned few minutes later, and our next stop was a nightclub.

"What are we doing here?" I asked with concern.

"We're going to eat something in here and watch a show and this nice gentleman is inviting us," Shoshana said.

"Oh yeah?" I said.

"Yeah," the driver said, pulling his chair close to mine, and with his offensive breath, he whispered into my ear: "We're going to have a great time."

I stood on my feet ready to run when Shoshana interfered, saying, "Cool it, she is just a kid!"

I sensed danger and I was scared. When I was offered a few drinks by Shoshana, I didn't refuse, and then everything around me started to lose its symmetrical shape. I woke up in a strange place with pain all over and I could hardly think. The last thing I could remember was the nightclub and the ugly driver with his suggestive remarks.

I wasn't naïve, but indeed, I was disturbingly stupid! Now, looking all around me I guessed I was in some sort of hotel. Suddenly like thunder, a thought hit me: I had been raped! At once, I uncovered myself searching for evidence of blood or broken bones or something!

"What are you doing? It's the middle of the night," Shoshana complained, half asleep.

"I am looking for blood!"

"What?"

"I am hurting all over, so I must have been raped!"

"Oh, shut up!" Shoshana said. "You are still dressed and no one has touched you!"

But still the sense of tragedy occupied my heart. Since then, I have learned to recognize the creative suffering of the Jewish nature. We are born like that! If we don't suffer, we will create something to suffer about, or for....just because! And of course, I can only speak for myself!

Oh God, I prayed, please forgive me for leaving Your presence. Please tell me who You are, so I can understand Your existence and mine. Are You really hiding behind the statues? How could I love You without love in my heart? Am I really so bad? Must all my desires be good and understood? Could You please just force me to do the right things? Oh, God, I don't know if I miss You or if I just seek the impossible. At times I know for sure of Your existence but immediately, dark clouds appear, erasing all hope, and once again, the sadness takes place and I'm lost and abandoned again. My heart cries in agony because I believed You hated me .....

I can't remember a night that I didn't call upon God, crying and begging, until I started to see myself through God's silence ..... Then the journey of destruction began again! First, I hated myself which was easy, knowing all the garbage in me, and then in fierce anger I announced: "I hate you, God"! Indeed, a deep darkness forced itself on me in the process to create my own destiny.

"I am going to be a prostitute like you," I said to Shoshana the next morning.

"I am not a prostitute; I am sick," Shoshana said.

"So go back to the hospital!" I said viciously, "and I will do what I want to do!"

Shoshana jumped from her chair in a fury and slapped me on the face. "Sit down," she whispered in rage, "and look at me! What do you see? A normal and attractive person? Beautiful and appealing to everyone? Well, little girl, that is a lie! I am miserable and cursed by my sickness because I am never satisfied! That is why I cannot be normal or beautiful, but you can! You are fourteen years old, and if you choose to be a prostitute, your life will end with your decision. You will sell your soul to the devil; your body will be a toy and you will be a joke. People will laugh in your face in disrespect! And condemnation will be your only friend, and when you finally realize the truth, it will be too late!"

It seemed that Shoshana told me all that in one breath, and now she was crying. I was deeply touched because it was the second time in my life that someone genuinely cared for me. First it was the priest and now it's Shoshana.

"I am sorry," I said sincerely. "I was angry with God, and somehow I thought if I sell myself, God would react, and He has!"

"Hasn't He?" Shoshana said.

After we left the hotel, we went to Shoshana's house. In my mind I saw her still living with her parents because of her disease. "How is it that you have your own house in your condition?" I asked.

"My condition?" Shoshana laughed. "When I take medications, I am fine, but then I can't deal with my apathy which is blocking my soul and my inspiration. My dear parents gave up on me because I'm no longer the cute reflection that used to dignify their boring life." Her eyes misted as she talked about her parents, and her pain had a fresh scent compared to mine. It is hard enough to be an orphan, but it is unspeakable to have parents that deny their own flesh and blood.

Shoshana opened the door to her house and darkness grabbed me by the throat. "Oh my God," I managed to say. "Why are the pictures so dark and scary?"

"These are the images that I fight, trying to erase them from my mind," she said sadly, "and basically that is how my disease looks. It's called schizophrenia and it expresses itself in many ways and it is different from one person to another."

"Are you in pain?" I asked.

"Like hell I am! But now sit down. I will draw you!"

"Oh no! I said, "don't even try! I don't want to look like your nightmares."

"Ha, Ha, Ha, very funny, just sit by the window."

So I did, and in no time I stared in amazement at my own image. "How did you do that?" I said.

"I don't know," Shoshana said. "I guess this is my talent. Do you like it?"

"I love it!" And I really did. Somehow, I looked beautiful in this black and white drawing. I put this portrait in my bag, with all the rest of my treasures that were forgotten anyway, but as long as I had the bag, I had it all.

As the evening approached, Shoshana informed me, with a smirk on her face, that she must take her medication which was in a different form than the doctor's prescription but very helpful: hashish.

"You think I am that stupid?" I said. "Hashish is a drug! Why do you do that?" I said in disappointment.

"You wouldn't understand, little girl," she said.

"Just try me," I challenged her.

"All right," Shoshana said, "come with me, and join the party." We were in the city called Jaffa which is by the seashore. Everything seemed festive and relaxed. Again I felt like I was betrayed by God. All the coffee shops were open, playing their ethnic music, and a thousand lights danced boastfully across the reflection of the water.

It could be me, sitting at the table with my family I thought to myself. I watched people walking on the sidewalk and they were happy and peaceful; some were holding hands, some were hugging and some kissing, but my heart was crying because I didn't remember the last time someone held me or hugged me.

Today as I look back, I can clearly see the dark cloud between me and God. Believing I was despised, I argued my case with God, and I begged to depart from this world as soon as right now. Anyone can endure pain and hunger in this world but it is nearly impossible to live without love. In order for me to survive, I transferred my needs by serving others, by loving them as much as I wished to be loved. When their satisfaction reflected back on me, I could breathe for a little while but the supply of oxygen was becoming depleted. I couldn't continue to lie to myself by giving to others what I didn't possess in the first place.

"Where are we going?" I asked Shoshana.

"To smoke hashish, of course," she said laughing.

"I am not going to do it," I said loudly.

"I did not offer it to you," Shoshana said.

"No, but you are taking me there!"

"Oh yes," she said, "and after that, I'm done with you, and you are on your own, little girl."

"Are you going to leave me?" I asked fearfully.

"I am not your mother!" Shoshana said in anger, "and I can't protect you from this world or from myself!" Once again, I felt like garbage that the world had spit out.

We arrived at Shoshana's destination. She banged on the door in a secretive manner, and few moments later the door was opened by an older man inviting us in. A strange smell welcomed us to a room full of smoke. Feelings of despair and fear began to crawl through the veins of my heart. As I looked around, I was lost in the fog of uncertainty.

I counted a few men sitting on the floor, smoking from a strange looking bottle with a long sniffing line and water on the bottom. "This is nargila," Shoshana told me. "Arabs like to smoke from that thing, but I like my hashish in the cigarette."

Who cares?

Shoshana smiled as she expressed her greetings to each and every man in the room. When no one bothered to respond, I felt foolishly safe.

We sat on the floor, and Shoshana was given a cigarette that was passed from one person to another around the room. After a while my head refused to stay on my shoulders, and I felt like I was nailed to the ground. I tried to stand up, but right then a man grabbed me and picked me up. I tried to kick and push. I even tried to bite him, but obviously, the man didn't care and I knew what was going to happen to me. After all, no one cared to say hi, so why should they see or understand anything? I decided to fight and this time I bit him exactly where my head was: close to his throat. The taste of his blood will be always a gruesome mark in my memory.

Following the bite, he threw me on the ground and I was paralyzed with fear. When he started to approach me with a threat, I opened my mouth and screamed with all the might that was within me and it was very loud! Suddenly, someone took my hand and dragged me out through the door.

"Relax," a man's voice said. "Come. You are not in danger. You can go now." Surprised and thankful from the new development, I start to walk into the night. The man stopped me, asking if I had any money.

"No," I shook my head.

"I can take you home if you like," he said.

   Home? Oh, how I craved in my heart for the warmth and security of a home.
Even though I did not trust this man, I did not trust myself either.
"My name is Arie," he said, "and if you don't want to go home for some reason, you can come home with me. I have six children and my wife needs help."

Chapter 9

A new chapter in my life opened. Arie introduced me to his wife, a small woman with dark hair and sharp eyes. Her name was Nurit, and of course, the names of the six children elude my mind. Nurit gave me instruction as to the work at her home which included cleaning and taking care of the kids twenty-four hours a day and seven days a week. I did it all while Nurit played cards with her friends.

The youngest child was two years old; he followed me everywhere I went. He cried and complained all the time. I had no clue what he wanted or what to do for him. I found some chocolate spread in the fridge, and every time he was crying, I gave him a spoonful of it. After a while, I adapted to his constant presence, but mostly to the fact that he needed me. At the same time strange new feelings took residence in the depth of my heart as I started to develop warm feelings for this small human. His tiny hand held desperately to my dress, and we became inseparable. The work at that house was hard enough, not to mention this small creature desperately clinging to me.

Today nothing seems strange or unusual because I see the plan of my Heavenly Father that showed me how to appreciate hard work and how to be thankful for the moments of rest. God also showed me the importance of selfless love and the understanding of sacrifice. Therefore, all the rejections in my life that I crowned in tears and protested against in rage reflected back on me.

Because I was the one that rejected the Lord, I was the one that chose to do everything against His will. Therefore, I had no excuses, not even one, because I was born with the knowledge of right and wrong and I was the one that refused God's love. The burden of my wounded soul distracted me from the truth of my Lord. In my weakness, the lies of the enemy overshadow the victory of the Light. I was in constant war, which I always stood to win, even though I had no tools and never had read God's Masterpiece. Yes, I stood to win because He chose me first and before I accepted His invitation.

So when the dark shadows of my past are taking possession of my life, I will remember the free gift and the power of the Holy

Spirit and the power of His Name. Blessedly, my spirit runs daily to the walls of perplexity, calling God's name with gratification. Oh, my God and Savior, my soul cries each day. Please make me strong at Your side, so I can see with Your wisdom and serve You with gladness.

Please let me be the instrument of Your will, completely cleansed from this world and from my will, so Your light will shine as a precious jewel in the depth of my heart forever. And please, My Lord, burn the memories of my past and put a wall of iron between me and the enemy. I found great hope and peace in your Word, my Lord, and as You removed the veil from my eyes, I could take the first step toward the truth because You unlocked the doors of my prison and I pray that I can gratefully honor You with the future.

Now let's come back to my testimony. Taking care of the house and the kids, Nurit occasionally approached me with the same questions time and time again: How did I meet her husband, did he touch me in any way, and did I like him. Frankly, at that point, I was tired of her suspicions and even more so from repeating her husband's version of how I was found desperate and crying on the street in the middle of the night and horribly terrified to be taken back to the mental hospital.

Well, I always knew that the smiling face of the serpent didn't deceive anyone as long as we see it as such, and Nurit didn't deceive me by her paradoxical personality. I was on guard and more vulnerable then ever as she promised to protect me, if I did all I was told to do!

All the physical work at home, including the kids, left me completely exhausted, and in my emotional state, I was broken. I did not dream anymore, and hope for a better tomorrow ceased to exist. By that time, I already realized that I was not born for a good fortune, but for the worst of it and even my tears lost their salty taste, but were sweet as honey in their comfort. My emotional pain accelerated vividly, and the essence of life began to vanish.

One day, as I cleaned the stairs by the apartment, a woman that lived next door greeted me with a smile: "You are working too hard for your age," she said. "What is your name?"

"Yona," I replied.

"I am Lora," she said warmly, and I liked her on the spot! "I have a daughter your age," she said. "Her name is Sara. Have you met her?"

"I don't think so," I said.

"Are you related to Nurit?" she inquired.

"No, I'm not. I'm just working here."

"And where are your parents?" she insisted.

"They died long ago in Poland."

"How long ago?" she asked.

"About five years ago," I said.

"Oh, you poor thing," she said, "all alone in the world!"

Wow... I was surprised! She is actually sorry for me, I thought, with a pinch of satisfaction. This woman must know pain, I concluded to myself.

"Listen," she said, "if you need anything, don't hesitate to come over, okay?"

"Okay," I promised with renewed hope.

Since this introduction, we had more and frequent discourse; therefore, Miss Lora knew everything already about my short life, and she gently encouraged me to come and live in her house.

Nurit was impossible; she hated me with a passion and didn't bother to hide it. I was her slave and she knew very well that I would do anything to not have to go back to the hospital; therefore, I couldn't entertain a thought of a better life. As for her friends, they were jealous because Nurit had such a good trained puppet. I could rest only when her husband came home; then, I was ordered to disappear and to go to sleep with the children.

One day Nurit and her husband took all the children shopping. "We would like to take you with us," Nurit said, "but as you see, there is not enough space in the car."

"It's okay," I said, relieved, because a moment later, I knocked on the neighbor's door, ready for a transformation.

Miss Lora opened the door, "Come in, come in," she said with a genuine smile. "Come in and meet my husband."

"Pleased to meet you, Yona," he said. "I'm Israel." He was tall and handsome for an old man, I thought. "Lora mentioned to me how hard you are working, and frankly, I was furious because I am a God-fearing man! And if I remember correctly, it is written in the Torah: "Anyone that saves one soul of Israel, it is as if he saved the whole Israel." *Hmm, I thought to myself this man really likes his name... Israel here.... Israel there... Israel is everywhere!*

"We have a daughter your age," he said. "She is visiting family at this time, but if you move in with us, you two will be friends in no time. You will be a part of our family."

"Do you have anything in Nurit's house?" Miss Lora asked, as I was still trying to recover from their gracious willingness.

"No," I answered, "just the things that she gave me to wear."

"Okay, then," Miss Lora said, "just leave them there."

A few hours later, I couldn't ignore the sharp echoes of noises as the children returned. I heard them calling for me, and I almost ran to do my work, but Miss Lora stopped me. "Just ignore it," she said. "They have a mother and it is about time she acts like one."

As my heart pounded in all its strength, I hardly could rest between my breaths. I almost fell to the floor at the sound of the doorbell.

Miss Lora opened the door as the accusing voice of Nurit reached me. "Can you believe it?" Nurit said furiously. "I opened my house to this little tramp and she left us! I will call the police and they will find her and put her back to where she came from!"

"And where is that?" Miss Lora asked.

"Well, she escaped from a mental hospital!" Nurit said victoriously.

"So you are saying she is crazy?" Miss Lora asked.

"She must be if she was there!" Nurit concluded.

"I personally don't think so," Miss Lora said. "But it is disturbing that you believe Yona is incapable, and you still allow her to be around your kids!"

"Never mind!" Nurit said. "I am calling the police, so this little tramp will know that there is no person born yet that can stab me in the back!" And indeed, she kept her word.

A few hours later, two policemen and three hospital personnel came to claim me, and there are no words to describe the mental anguish and the tremendous pain I experienced at those moments, as I gazed into my future, foreseeing the rest of my life in the hospital. I was paralyzed with uncertainty and knowing the sad reality that even God would not stand for me or protect me. In spite of pain and fear and all the doubts, God still was my only hope: "Pray Urshula, pray," I heard my mother's voice, and I sobbed for me and for her and for all the things I did not understand. I prayed, fighting the flame of anger that consumed me.

Oh God my Father, I cried. Remember me in Your protection, and see the pit of darkness that awaits me. Am I so bad in Your sight? Am I worthless to survive at your side? Are your heavens garnished with my sorrows and pain? Would You listen just once, and would You care? I prayed in such intensity that the painful pressure began to affect my stability.

"No! Please, no!" I cried at the sight of the officer reaching for my arm. I dropped in fear to my knees, holding desperately to Miss Lora's ankle. With tears and sobs, I kissed her feet, begging intensely for mercy. "Please don't let them take me... please..."

"Stand on your feet," Miss Lora said, wiping a stream of her own tears and scolding me loudly to never again put myself in as humiliating a position as that. "Don't worry any more, child. You are staying here!" she concluded.

"You cannot do that!" the police officer said. "We have official papers that allow us to take her away, and you cannot object because you are not related to her."

"Very well then," Miss Lora said, "You bring me signed documentation from her relatives that she is indeed mentally disabled, and that they gave her away for experimentation, and I will let her go!"

"Well, ma'am," the officer hesitated, "we don't have any family member registered here, but we must follow this order and she must come with us."

"Oh no! No!" Miss Lora said loudly, "This child is staying here! And at this moment I declare myself as her mother, and as such, I have all the rights until you prove otherwise!"

"We need to see proof," the officer said with evil satisfaction.

"And I need to see proof that her parents gave her away!" Miss Lora burst out victoriously.

"Ma'am, as far as I know," the officer said, "she has no one."

"She has me now," Miss Lora said, picking up the phone.

"What are you doing?" the officer inquired.

"I am calling the newspaper," Miss Lora said calmly. "If you can't help us, they will, and believe me, officer, the whole of Israel will read about the brutality to this orphan. It is unheard of!" Miss Lora shouted the last segment in the officer's face.

"Ma'am, please put the receiver down. I will talk to my superiors to find out how I can help. After all, I am a father too, and with a daughter as well. I am not without heart."

Miss Lora said nothing; she just held my hand in a comforting manner, and I knew in my heart, at that moment, I was in the midst of a supernatural intervention.

Thank you, my Lord, for saving me and comforting me once again. And to my relief, after a few phone calls, the officer did agree to leave me with Miss Lora, in addition to a few instructions.

I knew that Miss Lora gambled; I didn't know her plan, but somehow she had one indeed! As the officer left, she called her brother-in-law who was a big shot in the police department. She explained the situation, and he guided her through the legal proceedings in which Miss Lora became my foster parent. I was approaching fifteen, and I had been almost a year at Nurit's house.

I loved to be at Miss Lora's house, even after I met her daughter Sara who decided to be rude to me from the first time we met. She was a tall, beautiful girl with curly black hair and dark eyes. Her skin was darker than most Turkish immigrants, but I really loved the beauty of it. Contrary to her image, Sara was vicious in her nature.

"Don't you expect me to be her sister or her friend," she said to her father when he introduced us. "I do have friends and I don't need a sister!"

We became friends, sort of, as I did all her chores, and she took me along with her to a disco. It was then that the boys discovered me. Oh boy!

Miss Lora explained to me what the boys really wanted. She told me that, if I am looking for a good loving relationship, I must not comply with their requests. That was a very difficult goal because every boy that I went with wanted to kiss me, and according to Miss Lora, it was the first sign of disrespect because a boy won't kiss a girl on the first date, otherwise!

So I was searching for this boy with the gift of respect, and in the process, I dated someone different every day. On the other hand, I desperately wanted to be kissed, but I was afraid that Miss Lora would find out and I would be on the streets again.

Sara was mad with me most of the time, but when her boyfriend paid attention to me, she was infuriated. As we came home one night, she screamed at me, calling me horrible names, and she told me to leave her house and go to hell.

As I was sobbing on the way out, Sara's father woke up.

"Get the hell out of my house," Sara screamed. "Get out! Get out!"

"What is going on?" Mr. Israel demanded softly, but angrily.

"She wants to take my boyfriend from me!" Sara screamed.

Mr. Israel was silent for a long minute, and then he said calmly, "If your boyfriend prefers Yona, he is not really your boyfriend, don't you think so?"

"No, no!" Sara said. "He is my boyfriend and he loves me, but he is always so nice to her because she is always smiling at him!"

"Sara, you know Yona is always nice to everybody! Yona is always smiling and you can learn a lot from her."

"Like what?" Sara shouted back at her father.

"Like to be grateful and not complain so much."

"Yeah, yeah, poor little nice Yona," Sara screamed, throwing this punch of sarcasm strait into my face. "Dad, I bet you that the reason she is being so nice is because she is hiding something! No normal person is so nice all the time! And we all know why she is so nice. She is crazy!!! Don't you see it, Dad? That is why I want her out, Dad! I want her out now!!!"

"Sara!" Mr. Israel said loudly, "Go to your room and pack some of your belongings because you are the one to be leaving!"

"What?" Sara was dumbfounded, "I am your daughter not her!"

"Yes, indeed," Mr. Israel said, "but right now, I am deeply ashamed of you, Sara. How could you be so cruel and selfish! I want you to leave first thing in the morning, and please do not come back before you reconsider your character."

"Please, Mr. Israel," I said, "please don't send her away. I will go; this is her house, not mine."

"Child, this is your house as I decide, and you have no one to go to. Sara has a lot of family to go to."

I left in the midst of the night. I didn't want to be the reason for this family dispute. I was too exhausted to fight the rules of life, so I went to a police station and gave them the name of my social worker who came to collect me in the morning.

"Why did you leave those nice people?" she asked me.

"I do not want to talk about it," I replied.

"Very well then," she said, "you need to know that I have no other family available for you, so at this time, I will take you to a private school which thankfully has agreed to accept you. You must behave not to disappoint me or yourself."

Yeah, sure!!!! Like you really care, I thought in disrespect. Though the thoughts ran wild in my mind, I was still comforted by the fact that I didn't have to go back to the mental hospital.

The school was almost like a big village. I got a room with two more girls; Shula and Pnina were their names. In a short time, Pnina and I were the best of friends, and we are, even to this day. Instead of learning, however, we participated in many pranks, and because of that and our wild behavior, no one wanted to be in our company. This included Shula, the other girl in the room who asked to be transferred elsewhere.

The girls in this private school were from distinguished families; some of them had parents in the government and we were nothing compared to them. As the holidays approached, everyone was leaving to go home to their families, and Pnina invited me to hers. Pnina had lost her mother when she was seven years old; she had a father and two brothers. She was the only one that invited me to spend the holidays with her small family. That visit was not warm or inviting, by any means. We learned to support each other by surviving any hostile environments.

My curiosity for learning challenged me to stare in the face of inescapable reality. The things I yearned to understand were an unsolvable mystery. There was no place for me to go, or a person to confide in, except the silent hope wrapped in secrecy. I studied books, desperately and intently, in any subject and in all matters because books I understood. They were my simple answer, because the teachers' presentations in class were empty of all meaning, leading me to deep contempt and ultimate disregard for myself.

Today, as I am writing, I have a strong urge to address every word with a visual effect of the event. However, this urge is selfish, as I am led by the Holy Spirit, and acknowledging my lack of education, I do give all the recognition to my Lord and Savior. So, wherever I sway on the wave of the Spirit, I do recognize the necessity of the pain and trials.

Chapter 10

School became my enemy as I couldn't break through the thick fog of understanding. So once again, I escaped, going right back to the Turkish family which welcomed me with open arms.

I was so happy with their welcome that I forgot that my reappearance could create problems. They understood and reassured me that everything was going to be just fine. They called the social worker, and when she came over, I knew she was very upset and ready to take me to hell!

"We are so sorry for disturbing you so late," Miss Lora said, "but we are ready to take full responsibility for Yona and take her out of your hands."

"It won't be necessary," the social worker replied. "Yona has mental problems which must be addressed, otherwise, she will continue to escape without any cause or reason."

"I have my reasons," I said defensively.

"Don't you worry, Yona, all your reasons will be considered."

"That's right!" I exploded with rage and tears. "I will be a guinea pig like I was before and you know it!!!"

"Don't be ridiculous, Yona; you know that is a figment of your unusual imagination. It just proves that you need urgent help." I was beside myself, powerless and completely lonely.

"Don't you worry, Yona," Miss Lora said, "we will visit you and try to take custody of you, so you can come back to us. Just don't you worry."

I was taken to a private hospital, and without seeing a doctor, I was given injections that put me to sleep. When I woke up, I found out it was like a new world. Once again I was in pain all over and I could hardly stand on my feet. Some of the pain was familiar to me; it was from injections administered incorrectly into the muscle.

What have they done to me? I thought in desperation. Somehow I found the way out into a small garden, and to my surprise, the garden was fenceless! Anyone can escape, I thought to myself, but as I looked closely at the few people sitting around, I realized in fear that they looked more like dead corpses than people who would try to escape. Oh my God! I probably look like

them... I felt horrible, my head felt heavy and I was sick to my
stomach, and as I gazed on the front of my hospital dress, it was all
wet. I touched it and it felt sticky, so I peeked inside the dress and
there was a white liquid coming out of my breast. Oh my God, oh
my God... I panicked. What is happening? What have they done to
me???

At that point, I was struggling to stand up, and I needed desperately to go to someone for help and answers. I saw a nurse coming toward me. "Here you are," she said. "I have pills for you."

O yeah, I thought, just more poison! Instead I said pleasantly, "Thank you," pretending to swallow the pills.

"Open your mouth," the nurse asked, and I opened wide for her to check, "Good girl," she said, and as she turned away, I spit the pills into my hand. I had learned in the other hospital how to hide the pills in my mouth.

As I stood on my feet, I could hardly make it toward the nurse's desk. "Could I talk to the doctor?" I whispered to the nurse.

"And what is the matter?" she asked.

"I have milk coming out of my breast and a lot of it," I said, trying not to show how terrified I was.

She gazed at me suspiciously for a moment and then, disregarding the problem, she sent me away.

Then I saw a man in a white robe, so I approached him, "Are you the doctor?"

"Yes, I am, and you are...?"

"Yona," I said simply.

"So, Yona, how can I help?"

"I have milk coming out of my breast," I said.

"Oh, I see," he said without any concern, and as he gazed at me with his cold eyes, he said that I must be pregnant.

"I am not!" I almost screamed. "I cannot be; I never have been with anyone."

"Oh, come on, don't you lie to me. I am a doctor and I know these things." Well, he did not know and at this moment I had the urge to escape.

I was very weak, but slowly I was coming back to myself throwing away the medication I was given. I knew that there were many drugs in my system because I was weak and my body was shaking all over.

One day, when sitting outside enjoying the sunshine, I suddenly felt a horrible itch and burning all over. I started to itch everywhere and big, ugly, red spots appeared on my arms, and the burning sensation was overwhelming. I was careful not to show any panic, so they wouldn't give me any injections. I approached the nurse and I showed her the ugly spots. "They itch very badly," I said.

"Of course," she replied, "You shouldn't be in the sun with the medication you take!"

I take???? You stupid cow! I thought in deep anger I don't take medication. You inject them into me!!!

Thankfully, I was led supernaturally to behave and to be polite for my own safety. I did remember some time ago, another hospital but the same situation, and thanks be to God as He led me through that unspeakable ordeal, then and now. For clarity of things, the symptoms I experienced were the direct result of the new medications administered to me: first, there was Largectil meds and then, Torazin, which made me painfully weak to proceed but I was not discouraged. I talked to God because He was the only one approachable. I did not know God, so He was created in my mind, according to my needs, but regardless, He still was with me, yesterday, today and forever and in spite of my ignorance.

One more month passed, until I was able to think clearly for a longer periods. Physically, I was stronger, but I dragged myself through the corridors of the hospital, like other patients, pretending to be drugged and stupid. Sometimes, as I walked, I cried quietly because I needed to release all the baggage of unspeakable pain. As I cried, all of me was crying: my soul, my spirit, my heart. All this pain came out in silence.

My head nearly exploded as I kept my crying under control, but my whole being screamed to God, Who am I, Lord? Will You protect me? Will You hold my hand with love and acceptance? Will You wipe my tears? I am so lonely and so lost ... who am I, Lord?

When I realized the time and the year, I had lost almost a year. It was the month of June 1967 and I was approaching age 17. (The times are still confusing to me and so are some of the names.) It was painful to acknowledge the emptiness and the loss of so much time. I did not remember much and I was furious, but more than that, I was afraid because I could be so easily overpowered, and there was no person in this whole world that cared if I died or lived. To add to all the implications, I wasn't sure if I wanted to fight for myself.

I knew that I shouldn't feel as I felt and I was so afraid that the damage would be irreversible. I was almost in panic, barely able to breathe, when the anger stepped in. With that new energy, I was ready to leave right then.

Suddenly, I overheard from the nurses station that Israel was going to war with most of the Arab countries. The radio in the nurses' station was on full volume, and the reports indicated that there would be hundreds of Arabs solders against one Israeli solder!!!

"We need a miracle," the rabbi said on the radio. "God gave the land to the Jewish people, and He will sustain us as He did before."

"Those are nonsense words, Rabbi," the host of the radio shouted in fury. "Where is this God that allows children to die? Where is this God that prevented us from living in peace? Where was this God of yours when six million Jewish people were tortured and murdered?"

"He was always with us," the rabbi replied calmly, "and His presence honoring us in the heart of our existence, but only in our willingness to open our hearts can we understand the purity of a genuine love."

As the rabbi continued, I was puzzled, "Did we always know our earthly parents?" the rabbi continued. "Did we always agree with what they said? Did we reject the punishment and restrictions? Did we never resist or hate their corrections, just to find out that we take the same measures with our own children? So if we can't understand these earthly discomforts, how can we comprehend our Father in heaven?"

Very smart, Rabbi, I thought with amusement. Yeah, like all his words were going to mean something to anyone… I thought…I was wrong, because I did remember what he said and was haunted by it. I tried to calculate the simple logic of his wise comments. Nevertheless, I was concerned more about the multitude of Arabs killing us. How could something like that be possible, I thought: hundreds of Arabs against one Israeli? Well, I will die; we are all going to die.

God doesn't do miracles, not the God I created in my mind. Then a brilliant thought hit me; my God was weak because I was weak! To be precise: I could not see God beyond my negative experiences. At that point, I was afraid to hope, even though the light still shone in the depth of my soul. As I dared to hope, I saw Him, the God that is able to do anything, and everything, and not the God of convenience that I sheltered with decreased abilities, which justified my disabilities.

Suddenly the space all around filled with a noise of alarms. The voices in the radio almost screamed: "We are under attack! The Egyptian airplanes are bombing the city of Natania!"

Suddenly I remembered that this hospital is in the city of Natania. The nurses hurried to take the patients down to the basement. They pushed us to different rooms, latching us in. As I looked around, I saw an old man sitting in the corner of the room by a toilet. When our eyes met, he shushed me putting his finger to his mouth, showing me a little radio transistor. They put me with a man, I thought, puzzled, but I wasn't scared a bit because tremendous peace surrounded this old man.

"Come, come sit beside me, girl. It has been a long time since I had company."

"How come there are patients down here?" I commented.

He smiled as he whispered, "Secrets, secrets, little dear. Don't you have some of your own?"

"There is an awful odor in here. How can you stand it?" I said, changing the subject.

"Oh yes, indeed, it is awful and even after so long, I am not used to it. I clean it as much as I can when I get toothpaste. Some of it I use it to clean around and some I put in my nose against the odor. When they give me soap, I save it religiously for my private hygiene, thanks to a few humanitarian nurses that remember the lost puppies here in the basement."

"Do you have any family?" I inquired.

"Yes, yes, I do have family, and a very loving family that unfortunately sold me cheap. They did not have to put me in here. All I possessed was theirs anyway. They did not want to wait, and now they are ashamed to redeem themselves or to redeem me."

"You do not sound crazy," I said.

"Hmm…" he laughed, "and you do know why, don't you?"

It is a trap, I thought! He may be a doctor or something, and now he probably discovered that I stopped taking my medication! Oh! I am so stupid! Why did I take my guard off?

"Don't you worry," he said, as my distress was apparently obvious. "You don't want to develop paranoia in this place," he humored me lightly.

Very funny, I thought and without a word I kept my guard this time.

"Come on," he said softly, "you can trust me. I am too old to hurt you, and unfortunately, we are in the same pit. I think you are smart enough to figure out the danger and avoid it.

He knows that for sure, I thought, and he was right when he suggested that I could develop paranoia.

"Hey little dear, do you want to listen to the news? War is on, remember?"

"Yeah," I said, "we are going to lose. The rabbi said on the radio that there are hundreds of Arabs against one Israeli solder."

"Well," the old man said, "It may be so, but naturally your perspective is too simple in calculation as is mine; on the other hand, there is a supernatural fact."

"I don't understand," I said.

"We are God's chosen people, little dear."

"You are joking!" I said. "No one loves Jewish people! We don't even like each other! And we are prejudiced against each other. The ones that came from Europe are in the government's highest positions and the leftovers are just that! They are called *Frank* [Black] and other degrading names."

"Hmm…it is a very sad truth," the old man said. "Nevertheless, we always did wrong in the eyes of the Lord, and we are paying penalties for that, through all the wars with the Arabs. However, prejudice exists in every culture and every human heart. How we deal with it is up to us. Simple self-respect teaches us compassion, understanding, and the ability to forgive; all of us possess tools for discovery, which are the talents within, but it is up to us to develop them in the progress of this life tasks.

"The right recognition is never self-seeking monuments. However, selfless sacrifice for others in sincerity and truth will appear as noble gestures and those indeed are the greatest blessings of all. Unfortunately, none of us seeks them; we must realize that the prejudice is an obvious form of ignorance which has been shackled to the internal fire of self-imprisonment. Did you understand all this, little dear?" he inquired of me.

"Yes," I lied as I had lied so many times before to myself in order to survive. At that moment, the door opened wide and two nurses came in.

"Are you still talking to yourself, Yona?" one of them asked, as the other nurse laughed.

"Yes, I am, ma'am," I said, smiling at the direction of the old man who smiled right back at me.

"What is so funny?" the nurse asked.

"Nothing, ma'am. I'm just gazing at the beautiful animals crawling on the walls."

"Oh, I see," the nurse said.

"Do you really?" I asked.

"Here, take your medications," the nurse said impatiently, ignoring my question but she could not resist saying, "Go ahead and continue the conversation with yourself, Yona."

After both of nurses left, I flushed the pills into the toilet. The old man decided to take a break from me and went back to the depth of my imagination where he was born. I realized I was not at all crazy, but I refused to be painfully lonely; therefore, I chose my friends carefully. Now, if you like to know if this old man was real, I will say, "Yes, indeed, he was," as I put him there! What else could I do in this unbearable reality, who else could I talk to, and how otherwise could I sustain God-given sanity?

The reality in the basement was chaos, with many disturbed people in very little space. They cried and screamed, and some messed up on the floor. The smell was overwhelming, because instead of keeping us in closed rooms, they decided to keep us all together.

I felt a sudden urgency to ask the nurse for toothpaste; I was surprised to get it. I put some in my nose, feeling immediate relief from all the smells, and in order to draw some attention to myself, I smeared some of the toothpaste on my face. This was a very bad idea because it dried fast and I ended up with irritated skin. I learned very quickly not to take advice from any imaginary friends.

By late afternoon, we were emotionally drained. Some sat on the floor in silence, others rocked back and forth in obvious distress, but most just tried to survive in this confused and disconnected world.

The constant war reports continued. As I searched these poor people's faces for a sign or hopeful expression, there was nothing, nothing at all. They did not understand what was happening, but when the nurses expressed their feelings by clapping or hugging each other, the patients did the same, and eventually even I joined the party. *Israel is winning! Israel is winning!*

Everybody was lively in the chaos of the basement, because in this glorious day, the missing piece of Jerusalem returned. The heart of Israel was restored and the land of my Lord was reborn.

The radio was on full volume as I listened to a sobbing solder reporting the latest victory: "We are at the Lions' Gate in the old city of Jerusalem," he said with a broken voice. "I am not a believer but now, at this moment and in this spot, I am on my knees and I know that He is with us, because I know…" He did not finish the sentence as his sobs deepened, and I cried with him feeling almost what he had seen and experienced.

Beyond the walls of pain and fear,
There is a promise that shines within.
Beyond the darkness of this world,
There is a promise that I can hold.
Beyond the knowledge and beyond my sense,
There is an answer in that empty space.

Drunk with a victorious spirit, I snuck out and walked into freedom. After hours of walking, I found myself in the heart of the city called Natania. The first light of early morning gently brushed the darkness away. Through the misty veil of the morning fog, a single sunbeam broke through, reflecting into the gloss of the roaring sea. I sat on the bench near the water, aching with fear and loneliness. Furious waves splashed frantically on the stones, leaving an angry residue of salty water on my face against the anguish of all sorrows and against my tears that refused to cease.

I need to be angry to survive, I thought with urgency. I don't need to be sad or discouraged. I escaped to my freedom to sustain it because enough was done to me, and enough was taken from me. Valuable time was stolen from me, and all vanished into the dark and brutal experiments! No one had the right to take it! And no one will ever again!!!!

My heart was beating faster with an encouraging energy and I was almost ready to fight for this life. Once again, I was not sure of my sanity. My feelings worked fine, but my memories refused to come to the surface. Perhaps my shield of protection was impenetrable. Still, inflamed with the new power, I decided to open the door into my past to face it and to conquer the difficulties of life.

Facing my past, I was stripped bit by bit from all pretentiousness, and once again I gazed into the ugly frame of my persecutors and I was lost in the storm of unexplained hate. I remembered the unsettling sadness in my mom's and dad's eyes, and for a single moment I had a silent wish: If only we weren't Jewish. At that second of realization, a deep compassion was added into my soul, and I wept for these two strangers that just happened to be my parents.

Love is the main necessity to mold an appealing character; it is a positive enforcer and living water of never ending promises. Love is the most mysterious riddle when no one can say I have much of it, or just a little. It is divine in structure that ultimately leads us to our Lord, but if the walls of understanding are hard to break through, it is because we had used self-sufficient constructors of lesser blessings. Therefore, we must seek Him that knows all and to surrender willingly to Him that created us from the dust of the earth. Then and only then, He in His Love will grant us to possess the genuine freedom in its supernatural state of comprehension.

I was almost seventeen and all alone in this world; therefore, bitterness and anger befriended me. Afraid and hopeless, I knew that a lack of education was my number one enemy, but I was highly blessed with a healthy curiosity that led me to be informed about the events of the world, as well as in many social matters. I always rejoiced in any opportunity to learn anything that would establish the necessity to belong to a higher social status.

Believing there was no other alternative, I turned once again to the Turkish family that opened their arms with acceptance.

Unfortunately, I learned the reason when the ugly truth surfaced. I was asked to find out how much money I would receive from the government, in accordance with a program for Jewish people that came from other countries. I found out that I would receive about three thousand dollars, and in addition, I would receive tax-free most of the home furnishings. Therefore, without hesitation, the Turkish family introduced me to a colorful bunch of bachelors that subjected me to recurring investigations about the stupid money! In spite of my love for these people, I learned that their preferences were much different from my simple needs, so once again I tasted the bitterness of rejection.

Chapter 11

As my vision of the world expanded, I knew that I must seek promising opportunities. I did not know how but I decided to take responsibility for my own life. I found me a boyfriend who was simple enough to complement my insecurities and my lack of knowledge. He was a carpenter and he was a hard-working person; his name was Shlomo. Sadly, in my confused mind, I did not yet grasp the meaning a of relationship; this was a new responsibility and I perceived it as a kind of game.

As I look back, I do not understand why I did the things that I did, but now I know I was in constant molding by the hand of God, because in reality, God indeed was the only parent I missed and was trying to find. However, my confusion was much too deep to grasp. I refused to check my heart out of fear that I would face the dark truth. I knew about love and feelings, but those were not mine because I was nobody, without family or parents or anyone to claim me as their own.

At times, I considered myself a survivor, because in my struggles, I always managed to find a bit of hope. I cared for people sincerely but never desperately, and sometimes I missed someone to care for me. All the books I read were a strong shield against reality. The movies I chose to see were full of drama and desperation that reflected my life experiences, but their positive endings always gave me false hope and peace for a better future. Well, just for a little while, until the next ordeal.

Reflecting back, I can see my struggle within, as I couldn't break through the shadows in my mind. I was terrified of my own thoughts, and I couldn't trust or give myself to anyone. It was always safe to cry for someone in the book or movie, but I rarely cried for myself. I knew I should not show any weakness in order to build effective power and significant character and *I had a few of those* ... as long as I was not myself.

I was the daughter of an American ambassador, and in different settings, I was the niece of an Israeli president, and sometimes I was the daughter of a heart surgeon. However, my lies were effective and I got a lot of attention and admiration, with one exception; my conscience always bothered me.

Shlomo was a good man in the beginning, but at the first disagreement, he told me I needed to be thankful that he married me because no one else would. "You know you are nobody," he said. "You don't even have a family tree, and who knows who your mother was!"

"Don't talk about my mom!" I said loudly. "I respect your family, and you will do the same!" I said in a threatening manner.

I was angry and tired of defending myself. Israel that promised me shelter forced me already to the highest level of hell. It was easy to blame Israel or different settings in my miserable life, so I did not have to take responsibility for my action.

"And you may not even be Jewish," I heard him saying in disgrace.

This remark brought me back to the time of our arrival to Israel and the kibbutz when they couldn't find all the documentation about my mother so we were instructed how to become legally a converted Jew. I did not like that, not after what we experienced in Poland, but we had to do what we had to do. My brother, on the other hand, received his papers plus his circumcision, and he legally became a Jew!

But as for me, I had to continue studying the Torah and memorizing what I was told, and every three months I came before three rabbis for a test which I constantly failed because they always found something that I did not know.

Eventually, at the age of eighteen, and with my own ammunition, I promised myself that this would be the last time I would stand before those hypocrites.

They entered the room with their black costumes that had intimidated me every time, but not that day. "Are you ready, Yona?" one of them asked me.

"Yes, I am," I said with rising confidence. It seemed like forever when I was answering their questions, without even one mistake!

"You did well," the rabbi said, "but we have just one more question that must be addressed."

I knew in that moment that they were fixing to fail me.

"I am ready," I said with a strong voice, as one of them presented the question.

"Which fish are we the Jewish people permitted to eat?"

"I do not know," I said. "I do not eat fish!"

"Well," the rabbi said, "We will see you in three months."

"Oh, you will NOT!" I said, raising my voice. I picked up a chair, and with all my strength, I threw it into the wall. "How dare you to tell me who I am or am not! Poland already told me! I was beaten and ridiculed because I am a Jew, a DIRTY JEW, and I never wanted to be Jewish anyway, and especially now! Both of my parents were in Auschwitz, and most of my family was murdered there!

"And you know what?!" I said, "My grandfather's beard was longer than yours!! And white as a bright light!! He was a Jew and he died because he was a Jew, and I have his blood! And my blood was shed on Poland's streets, on courtyards, on stairways, and in many dark corners, but mostly anywhere they could catch me!

"Me! 'The little defenseless dirty Jew!' So, you see, your piece of paper cannot change all that!"

At that point, two security men entered to remove me, and as I was ready to submit myself, one of the rabbis asked me, "Did you just say that both of your parents were in Auschwitz?"

"Yes, that's what I said, and you will find confirmation in the concentration camp's records."

"Wait, please," he said to the security man. "If your mom was in Auschwitz, she must have been Jewish because this was a death camp for the Jews. We will recheck the records, and for the time being, here are the papers that prove that you are born Jewish, and not a convert."

Who cares? I thought in anger, as I took the paper from his hand. But I could not let it go, and in anguish, I asked if I could say something, "Go ahead," they said in unison.

"Why is it," I said in irony, "that now, more than ever, I feel like a dirty Jew?" They just gazed at me without a word said.

My social worker waited for me. "Why are you crying?" she asked. "Did you fail again?"

"No, I did not fail this time, but they did and you did!" I said, in angry confrontation.

"I failed you?" She really seemed surprised.

"Yes, you did! At least in Poland I knew why I was hated, but what was your excuse? What was your reason to put me through hell? Why did you put me in the crazy hospitals? There were no children in there! I was the only child! Why would you do this?"

"I am truly sorry, Yona. I did not know."

"Yes, you did! You just did not care," I said with bitterness. With evil spiritedness, I added: "I wish that the money you got to care for kids like me you would spend for medications to relieve you just from half the pain you caused me!" It was a vindictive remark, and I felt a pinch of regret as I watched her surprised face but I did not apologize.

I was eighteen years old and legally free, so a new chapter in my life was in order.

Shlomo brought to the surface all the things I wanted to forget: he betrayed my trust in him, as he twisted the truth to form a weapon against me. "Look at yourself," he said. "You even don't look like a Jew!"

"You are right," I screamed. "I do not, but you do! As he raised his hand to hit me, I added in provocation, "And you're acting like one too!"

Shlomo did not hit me, but somehow I realized that that was just what I was asking for, but why? *Did I have to see myself through the eyes of my enemies? How can it be, I thought in perplexity, that there were moments in the argument that I wanted to be punished? Suddenly I knew: no one can hate me more than I hate myself already.*

Shlomo's family was rich in siblings which I found odd at that time. They often got together, even for the smallest events like to watch special programs on the television. Their origin was the mountains of Tripoli (near Iraq), but in Israel and among the Jewish people they were in the category of second class citizens, so, in my subconscious, I'd try to assure my European superiority because I needed to be something or someone and with a family tree of some kind.

My wedding was a big event, and in my non-existent maturity, I did not comprehend in depth the importance of it. I felt like a princess that was still searching for her prince. I wore a princess gown and a sparkling tiara on my head. I played along, pretending I was happy, pretending I was strong, and pretending I was loved.

I was smiling for everyone with a pain in my heart that tore me apart because I was different, because I didn't belong, and because I didn't have a home address. I was like a garbage dog that wiggled its tail to everyone and for no reason at all.

About two hundred people attended my wedding and 99 percent were from Shlomo's side of the family. I was kissed and hugged and told time and time again how beautiful I was, but in the depth of my soul, I'd ask myself repeatedly if seven heavens were nearly enough.

In the midst of all these enchanting moments, I recognized my brother in the crowd with his adoptive parents. Once again, the feelings of insignificance engulfed me against the cold blessings of his adoptive mother. It reminded me vividly that I was not adoptable. Her rejection was still alive in my whole being. "I hope for you a normal and productive life," she said with a handshake.

She thinks I am crazy, I screamed in my inner thoughts. She doesn't wish me a normal life. She is telling me that I'm worthless and crazy! I gazed at my brother who sat silently with a frozen smile glued on his face. Oh well, I thought, he is protecting whatever he thinks he has, and I do want him to be happy. I refused to confront my problems because I pretended to be someone else anyway.

I refused to exist in my reality and to see myself through some people's eyes. I knew what it meant to be chased and ridiculed and to be called stupid, so no wonder I was terrified to be myself.

After a few months of marriage, I walked out. The constant confusion and self-expectations overwhelmed me. I felt lost in the midst of life's whirlpool. I wanted to scream out to the echoing pain of my soul. I knew that something was wrong with me, the brutal time I spent in the mental hospitals left me scarred and in constant fear. The damage seemed irreversible. I felt like a caged animal. My thoughts reflected destructive images of myself as a sick shell of insignificance.

If I just had family, everything else would fall into its place. Disregard for myself implied disregard of God for me; therefore constantly I dug into my actions just to find a leading pointer of God's hate for me.

I tried to make peace with the Turkish family, but this time I had nothing to offer, so the good will was absent and so were the warm smiles. I was lonely and discouraged, so I decided to go into the army, but my childhood mental hospitalization did not escape them, and I was rejected. It was the last stroke that broke me mentally and then, suddenly, an unconventional organization surfaced, along with a new game and a new name.

They promised me that I would be educated, trained, and needed for the right situations. I was more than grateful and very happy. However, many things turned into a vicious encounter of twisted fate, and as a result, I was never the same. My heart froze in the face of all I experienced, and for a long time, I was cautious and suspicious of everyone that crossed my way. My journey to self-destruction had barely begun.

Chapter 12

I was in great physical shape as a result of many hours of
training, but mentally I was chained to a self-built prison with
voices running through my head: *You're not good... you will fail,
no one wants you, you are ugly, and you are stupid... You! You!
You are nobody!*

I was too submissive and I eagerly volunteered to please
everyone. In spite all of my weaknesses, I learned a lot but faced
nothing. The future was in the shadows and only half-truths
surfaced in my sick mind. The fear of insanity was burning me to
ashes, and reality did not belong to me anymore.

It was then that I was placed to work with Tommy Diablo
whose real name was Zwi Holtzer. He was a multi-talent trainer
and a professional manipulator; however, he was also a good
acrobat, and he trained me for his magic show with reptiles, doves
and dogs. He trained them and I performed with them; he trained
me, and I did better than the dogs. I was like a puppet in the devil's
den.

Tommy's house was right on the beach and it was my
temporary home as well. He was old enough to be my grandfather;
nevertheless, I became his lover, or perhaps I should say a pleaser,
because love had no part of this strange relationship.

Secretly, I gave my heart to a fellow colleague named
Moshe. We did our duties together, and for some reason, he called
me by the name Cloudy. Sadly, though, I was with Tommy, and he
knew how to use my insecurities. In moments of clarity, I hated my
actions with pain and regret, and I wished to tear my soul out.

Every night I ran to my special place on the seashore where
I found some freedom. It was also a place where I talked to God,
pleading with Him selfishly, *Please, God, if you are really up there
or anywhere, help me to die. I don't want to do what I am doing,
but I don't know how to say no, because of the fear of rejection or
even punishment. Oh God, please help me, lonely and abandoned,
I pleaded with someone or something that I did not know. Still, I
called Him God.*

*I created my god of convenience, a god that would meet my
needs, but he did not, and in his silence, I felt rejected time and
time again. However, in those lonely nights, something was*

changing in me, and as I began to recognize my handicapped personality, I cried until I dropped exhausted on the rocks of the seashore.

I loved the sounds of the sea and the splashing waves washing the rocks at my feet. At times I spent all night on the seashore. Opening my eyes to a colorful sunrise, I used to blink my eyes and gaze straight at the sun, and through my eyelashes I was able to see all the colors moving and blinking back in unison and in those small moments I was grateful for my life. I loved the clear air of the sea against the pollution of my soul. I loved the gentle caress of the wind and the powerful illustration of the waves. Most of all, I appreciated the depth of this incredible beauty, even though I did not know much about life, and most definitely, not about God, but in some awkward way my conscious always reminded me of His supernatural presence.

For three years I was in the service of my different personalities and in the service of Tommy Diablo. We traveled to many places in Europe and other continents, performing on stage. I loved to be on the stage because it allowed me to be someone I wasn't, and indeed I was someone else every night. I did three different performances every night, and for each performance, I was introduced by a different name and no one ever guessed that one person did the three different shows.

With different accessories, makeup and wigs, I found a shelter from myself, as I cheated the moments, believing that I was beautiful, strong, and self-confident. However, fractures of my past always broke through, forcing me to face the inescapable truth.

At times I remembered the teacher from the orphanage and her incredible courage. She taught me a lot in the middle of many nights, pointing out the importance of my capabilities and the acceptance of my Jewish heritage, so indeed there were moments that I dared to be the person that she taught me to be, with confidence, courage, and integrity.

I never felt comfortable with Tommy, and I despised the occasional duties that sent us overseas. After three long years, I was tired of everything, and I was at a breaking point. My weaknesses reflected back to my self-hated personality and my capabilities were frozen in the past realities. Nevertheless, God was watching over me. I wished painfully to be free, and I yearned to walk taller in the light of self-respect.

Tired of the falsehood in my life, a new power ignited in me, so I dared to stand taller and stronger to eliminate everything wrong in my life, especially Tommy. I believed that I was a small part of a big and illegal project that helped Israel against the regulations of the United Nations, which continually prevented Israel from defending herself. We were informed that, if we were caught, Israel would never acknowledge us. Our trainings were in accordance with our intellectual and psychological capabilities. We learned how to adapt to cultural differences and informatively benefit from it. The rest I will leave to your imagination because, sadly enough, all I had built in my mind shielded my reality.

I wish I could take you through the roads of my desperation, holding onto every drop of clear sanity. I wish I could show you all the dark places of fear and regret. I wish you could see the showers of pain and tears that burned all the parts of my soul. Dark and dreary was my world and only a single beam of light sustained me, as I allowed myself to remember Christ. If I had just known that He remembered me.

Every night after my performance, I watched a man performing with fire, and I just knew that I had to do that! I asked Tommy to show me how to work with fire, but he refused, pointing to a danger in the smallest mistake, and he said that my teeth would turn black. However, I was determined in my decision, believing this was my only way to freedom. At that time, we performed in the old city of Jerusalem in a prestigious club named Taverna. Many important people from the Arabic Palestinian society were among the guests, but when the show began, the club was filled with Israelis as well.

After the show, I approached the person that performed with fire: "I will reveal to you some of our magic secrets, if you will teach me all about the fire," I said, flirting a little.

He stared at me as if he was seeing me for the first time and then he laughed. "I will teach you anything you want," he said, between his ugly giggles, "if you sleep with me!"

Yuck! Blech! I was furious, forgetting that I had flirted with him first. Still, how dare he speak to me like that!

"Fine!" I said, not hiding my fury. "Your disrespect defeated you, and I am desperate enough to learn to eat fire on my own, so you can wipe that ugly smirk off your face because tomorrow I will be your replacement!"

"Help yourself, if you can! Ha, Ha," he laughed, as his challenge rang all over me. The same night, as he performed, I watched him closely, carefully remembering every detail.

The next step was to inform Tommy I was leaving him. At first he was in shock and then he burst into rage, almost reaching the point of madness. He called me all the nasty names he could think of, and for a moment, I feared that he would hurt me.

"Relax, Tommy!" I screamed. "I resigned from the organization, so there is no point or reason for me to stay with you."

Tommy was dumbfounded, "You did what?!"

"I resigned from the organization," I said calmly.

"What the hell are you talking about, Yona?!"

I laughed at his outburst, "It doesn't matter, Tommy, I'm not interrogating you, so it's needless to play this game, and as I said to our friends, 'I already forgot the past three years.'"
As I walked away, I heard him say: "You will be begging me to take you back."

Chapter 13

Finally I was in charge of my life; well, at least that's what I thought. The next day I started to practice the secrets of the fire; I did not know much, but I was determined to succeed. I did know that simple gasoline would produce an orange red-color in the fire, but the alcohol would create the illusion of blue, so I mixed the two. I practiced all afternoon. I was burned, scratched, and covered with black residue, but I got it! I was able to put the fire in my mouth on my arms, my belly, and my legs! The rest was not important because I did have a few acrobatic talents and I could dance and perform.

In the evening, before the club opened, I approached the owner who was an Arab Palestinian. "Hey, Yona," he greeted me pleasantly. "I heard that you left Tommy."

"Yes, I did," I said. I was still in a fog of disbelief but strong enough to shed the slavery shackles.

"Do you want to perform for us?" he asked.

"Maybe," I said.

"I will pay you well and even more than we paid you before."

At that point, I did not want him to know that I never received any money from Tommy, so instead I said, "Fine, I will work for you but with new terms."

"Whatever you want," he said.

"I'd like to dance with fire and each night I'd like you to pay me in cash."

The owner of the club smiled as he said sarcastically, "And what am I supposed to do with the other performer? People are mesmerized as they watch him."

"I know," I said, "but he is also performing with knives and reptiles, and you know that I will bring more customers that will appreciate your taste in quality."

At that time, and specifically at that club, there were not contracts to consider, so the owner of the club happily gave me the job.

The guy that I hurt purposely surprised me in my dressing room, and before I realized what was happening, there was a knife around my neck, and vicious words were spitting into my ear.

"I promise you," he said, "one way or another, you will pay for the nasty number you pulled on me!"

I was completely frozen. He was just slightly taller than myself, an ugly little creature that used to put small reptiles into his nose and take them out of his ears or his mouth, and against all odds, he was a big hit onstage.

He smelled so bad, I almost vomited and there was not a chance in hell that he would release me from his clutch. He did not know that my life was one big bleeding wound, and death was more welcome for me than this life.

So with strange courage, I challenged him to act. "Go ahead, you coward," I said. "Go ahead and slash my throat!"

At the same moment as I spoke, I moved my head backward, with all my strength, planning to hit him straight on his nose! Drops of red splashed all over my eyes like rain and I slid down into unconsciousness.

When I woke up in the hospital, I was told that I almost fractured my skull. The rain of red I saw was probably an illusion just before I passed out. Apparently, I hit an iron pole and not his nose. I do not know how it happened, but the ugly creature vanished, though, not before I experienced jumpy days and sleepless nights out of fear that he might return to claim his revenge.

I remember my past actions with deep regret and disrespect for myself, realizing most of the choices I made were out of self-hatred. The established personalities that I created as a shield were robbing me from the truth. I prayed to God to help me, so I could break through the walls of depression. I begged Him to surround me with His protective power, and I even dared to ask Him to be His beloved child. Somewhere in my soul I knew Him strongly and profoundly. I knew that He could heal me and save me and He could lead me to His victory. I knew for sure that only God could love me so completely.

Yes, indeed, I knew that He is and He was and He will always be, but who is He? I did not know. I buried myself so deep in the lie that I even forgot who I was.

*The children that chased me in Poland and called me a
dirty Jew were still very much alive. They followed me everywhere:
in my nightmares, in human interactions, and in the still of many
nights. I could hear them calling me and once again I am a little
girl trying to hide from the whole world. Get her! Get her! I can
still hear their victory cries, and I am out of breath running and
shivering with fear and despair. I am covering my head with my
hands, from the stones they are throwing at me. The sticky blood
runs through my fingers into my eyes, disabling my sight, and they
get me. They always get me in the end, until the next nightmare.
Then and today, I do feel weakness when I allow the past to step in
with that significant torture into my world.*

I got a different room in the same hotel where I had stayed
with Tommy, but this time I shared the room with a belly dancer
from Turkey. She was a very nice girl and I befriended her. She
had a purpose in her life, not like me who was living from day to
day, and pretending to be someone else.

The fire performance was a big success; I used some
improvisation for my new fire personality, and I was excited to
create my own choreography. The club was full every night, and I
was satisfied because I told myself that they came to see me. Other
club owners approached me to work for them, and I walked on
clouds. When my boss found out about it, he began to pay me
more, imploring me not to leave his club.

"Don't be ridiculous," I used to tell him, feeling good about
myself.

"What do you mean by that?" he asked me.

"Nothing, nothing at all," I used to answer.

"You aren't going to leave me, are you?"

*I must admit that I really liked his repeated concern, not
only because it made me feel like somebody important, but it was
another lie adopted by me to survive. The awareness of the truth
and the cloud of insecurity never left me, and I was aware that my
seductive costume and sensual performance were the reasons for
my success, not necessarily my talents. Even when the truth hit the
core of my soul, I continued lying to myself.*

The first show started at 5 p.m. and ended about 8 p.m.
followed by a dinner, and then another show began at midnight and
ended about 3 AM.

After work, the Turkish girl and I arrived at the hotel very tired. We had barely closed our eyes, when the Muslim caller came on all over Jerusalem, calling Muslims to pray. The speakers echoed all over, in the loudest sound.

"Stupid Muslims," I remarked in anger. "Why does everything in their world have to be so loud?"

"On the contrary," my new friend said, "the Jews are the ones that make all the chaos in the world!"

"Oh, really!?" I said, standing up, all energized and ready to fight. "Listen," I told her, "We the Jewish people are not bad; we are just misunderstood. If we are as you are implying, this horrible noise would have been cut off a long time ago! Anyway, this loud calling for a Muslim prayer has just one purpose: to intimidate all other religions here in Israel!"

"Not true," my friend commented, irritating me once more with her remarks.

"What do you mean, not true?"

"Well," she hesitated for a moment before she said what I already knew, "the whole world hates Jews!"

"That includes you!" I threw into her face.

"I am trying not to hate anyone," she said, "but you cannot ignore the history of all the horrible things that the Jews did."

"Name just one!" I challenged her.

"If I repeat, I am afraid that I will hurt you."

"Please, do not hesitate," I said in irony. "There is nothing you can add I have not heard before."

"So you must know all about your race," she whispered viciously under her nose.

"Yeah, I know what you know, but I also know the truth that not many want to hear. Are you a Muslim?" I asked her.

"Yes, I am," she said, "and I am proud of it too!"

"So you were born to Muslim parents, am I right?"

"Why do you ask that?" she said.

"Well, I do not see you practicing Islam. You're not praying, not covering, and you are a belly dancer, so which one of these are you most proud of?"

She was silent for a long moment and then she burst out: "I do not know what all this has to do with anything!"

I understood her with the fierce anger that I carried as a possession from Poland. "Listen to me," I said. "You were the one to open the subject of pride and destruction by the Jewish people, so please, name one Muslim person that contributed something to society and I will give you names of hundreds of Jews who did just that."

She stared at me for a while and then she said a name: "Inkoltum."

"The Arabic singer?" I asked.

"Yes!" She said in victory.

I realized that I could put her and her Islam as a mere shadow against the things that the Jewish people accomplished, not only for themselves, but mostly for others. However, I was silent because at that special moment something moved me..... Once again and only for a short second, I relaxed in the knowledge of God's presence. He was watching and guiding me always, but this time in a clear realization I knew that I needed much more to survive, I needed to know Him in order to understand His language.

"Yona," my Turkish friend called, "it is your turn to give me a name of a famous Jew." I saw anticipation and desperation in her eyes and I decided to be kind.

"You win," I said, "No one is good as Inkoltum."

"What?" she said suspiciously. "Are you mocking me?"

"No, I am not," I said, "I like you, so let us go to sleep, goodnight."

"Okay, goodnight," she said, and under her breath, she added, "I am still proud to be a Muslim."

I acknowledged many Jewish accomplishments, and I wanted to be proud of my people, but I could not because the words *Jew* and *Jewish* had scarred me and burned me; the wounds were tender to the touch. Nevertheless, my new Turkish friend adopted a new habit of pointing out my weaknesses, and in that, she challenged me. We argued almost daily. We never hated each other, but somehow it was an emotional necessity to elevate ourselves culturally and intellectually. I don't know about her, but her challenge did just that, and I started to see myself in lesser judgment.

I was free and no one was telling me what to do or how to do it. My performance on stage was always the pick of the show, and I did enjoy the attention, but the truth I possessed pierced my soul regrettably. My feelings were a crown of destruction that consumed me, gradually to the point of death, and I knew if I didn't face the past, I would have no future.

One night, as I performed, a man jumped on the stage to save me, "Don't burn your body!" he screamed. He took the burning skewer out of my hand and his sleeve was caught on fire. As I tried to help him, I was burned as well.

Later that evening, I realized something important: this man didn't scream, "Don't burn yourself!" He screamed, "Don't burn your body!" My body and I were completely two separate issues and I did not dare, in my mind, to put them together.

I used to get invitations and gifts all the time. I always returned them, as I knew better than to keep them, well, at least I thought that was better. The projectors flashed their lights very brightly at the time of the performance, so I was not able to see the faces of the crowd. Even so, I could not ignore the handsome policeman that sat close to the stage every night. Secretly, I wished that I was the reason. I was too shy to make the first move; however, destiny had already knocked on my door.

After my shows, in the early morning, a big Arab man approached me in an accusatory manner. "I was the one that honored you with flowers," he said, "and you refused my friendship attempts." I tried to explain that I refused everyone's gifts, but he dismissed my explanation.

He grabbed my arm, pulling me closer to his chest, and that got me mad! I was not afraid because my anger took over, and I had had it with this life. I picked up a heavy beer glass, and I hit him with all my might. I was so surprised when he dropped on the ground. First, I couldn't move, and then I start to laugh, and I couldn't stop laughing. I just laughed and laughed until I heard the club owner's voice.

"He is one of my best costumers," he said with deep disapproval. "What did you hit him for?"

"Maybe to protect myself," I told him in sarcasm.

"Well, I need to call the police and an ambulance, and don't expect me to stand by you."

Before I targeted him with a nasty insult, the handsome policeman splashed water on the face of the unconscious man who came to life at once. "Do you want to press charges against this young woman?" the handsome officer asked.

"Yes, I do," he said, sitting up.

Then something unreal happened; the police officer hit the man three times on the face, and then he asked again, "Would you like to press charges against this woman?"

"No… no, I don't think so."

"Do you know this woman?" the police officer continued with his persuasive interrogation.

"No, I never saw her before."

"Okay," the police officer concluded, "you are free to go." He helped him to stand up and even opened the door for him. Then he turned to me, "Come, I will buy you something to drink. You are still shaking."

"By the way," he said, "My name is Eli.

"…Yona," I said.

We continued to see each other every day, and I liked him!

Chapter 14

One late afternoon, as I got ready to go to the club, a familiar face appeared at the door. It was a moment of joy and surprise. "Get out of here," I teased him jokingly. It was Moshe, a good friend from days past. We had done many things together: a solid group of four men and three women in unconventional service. Moshe held a special place in my heart, as he constantly came to my rescue, and naturally, I had had a secret crush on him for a long time. Nevertheless, in order to conceal my weakness, I always maneuvered my actions, so he would not suspect my feelings for him.

"I am happy to see you, Cloudy," he smiled, as he pulled me into his arms. (Cloudy was his pet name for me.)

"What do you want, Moshe?" I asked.

"A big favor," he replied.

"Do the filthy jobs yourself," I said jokingly.

"I just did when I came to see you." He said it in such a low voice that I could hardly hear him. "Believe me, Cloudy, I didn't want to come here, but in this case you are already involved."

I was puzzled, "What do you mean?"

"It is about your boyfriend,

"Eli?" I said surprised.

"Not Eli...but Ali," Moshe said, "he is an Arab, Cloudy, and I am sorry to be the one to tell you that."

I stood still, and the world stood still. How is it possible? I thought I possessed the ability to recognize an Arab, even if he had blond hair and blue eyes. I could recognize a Jewish person as well, just by looking in their eyes, but this time someone actually fooled me and my self-ammunition did not work anymore.

"Are you okay, Cloudy?" Moshe asked in concern.

"I am fine; don't worry. I just remembered when you told me not to play with fire, guessing who is what, because Nazis used to target the Jewish people by pointing out different characteristics about them. I remember that, Moshe, because you made a good point of it and I was ashamed of myself."

"Oh, no, no," Moshe hurried to my defense. "You also said something at that time that was profoundly true as a response to my remark."

"Did I really? What did I say?"

"You said that the Nazis were in the bottom of human intelligence; therefore, you were not surprised that their power came out of united hate, and there is always power in unity, positive or negative. The Nazis lived by other people's accomplishments, so there was not a problem for them to recognize a Jewish person because we were, and are, a proud nation which is our number one disability, then and today.

"When Hitler came to power, most of the intellectuals and business owners were Jewish; therefore, their confidence reflected on their external image. They walked tall and spoke with authority, so it was easy to recognize them. The other kind of Jews were the religious ones that could be recognized by their traditional clothing. We the Jewish people carry a lot of pride, and that is the reason that the Nazis recognized us: our pride killed us and prosecuted us and made us blind! That is what you said to me. Do you remember now?"

"No, I said, "but it sounded good!"

"Moshe, what about Eli?" I asked in concern.

"His name is Ali, Ali Rabia," Moshe repeated calmly.

For a moment, I felt deep sadness, and I wondered when the anger would move in, so I could function and think. Somehow the negative emotion of anger always gave me a push of strength. Moshe opened his arms to comfort me, but I rejected his sympathy,

"Go to hell! I'm not doing any favors anymore. I resigned remember?"

He looked at me with understanding. "You don't have to," he said, "but at least read this file and think about it and I'll see you sometime tomorrow."

After Moshe left, I opened the file, and two pictures stared back at me: one of Ali and the other of his brother Muhammad. Apparently, there was some link between Muhammad and a terrorist organization. Ali was notified about the implications upon Muhammad's arrest, but the highlights of suspicion fell on Ali after he visited his brother.

The moment Ali entered his brother's cell, he had started to hit him, shouting in his face: "Who are the people you are involved with?! You must talk; otherwise, you will be in big trouble with me and with the police!" Muhammad was under his brother's interrogation for ten long minutes, but he said nothing. When Ali left the cell, Muhammad was obviously shaken up and bleeding. That scenario made Ali a suspect. In fact, a few Palestinians had already been arrested after applying for the Israeli police force, and Israeli intelligence discovered that the orders had come from terrorist organizations.

I must say Israel had gone out of the way to provide for the Palestinian Arabs. After the Six Day War, Israel connected them to water and electricity. Special Arabic speaking groups were formed to encourage women's education. Housing was given to widows and divorced women that lingered on the streets with their children. They got money every month for each child, plus they got food and health insurance and a lot of consideration. All of that was given free of charge.

Nevertheless, they hated us; the more we gave, the more they hated us. All our generosity was translated as weakness. Israel opened doors for citizenship, education, and progress, including various opportunities for work, but underneath all that good will, terror was formed. It silently crawled into the heart of Israel, spreading its venom sufficiently, and the world was deceived and robbed of the truth. Israel was despised on account of the so-called disadvantaged Palestinians.

It was at that time that Israel had not yet recovered from the miraculous victory of the Six Day War. This victory brought arrogance and self-sufficiency to the soul of Israel. At that time also, I was willing to give my life for my beloved Israel but looking back, I was willing to do almost anything for just one drop of love and acceptance.

When I found out about Ali's Arabic identity, I stood against a difficult situation. I knew that I had sufficient intelligence; after all, it was in use by experts. However, I myself did not know how to benefit from that because all my focus was on personalities I created to overcome the fear of myself. I recognized my weaknesses, but myself I did not know, not anymore.

I lied to myself, believing that Ali wanted to impress me, even when all my senses screamed otherwise. Paralyzed in the face of the truth, I forcefully held on to a false image of love. I sincerely believed that no one else would want me, as I did not want me. I was what I was: a cheap imitation of everything I wished to be, my self-image reflected clearly all the lies I lived by. I was fading away.

Ali? He pampered and complimented me constantly, and I was on Cloud *SEVENTY-SEVEN*. He was highly impressed when I read him my poems, and he listened intently. I conveniently translated his good manners into intelligence. He was still playing his game as a Jewish officer, and I tried very hard not to say a word, but it began to irritate me.

Moshe came back as promised, greeting me with a light kiss on the cheek, and without hesitation, he went right to the point. "Have you read the file?" he asked.

"Yes, I did, and I think Ali is hiding something."

"So you are going to help us?" He gazed at me like a puppy waiting for a treat."

"No, I do not trust myself to do the job objectively," I said.

"And why not?" Moshe asked.

"I happen to like Eli/Ali and I refuse to manipulate him!"

"Fine with me," Moshe said. "Leave manipulation out of the picture, but cut the truth out of him!"

"What will you do if I refuse?" I asked in confrontation.

"Would you really refuse me, Cloudy?"

"Yes, Moshe, I just did."

Moshe was dumbfounded. "What is wrong with you, Cloudy? You were always the first to help."

"I am weak, Moshe, and I lost my mental stability, you see?"

I started to blink my eyes as fast as I could, and I was hearing voices and echoes from the past... whooooo, whooo... And the current reality was killing the core of my reasoning.

"Are you on something?" Moshe asked me in concern.

"You tell me, Moshe. Am I? I cannot ignore, with jokes, the reality of my emotional state," I said. "I am confused and sad. I dreamed of finding shelter from my nightmares in Israel, but instead I found condemnation. I hoped to find my identity, but even that was in question. So tell me, Moshe, why should I ignore the match between me and the Arabs?"

"You should not," Moshe said seriously. "You are one of us."

"Who is *us*?" I asked sarcastically.

"Us are the Jewish people and you are one of us."

"Thank you," I said, as my eyes started to tear, but just for a moment. "You see, Moshe, I thought that I was smart enough to put the past behind me, but I realized that it is beyond my power to do so. Therefore, I can only acknowledge my weaknesses but never my strength.

"Facing my past and my heritage, I feel controlled and vulnerable by it, so for self-preservation, I ran to the safety of a new personality. Moreover, this disability was turned to an advantage for our services without considering the fact that I created the personalities knowingly, not subconsciously. I was the one that led you to think that I am mentally disabled because I needed to know how far you will go in using me. Nevertheless, I am still a servant to all, but never to myself."

"I am sorry, Cloudy," Moshe said in sympathy, "but all of us gave something for a cause or for personal reasons. I am fighting demons as well every day. Cloudy, I want you to try to see yourself through my eyes, knowing always that you are one of very few people that I trust."

"Do you really?" I said, not hiding my doubts.

"Of course, Cloudy, I never believed in information reinforcement, from people or circumstances. I learned to be strong and on guard. That is why I chose you to help me."

And before I realized what was happening, he snatched me into his arms. "You will do just fine," he whispered into my ear, and my heart skipped a beat, as I wondered if he ever guessed how I felt about him, and that he was using it as a tool of manipulation.

"Okay," he said, "time to go, Cloudy. Please, consider our little talk. He lingered for a second by the door and with an amused smirk, he announced, "I love you, Cloudy."

"I love you too," I said as a common response. "And for your information, Moshe, I was the one that allowed you to manipulate me, not otherwise!"

Moshe stopped for a second, stepping back into the room. He moved closer to me; I could feel his heavy breath on my forehead, and before I took another breath, he kissed me like no one before, softy and sensitively, yet with passion and desperation. I almost lost my balance when he let me go, and when our eyes met, it was an electrifying moment, and we acknowledged our feelings.

"You have no idea, Cloudy, how long I wanted to kiss you," he said, short of breath, "but we worked together and..." he hesitated for a moment, "you know the rest."

I heard his voice in the distance, as I was still overwhelmed, and I did not know how to react so I fired at him, "Why do you call me Cloudy? It is not my name!!!"

"Oh yeah," Moshe sighed loudly, "get mad, get feisty, defend your territory. That is how I know you best, and I know you better than anyone!"

Yeah, I thought in disappointment, you know me, you desire me, but still I am #2 on your scales... after your illegal duties!

"I promise you, Cloudy, that if you learn to like yourself, and learn to laugh at your mistakes, others will do the same. And yes, I call you Cloudy because of the rare moments you were yourself, you were gazing at the clouds and dreaming, not acting and not pretending. I remember one day, when I woke you up from such a dream, you told me that you were praying, remember?"

"Yes, I do," I said. "You are right, Moshe. I did not lose myself completely because I am still praying like a little insignificant worm, and I don't know, for sure, who or what, I am praying to!"

"It is common, Cloudy; it is human nature to call upon God in times of distress," Moshe said, "and I'm glad that you have a higher power to rely on."

"You don't understand, Moshe, I feel like I lost a very important part of myself, and I need to find it to be complete. I believe if I find God, I will find this missing part of myself. Does this make any sense to you Moshe?"

"Maybe," Moshe said. "But what really matters is that you would make sense of it."

"Oh, I wish I just knew," I said, "so I can crawl out of my perplexity."

Moshe locked his arms around me in a comforting gesture as he always did.

"Cloudy, please," he said, "be proud of yourself and your accomplishments, as we are proud of you. We traveled the world together, and we experienced things that many people can only dream about. Please remember all that, not the duties but the accomplishments."

"You are right, Moshe. I need to forget, because all that could be another figment of my imagination, including you, Moshe! I am sad and mad because I lost the privilege to serve Israel in uniform. Instead I serve my country like a terrorist, and worst of all, I cannot talk about it because, if I do, I would be pronounced *crazy*, remember? I do believe that the mental hospital was a bargaining tool of the organization to control me and I think you had a hand in it! So Moshe, do you believe that I am crazy?"

"No, I do not, Cloudy, and I never did. You are very sane, believe me, and you are beautiful and funny and you are very intelligent! Nevertheless, you accepted all the terms and you never protested. So what happened?"

"I hate the fact of being a tool of manipulation, but mostly I hate my childhood mental incarcerations and the experiments. All of that robbed from me what was left of my childhood and from having a normal life. I could be very beautiful and very intelligent, I could possess great talents and I could be admired for all these things, but only one whisper that I was in a mental hospital and all the lights will go off. No one will think anymore that I possess wisdom; they will say it is madness for sure! No one will see innocence or beauty because one unjust whisper accumulates more power than ten thousand talents, and that is how I will lose all my credibility."

"I am sorry, Cloudy, that you feel so betrayed; however, I will tell you this one thing, your mental history was indeed a tool of negotiation in which I had no part. Nevertheless, at that time, I agreed with the legitimacy and the reasons. It was explained to me that you, in your gratitude, would be more efficient and more prone to follow orders, and who am I to dismiss experts' opinion?"

"Yeah, sure," I said. "I bet you that you as well were manipulated," I said bitterly.

"So what?" Moshe said, laughing. "I was happy to be chosen and you were chosen, Cloudy, because you are like a rare diamond with many facets. You were chosen for the same reason that I was chosen."

"Oh, shut up, Moshe. I am tired of everything."

"I know, Cloudy. Sometimes it is hard on me too, but then I remember all we have done, and I am proud because we did it for our country; we did it for Israel! Moreover, and most importantly, we prevented many disasters and in that, we saved many lives. It does not matter if it was legal or not, or if it is the truth or a lie, or even if it is a figment of our imagination. But, I promise you, Cloudy, that one day your children will listen in fascination to all your stories, and when they asked you if it is the truth, you just tell them, that the combination of courage and sacrifice never comes from madness but from crazy moms."

"You are smart and funny, Moshe," I said. "You always make me feel so much better, and I thank you for that. Nevertheless, I would never share with my children all we did or accomplished."

"And why not?" Moshe asked.

"Because I would never bring children to the misery of this world. I have no right to do so!"

"You will change your mind," Moshe said, before he shut the door behind him.

Chapter 15

After the early evening performance in the nightclub, Ali took me to an Arab bakery where we tasted different breads and bagels. I had about two hours until my next performance, and I was ready for a small attack concerning his identity. Before I said anything, Ali spoke, "I want you to stop working in the club!"

"And why is that?" I asked.

"Because I want to marry you."

"Is this a proposal?" I asked.

"Yes, it is," he said.

"So?" he asked.

"So what?" I said.

"Are you going to marry me?" Ali asked again.

"I do not know. I need to think about it," I said.

"Why do you need to think about it? Is there something wrong with me?"

"You tell me," I said.

"Tell you what?" he said uncomfortably.

"Your whole name!"

"Ali Ahmad Rabia," he said, "and I hope it will not make any difference that I am not Jewish."

"Oh that! Don't be silly," I said, lying. "I have known about your Arabic heritage from the beginning."

"How did you know?" he asked, surprised.

"You were too nice to be Jewish," and in my heart, I thought, *and too stupid to be with me*.

"So, Yona, will you marry me?"

"Maybe," I said, "Just give me a few days to think about it."

The next day I called Moshe, and when he arrived, I told him about the proposal, hoping for a personal reaction.

"Take it," he said. "We need people in west Jerusalem."

His answer infuriated me, so I backed up a few steps, enough to level the difference in our heights, so I could look straight into his eyes. Fire was burning in my heart, along with a deep yearning for a word of caring or perhaps love, but instead I said coldly, "I refuse to work for you, Moshe, or anyone else, so any suggestions you may have or any compromises, flush them into a toilet!"

"It is fine with me, Cloudy," Moshe reacted with calming self-control. "I will never force you to do anything for me or your country; it is strictly between you and your conscience. However, in the future, if for any reason you need me, here are all my personal contact numbers."

He handed me a piece of paper with numbers, and at the end of it, was his recent address marked with a smiley face. He always knew how to soften me with his manipulations and that was a reminder of weakness into my character. However, the knowledge that Moshe needed me was always a fresh breeze of self-appreciation.

"Fine!" I said loudly. "If I do witness or suspect anything I will let you know, but as to your patriotic manipulation, Moshe, just to let you know that there is no conscience between my country and me, or between YOU and me!"

My Jewish identity held roots of disgrace that challenged me to learn and to study the history of the Chosen, so I could accept it and embrace it. My positive attitude led me to many unbelievable studies; the more I learned, the more I was enticed to believe in the miracle of creation and in the God of the universe. However, as I learned about all the rules and the commandments, I left it alone because I refused to be a prisoner to more rules and to be shackled to cold ritualistic ceremonies that had no reason whatsoever in my understandings.

I felt that I already paid the price of redemption, so why the rituals?

I liked Ali okay, but I also knew that a decent man would not marry someone like me: all alone in the world and stripped of a heritage and the family tree. I was like a lost dog that wiggles his tail at all times and to anyone, a dirty animal rather than a human. I was always available to do any task required and all my duties were done with forced cheerfulness, only to hear a word of approval, to see a warm smile of acceptance, or just to be noticed. These moments were the fuel that kept me alive. However, one day all that ended.

Drained physically and emotionally, I wished to die.

I cried to God to free me from the torture of days gone past. I begged God for mercy and for a fraction of His wisdom. I begged Him to show me the garden of His love, so I could win this life and survive. I was barely breathing an existence, and hope was just a word written in black and white. I did not plan for the future because I feared it would collide with my past. I was very careful not to be trapped emotionally; therefore, I loved everyone and no one. I felt a lot and nothing; yet, in all that confusion, I always craved to experience love. Therefore, I would never give myself completely to anyone.

All the treatments I received and the events of my short life did not carry a positive outcome. I was young and already broken. I wished for a sliver of light that would lead the way and pull me out from the deep dark hole. I could not find even one door to knock on, as a painful loneliness sat on the edge of my throat. I was lost because I did not find sincerity in anyone, even in me. All of my lies and acts exhausted me, and I could not separate the truth from the lie.

I experienced normal encounters, only through mimicking other people's behavior patterns. I dreamed because it was the only thing among my possessions that no one could take away. In this God-forsaken land, God still could grant me this gift of pure love; otherwise, I would just have to wait to receive it in the heavenly realm of freedom and peace, if indeed it is... I knew that my false reality must end, so I tried to end my life. I did not care where I would go after I died; I just believed that anything must be better than this life. I took sleeping pills, put on a Connie Francis record to dramatize the event, and I went to sleep.

However, Ali found me and took me to the hospital, "Why would you do something like that?" he asked me. "I do not know why," I said, *and for a short moment, I thought that it might be the truth, but suddenly a thought flashed through my mind: Indeed... without hope there is only death, and I did not have anything to hope for. After I experienced the false grasp of death, the pain of rejection intensified.*

Even God does not want me, I cried to myself, and why would He? After all, I tried to sneak in the back door into His kingdom, and He threw me right back into my hell. How funny! I dared to entertain myself. I knew that God was not happy with me, and somehow I always managed to do everything against my better judgment. I did not want to care or shed tears because I truly and sincerely wanted to die; therefore, to be married to Ali or to die, it was one and the same.

Ali drew a map for me to get to his house and to officially meet his parents. They lived in the heart of the old city of Jerusalem.

I remembered the old city, and the first time I had beheld this magnificent jewel, I acknowledged the divine privilege that was given to me. As I stepped into the holiness of God's majestic possession, I was instantly wrapped with God's presence, yet fear beseeched me to run to the shelter of my grieved reality.

I walked with the map in my hand, following the directions precisely, but nothing resembled human living quarters. Discouraged, I asked someone for directions, showing him the map. Immediately the person recognized it. "Ali," he said with a smile. "I know Ali," he said.

I followed him as we went the same way I had walked three times before, and I could not understand what I had missed. He stopped by a very small wooden door, pointing at it, and before I could thank him, he disappeared. I knocked on the door a few times, and when no one responded, I bent my head down and entered to a tiny yard. In the corner stood a large barrel, and I saw Ali pouring water from it into a small basin. He did not see me at first, as I watched him wash his face. *My God, I thought to myself, how is it possible that there are still people living like this?*

"You are here," Ali greeted me, wiping his face with a white cloth. "Come on and meet my mom. She cooked food for you that we serve only for special occasions."

I bent my head again as I entered a small room. Everything was built from Jerusalem stone: the floor and the walls, even the small yard. It felt like I was in a small cave, but the room was cool and refreshing against the heavy heat outside.

One huge plate with a mountain of rice and chicken took up a lot of space of the room, I noticed. Then a small woman approached me and embraced me with a strange force. I was shocked when I realized that she was checking me out.

"She is so thin. Don't the Jews know how to cook?!"

"What did she say?" I asked, pretending not to know their language.

"It was nothing," Ali said, laughing. "She is just concerned for me. If you become my wife, you will need to put some meat on your bones."

"Fine with me," I said. "I really like to eat!"

"Good," Ali said, "because this plate is just for you. It is one of our traditions that the bride-to-be must eat all of it!!"

"You are not serious," I said.

"Yes, I am serious. It is the tradition."

"You can feed at least ten people with all this food," I said in desperation.

Ali looked at me seriously, adding, "If you don't finish, we can't be married!" Therefore, I began to eat.

My first thought was to leave, but I was a fighter and I thought, if their Arabic women can do it, I should show them what I can do! I started with the chicken and then little rice, chicken again and a little rice. I could not eat anymore, so it was time for me to leave.

"Thank you for the food," I said politely, holding my cool in the midst of this irritating circumstance.

"Please don't leave," Ali said, "You just passed the test to be an obedient wife, and we were joking with you anyway."

I did not feel like laughing, and I didn't feel any relief. As usual, I just hated myself with a passion. Anything that happened was an indication that God Himself conspired against me with these people. God was always on my mind, even though I did not know Him.

By now, Ali was fully dressed in his police uniform. "I must go to work," he said. "Stay with Mom so you two can learn to know each other."

What?! I thought to myself, how are we going to communicate? After Ali left, she removed the food, smiling every time our eyes met. I wondered what was coming next!

When she came back, she carried a pot of tea and two small glasses. *Great, I thought, we are going to have an Arabic tea party!* "You like Chai with nana [tea with mint]?"

She showed me green leaves and I just smiled and politely said, "Shukran [thanks, in Arabic]." Her face immediately lightened up with a big and sincere smile, "Afwon [You're welcome]!" she said.

I knew Arabic for spoken communication and only few people knew I knew this language, and I intended to leave it that way. Ali was so happy when he thought that I had learned two words in Arabic, *thanks* and *you're welcome*, but he did not know that my knowledge was my ammunition. Ali's mom was checking me out as I sipped from the tea. "Is it good?" she asked. I just smiled and said *thanks* in Arabic.

I was ready to leave when two women came for a visit. They were smiling but curious, and for a moment, I felt uncomfortable as I continued to pretend to be clueless about their language.

"She doesn't look like a Jew," one of them said. *I like her,* I thought in amusement.

"She has beautiful eyes, and her skin is like marble," the other woman said.

"Yes," Ali's mom sighed deeply, "I thought I would die when I heard that Ali wanted to marry a Jew! He is my firstborn," she said in deep sorrow, adding, "and I am losing him to a Jew."

When she said that, she looked at me and I smiled, but it wasn't fun anymore to know Ali's mom's opinion, and especially when the word JEW reappeared! However, before the guilt surfaced, I reminded myself that my knowledge was my advantage and my weapon. I didn't need to know more, so I stood up to go, but Ali's mom stopped me.

"Wait," she said in Arabic. She handed me a box with food to take with me. "You need to eat," she said.

"Thank you," I said with gratitude, knowing that she probably wished me death. Yet, I sensed something was very special about her: motherhood, perhaps?

I visited again to meet all the family. There were nine children altogether. I met six of them, including Ali. Everyone was checking me out, and I found it quite entertaining. "Son," Ali's father said, "she needs to be a Muslim to marry you."

"She will never agree to that," Ali said, "and I already told her that in Islam we can marry anyone we choose and from any religion."

"You need to trick her to accept Islam as Prophet Muhammad, peace be with him, ordered!"

Wow! I thought in amusement, I am the mother of all tricks, so I wanted to see how he would trick me... From this point and on all the preparations for the wedding picked up speed.

I went with Ali's mom to Ramallah (an Arabic populated city). She chose the wedding dress for me, plus another seven dresses. She tried to explain that, after I was married, I would come to her house, and for seven days, people would come to congratulate us, and I'd have to wear the seven dresses for them, so they will see that I am not poor and also admire my dowry.

As for me, I just smiled, leaving her dissatisfied for my lack of knowledge. If she only knew that I understood all she said. Surprisingly she did not say any bad words in all that time she talked to me. From time to time, I let her know that some things I did understand and it made her very happy.

As I proceeded digging my grave, everywhere I turned, there was someone warning me not to marry Ali. I was told repeatedly, if I married Ali, I would be his property and I would lose all my rights. I did not believe it because, to the contrary, I believed that I was the one fooling everybody!

The day came when we were ready to go from Jerusalem to Jaffa, a town near the seashore and partially populated with Israeli Arabs. It was the day when I would marry Ali in the Arabic way and by an Arabic sheikh.

Ali came to the hotel to pick me up with a big red car, a Chevrolet Impala. "My friend gave it to me," Ali said, "so we will go in style. We will be married legally, and after a week, there will be a wedding party."

The road from Jerusalem to Jaffa is all the way downhill; it always scared me to look down, as it was so high and the pit was so deep! We left in a good mood, and as we started to go down, the car lost its brakes! Oh my God! I was terrified, praying to my God and his god and all the gods in the universe, as Ali struggled with the car to stop it. I already saw myself going to the pit, broken and hurting but not dead, because I already established that God didn't want me.

Ali hit a protective stone fence and we stopped. I got out of the car, shaking from that terrifying ordeal. "We need to go back," I said to Ali.

"No! No!" Ali said. "There is something trying to stop us, but I will continue to drive in spite the brakes!"

"Without brakes?" I almost screamed.

"Yes! Without brakes!" Ali said.

Now, when I look back, I know that indeed this Something that tried to stopped us, was no other than my Heavenly Father, my God. If I had only known then that I wasn't abandoned; if I only understood with my heart that I was not alone...

When we arrived in Jaffa, I was half dead with fear. Ali left the car with a mechanic, and then we walked to the Muslim quarters to be married.

"Listen," Ali said. "You are going to live among us, so you will need a new name."

Great! I thought to myself, one more name could not do any damage.

"Do you have any name in mind?" I asked Ali.

"What about Shadia?" he asked.

"Nadia is much better and more international," I said.

"So be it," Ali said, satisfied.

"Are you a Muslim?" the sheikh asked me in Hebrew.

"No," I said.

"Would you like to be?" he asked.

"No, I am Jewish."

"Never mind," Ali said in Arabic, so I would not understand, "just make her a Muslim, so legally she will never take my children from me."

"You have children with her?" the sheikh asked.

"No, no, but I want to cover all the bases."

"Okay," the sheikh agreed, and looking at me he said: "Repeat after me all I say."

Stupid, I thought to myself.

Instead I said, "Okay." Every word that he told me to repeat I twisted and said wrong, but he did not mind. After that, he gave Ali the papers, and it was done. I did not know that the grave I had dug for myself was ready to cave in.

When we came back, Ali was telling the brakes story to everyone that was willing to listen.

"She is now a Muslim," he said, "Congratulate us!"

"Mabruk! Mabruk [Congratulations]!" everyone said.

I was beside myself. I could not scream that I was not Muslim because I did not want them to know my secret. I just comforted myself by remembering that in the Jewish Torah somewhere somehow is written that a Jew cannot change his religion. On Judgment Day, every Jew will be judged as a Jew, as every Gentile will be judged as a Gentile. Today I know much more.

Nevertheless, a good thing came out of this entire scenario: when I thought that I lost my Jewish identity, I found it and for the first time in my life, I did not want to lose it. Still, though, I did not know what I would do with it, especially among the Arabs.

The official day of the wedding came like a storm. Ali's three sisters came from overseas with all their children and other extended family. Everyone was busy with cooking and preparations. I was itching all over my body from the treatment I received a few days previously from Ali's mom. She waxed all the hair on my body, and afterwards it looked like I had chicken pox.

"It will heal by your wedding day," Ali's mom said, but I was happy that at least my face cleared.

Everything was very strange, and suddenly it was frightening as I dared to face the truth. I searched desperately for a shelter, a fortress of care and security to fill the void in my soul. I felt alone like never before, and I wondered how many more levels of loneliness I would have to experience until I found peace.

The celebration took place at Ali's aunt's house because she had more space. In the morning, I went to a salon for the final preparations and I was ready in two hours. Once again, in a white dress, completely disconnected from myself, it was as if I was watching a senseless movie. At Ali's aunt's house, two tables were put together, and on the top of the tables, two chairs were placed for Ali and me to sit above all others. The chairs were very uncomfortable and I was afraid to move, lest I would fall, providing free entertainment to the delight of all the celebrating women. The room was full of women. Ali was the only man.

The women put their right hands close to their mouths, and with their tongues, they created loud noises: a kind of *LuLuLuLu*. One woman stood and began to scream sentences directed to Ali. She did it playfully but sarcastically, and the spiced sentences were aimed specifically to the wedding night. Everyone was laughing and screaming *LuluLulu*. Ali was blushing, and I was surprised that women in this culture dared to use suggestive and expletive language as this. I found out that this specific one woman was hired for one purpose only: to embarrass the groom.

The chair was uncomfortable, but worse than that were the women that touched me and checked me out, without shame. I held on desperately to the chair as Ali's mom poked me on my back every time that I sank into it. "Sit straight," she said, "so they can see you!" It was senseless pretending that I didn't understand their language because Ali's mom had already found a way to communicate with me: one poke on my back and it straightened me up--well, at least in the chair! She talked to me mostly with her hands, and I intended to leave it that way, as I felt security in what I knew and they did not.

Everyone was dancing and celebrating, and from time to time, a man entered the room, handing a money gift to Ali. After four hours or so, we were free at last.

Ali's mom was very sad because we were leaving to our rented apartment. According to Arabic tradition, the firstborn son brings his wife to his mother's house to take over the work, so the mother can rest. However, if the house is big enough, all the sons will stay with the mother, and their wives will serve and help follow the instructions and requests of the mother-in-law.

As for Ali and me, obviously, everyone thought that I was the reason for breaking this tradition. Nevertheless, I suspected that Ali as well wanted to be some distance from his family.

On our wedding night, Ali gave me a gold pendant and French perfume. He did not force himself on me, and he was very gentle. I almost believed that God loved me after all. The next morning, Ali woke me at sunrise. "Wake up, wake up," he whispered. "We need to prepare for visitors."

"Why so early?" I asked.

"Remember what I told you," Ali said. "They are going to check to see if there is blood. I told them that you are a virgin."

I jumped out of bed, all mad and confused.

"Do not worry," Ali reassured me. "Just straighten the bed so it will look nice. I already staged the rest."

Before I asked for an explanation, there was a loud knock on the door. I ran fast to the bathroom to fix myself up a little, and when I came back, the bedroom was full of people.

Again, and without shame, or permission, these unwanted guests started to open everything that had a handle on it. One of the women stood by the bed for a second and then, in just one movement, she uncovered the bed and time stood still; everyone in the room stopped what they were doing, and all eyes froze on the bed. I, of course, knew that they were looking for blood, but the bed was clean!

Soon enough, my disgrace was written on their faces with great contempt, and I was amused. I couldn't believe I was part of this comedy club, and I could barely keep myself from laughing out loud. Then I heard the celebration triumph with the tongue composition, *LuluLulu*, when one of the women held up a sheet in her hand that was smeared with blood! *LuluLulu*!

Oh! Shut up! I wanted to shout back, as the woman's screams had aggravated every string of my nerves. The men, on the other hand, were congratulating Ali on his successful manhood.

Ali's father approached me and shamelessly he asked me if Ali's performance was good. What?! I thought to myself offended, how dare he ask me such a personal question? However, soon enough, I reminded myself to relax, lest they find out that I know their language.

"What did he say?" I asked Ali, as he joined us.

"He asked if I was good last night," Ali said in self-satisfaction.

"Well," I said, smiling to his father, "you tell him that I wouldn't know; after all I was a virgin, remember?"

After a very long hour, everyone left and Ali cooked for me a wonderful breakfast with the inner part of the lamb: the heart and the liver. I made Turkish coffee and we enjoyed each other's company, laughing at the trick that Ali pulled with the blood.

"How did you do it?" I asked him.

"It was not easy," he said. "These women are professional in checking the blood of the virgin. They say that this kind of blood doesn't wash easy, so I got help from an old friend, and as you witnessed, you passed as a virgin."

"I do not understand," I said, "how a personal issue as my virginity had to dignify me publicly."

"This is our culture," Ali said.

For the next seven days, I went to Ali's mom's house and stayed there all day. Friends and family, women only, were visiting all seven days, and I was asked to wear all the different dresses that Ali's mom had bought for me.

I also danced at the request of Ali's mom; she did not know that dancing was what I did when I met her son. Therefore, I danced for them repeatedly. For each and everyone that visited, I danced slowly and properly, like a virgin should. Well, at least that's what I thought. However, all of the Arabic traditions and rituals plus all of my pretending became emotionally exhausting, and when the seven days came to the end, I began to observe and learn all the customs in my new life.

One day Ali came back from work, and as he shed his police uniform to wear regular clothes, he asked me if I would like to join him to buy a chicken.

"Of course," I said. We went to a small place with many caged chickens.

"Which chicken do you like?" Ali asked.

I looked carefully and then I saw a beautiful red one: "This one." I pointed it out with excitement.

Ali nodded his head to the owner who took the chicken out of the cage, and in a blink of an eye, he cut the chicken's head right off!

I was not expecting that; it shook me up terribly and I started to cry. *What was I thinking? That he is buying the chicken so I could play with it.*

"Why are you crying?" Ali asked. I looked at him and I was convinced that a cold-blooded killer stood before me. "Why are you crying?" I heard Ali asking again.

"I am crying for the chicken; I did not know she was going to be executed!"

"It is stupid!" Ali said through his clenched teeth. "Stop crying," he said angrily, "or I will give you a good reason to cry!"

However, for some strange reason, I could not stop crying. Ali was so furious, I could see fire flashing out of his eyes. He whispered something to the owner of the store, and the man moved out of the way.

Ali pushed me inside with all the caged chickens. He pushed me against a wall and hit me with his fist in my stomach, and for a moment, I could not breathe

"Why? Why?" I managed to say.

"So never again will you embarrass me as you just did," and before I could say anything, he hit me again in the same place. The intensity of the pain brought me down to my knees.

"That is how I want you always, on your knees!" he said.

...and it seemed like my heart froze forever. I chose to believe that God's power worked against me, and Ali's cruelty just reflected God's disregard for me. Nevertheless, I probably would not have survived if I had blamed Ali or God, or even circumstances. Sadly, I blamed myself, the person that I was hiding from, the person who saw herself through the eyes of her persecutors, and justified their actions. There were two of us: the real me that I nearly forgot, and there was "she," with different names and characters that I created and recreated, and I called her the "want-to-be."

Today I know that God was always right there, guiding me patiently by extending His comforting presence. As to Ali's actions, I could not believe what had happened. Why so soon? I thought. It was almost as if I believed that I deserved to be beaten, but not yet and not so soon.

Ali pushed me into the car and as we drove, I started to cry again, quietly, lest he would see. It was painful to face again the unspeakable hate and the pain that came along with it, not so much the physical pain, but the emotional. It was so painful that I couldn't take a whole breath but I could breathe only in short waves. *Today I know that it was my soul that cried within me.*

"Are you crying again?" I heard Ali's voice.

I said nothing as his hand flew across my face. He stopped the car, and without a word said, he started to punch me again, and again, and everywhere possible, and I let him.

"Remember," he said, "I can kill you and no one will even ask about you so, if you are thinking to leave anywhere, forget it!

You are good as dead! Remember," he said, "This was just a small reminder of what will happen if you disobey me in the future!"

When we arrived home, I was in shock, feeling nothing at all, as if I was ready to die. "You can kill me if you want," I said, "but I would like you to know that I am deeply ashamed that you are my husband. You can control me as you like," I said calmly, "but you have lost my respect forever."

As I stood to clean myself from all the blood, Ali collapsed into a chair, sobbing, "I am so sorry," he cried. "I don't know what had possessed me. Please forgive me, Nadia, please forgive me. I promise I will never touch you like that again."

After I washed, he made coffee, and we smoked a cigarette. Everything was forgotten and forgiven because I always forgave. I just had a hard time forgetting, and for this reason, my defenses were shutting off.

I had a new name now, Nadia Rabia, and I got used to it very fast, as I got used to other changes in my life. Two days after the beatings, Ali's mom came for a visit, and when I opened the door, she backed off when she saw the bruises on my face.

"Did Ali hit you?" she asked, but I said nothing, even though I wanted to say he did not mean it, but I kept on pretending that I did not understand. Nevertheless, the purpose of her visit was to teach me Arabic cooking, so we cooked together. She showed me everything so I would remember,

After we ate, I lighted a cigarette, but she took it from me, and in the nicest manner, she explained that I would feel better if I washed the dishes first and then I would enjoy the coffee and the cigarette much more. She was right. She was not pushy but very gentle, and I truly liked her. She explained words to me by showing me different elements in the room, and I enjoyed my time with her. At times, I felt guilty pretending that I didn't know her language; on the other hand, I truly believed that she started to like me because she believed my vulnerability. She felt valuable and strong at her ability to teach me Arabic at such a speed that no one else could.

As we sipped from the coffee, Ali came home. He approached his mother to kiss her hand in the Arabic tradition, but she pulled her hand from his.

"What is the matter?" he asked, concerned.

Rising up from the chair, she said, "I will show you what the matter is!" She took off her shoe and began to hit him with it anywhere she could reach… "You coward!" she screamed at him. "You are not a man," she continued to hit him with the shoe.

I was amazed how a small woman like her could reach his head, and it was the one point where the shoe mostly ended up. I was also surprised that Ali did nothing, and said nothing to defend himself. Furthermore, I could not believe that someone in this world actually took a stand for me, and in that moment, I knew that my gratitude for her would last forever.

The same day, before she left, she ordered Ali to translate for me what she was about to say. "I know you are lonely in the world," she said. "Unfortunately, in our culture, your situation is less than respectable because we are proud of our family tree and we boast in our heritage and you have none. Long ago, they used to kill orphans but not since our prophet who was an orphan also. Contrary to you, he had a heritage…"

I wanted to jump and scream, I have a heritage, but I did not dare to look back to my cursed past. I just remembered a foggy picture of my father's parents, the only possession left after the extermination of his whole family in the concentration camps. My mom had no pictures but one surviving sister that grabbed life by its horns and lived it to the fullest. I remember her clearly because of her beauty and her passion for life.

Ali's mom was correct. I exterminated my heritage with shame and pain, and I was barely coping with all the lies I created, but at that moment, I wanted to defend my Jewish heritage because I needed to defend myself.

"I talked to Abu-Ali" [Ali's father], she said, "and we want you to call us Mom and Dad, if it is okay with you."

I felt like a big rock blocked my airways, and I could not stop the tears that burst without restraint. I was crying for my family that I never met, for the poor souls that so courageously marched to their deaths. I was crying for them because they were part of me, and I a part of them. How long will I continue to escape the truth hiding from myself? How dare I hide from their legacy? They died so I can live. All these thoughts flashed through my head like lightning.

"Why is she crying?" Ali's mom asked with concern. "Did you translate everything exactly as I said?"

"Yes, I did," Ali replied.

"Why are you crying?" she asked me.

But I could not talk; instead I kissed her hand, and then put her hand onto my forehead, according to their tradition of respect, and then I said, "Thank you."

There wasn't any need to explain my heritage; they would not understand. I didn't understand as I did not want to; after all, who can comprehend darkness but the evil?

A few months after our marriage, Ali's mom became sick, diagnosed with stomach cancer, and I was crushed. Nevertheless, in spite of her sickness, she never ceased to teach me all I needed to know about her culture. She taught me how to crochet and how to prepare Arabic food; she taught me also how to talk to people.

"Listen," she used to tell me. "Listen and learn, but never give it away." Basically, she told me not to participate in gossip. "Even if you are asked for your opinion," she used to say, "smile and say, 'I do not know this person well enough to establish an opinion about him or this subject or another.'"

I used to take her to an Israeli hospital in Jerusalem for treatments, and everyone loved her there. A year later, I was conversing with her in Arabic, but I also convinced her that she was the only one who understood me and it really complimented her. I used to translate what she said to the doctors and vice versa.

Moreover, the personnel of the hospital who treated her said she was the best patient, as she hardly complained. With Ali and among the family, I spoke Hebrew, but if someone addressed me in Arabic, I pretended that I had no clue what they were saying. Then Ali's mom would tell me the same thing, and miraculously, I understood!

"Why does she not understand us?" everyone protested.

"I know Nadia," she used to say. "Therefore, I know how to talk to her."

When I spoke to her, I whispered, so no one will hear my Arabic and know the truth. "Why does she whisper to you?" family and friends complained.

"She is shy," Ali's mom used to say. "She doesn't want you to laugh at her, if you hear how she speaks Arabic. Only I understand her perfectly," she always concluded with great pride.

One day as she lay in the hospital, she decided that, after her release, we would go to a village name Samua to meet a good family with a good-looking daughter ready to be married, and if suitable, Ali's mom said, "We will take her for my son Muhammad."

"What about Muhammad?" I asked. "Did you inform him?"

"Yes, I did and he agreed; he will come with us."

I knew about Muhammad because of the interrogation in the police quarters. Although released from jail, he was still not free of suspicion. Nevertheless, Muhammad was as a wild bird; he worked for the Israeli Museum, plus he managed meetings with beautiful fruit arrangements for high officials in the Israeli government, not bad jobs for a terrorism suspect. Muhammad expressed his talents in variety of ways, but mostly by dating Jewish and American girls. It would be very interesting to see him with an unsophisticated and innocent girl from a faraway village.

I found out Muhammad was willing to sacrifice his freedom for his sick mother who needed someone attending to her in all times. I experienced a bit of jealousy as I wanted to be the only one caring for her. Doctors did not predict good news, and the cancer tormented Ali's mom and the family; for that reason, new measures took place and a modern home was rented with comfortable lavatories and much more space that included extra rooms.

Part of all these quick arrangements was to marry Muhammad, so it was exciting to go along with Ali's mom and Muhammad to see the new bride. I was very curious to see the new interactions of the Arabic Palestinian culture. I hoped Muhammad would like her in spite of all his experiences as a lady's man.

"Thank you for inviting me to go with you," I whispered to Ali's mom's ear.

"But of course," she said. "You are the wife of the oldest and your opinion counts!"

"Thank you," I said, smiling in gratitude, which aggravated Muhammad.

"What are you smiling about?" he said angrily in Hebrew. "You don't know nothing about us or our culture!" he remarked in sarcasm. "You even can't speak our language!"

"Relax, Muhammad," I said in Hebrew, and in the same manner, I added, "You know I am not very smart."

Muhammad did not like me because I was Jewish. He also knew about my work at the nightclub, which he kept secret from his parents. Nevertheless, in Muhammad's philosophy, you play with the Jew, you manipulate the Jew, and you kill the Jew for the glory of Allah. Not being able to do any of it, he spattered me with his venom!

I knew exactly what he was thinking, and I remembered the animosity and the hate that targeted me most of my life. I had already reached the point of complete numbness, and it felt like a mosquito bite that did not itch anymore.

After an hour or so we arrived at a place called Samua. It was a beautiful, peaceful place with fruits, trees, and green pastures. We stopped by a white painted house and an older woman, the bride's mother, I thought, greeted us. "Welcome, welcome," she said with pleasant smile.

We entered a large guest room, and as I looked around, I realized how clean everything was. There were no pictures on the wall, and no books, only a china cabinet with beautiful cups and dishes. A young woman entered the room carrying a tray with small cups of coffee. She gazed shyly at Muhammad, and I wondered if she liked him.

All eyes were on her to see if she would spill the coffee, and if she was clumsy, but she did well. People were talking about her and about her future like she was not in the room, and surprisingly, she did not mind, but I did!

I asked her to come with me outside, so we could talk. She hesitated for a moment, but she got permission to join me.

"Do you like Muhammad?" I shot straight to the point. She did not answer; instead, she pulled a scarf over her face in a shy manner. I tried not to use too much of the Arabic language. After all, my secret was my advantage. I used simple words, and she warmed to me, knowing that I was a stranger. "Do you like him?" I asked again.

"Yes," she nodded her head.

"Do you want to marry him," I continued to push.

"Whatever my father decides," she said.

"This is your decision!" I said angrily.

"No, it is my father's decision," she said.

Now I was furious. "You are the one who's going to marry and you must decide," I said.

She was a little surprised at my outburst because, obviously, I had used my better lexicon of the Arabic language. "Did you decide?" she asked me.

"Yes, I did," I said.

However, in that strange moment I realized that I would like to stand in her place and have my father make all my life decisions. There is much to say about this culture, and there is much more to understand, but I don't want to prolong my life story with cultural details.

Muhammad married Huda, and a new chapter began. Their wedding was bigger and much nicer that mine was. Combining two families was more appealing and the celebrations brought more, many more, people.

Ali offered his brother our apartment for the first night with his virgin wife and he gladly accepted; otherwise, family would sit by the bedroom door, until he would successfully break through the virginity of his innocent wife.

I thought that it was a barbaric ritual; however, at that time, and with the western influence, many things were changing, but in one exception, the blind hate against the Jewish nation. I learned all I could handle in this matter, as I pretended not knowing their language. I learned their slang and body gestures that, many times, were contrary to the words used, and most of the time, I enjoyed my secret mischief because it gave me power and security.

The morning after Muhammad and Huda married, I joined the moral expedition that included both of the families to see the virgin blood! Opening the door halfway, Muhammad announced that nothing happened yet.

"Why not?" his father demanded. At that point, Ali interfered, asking everyone to leave, but the father demanded that Muhammad and his wife would return to the house where everyone was, according to the proper tradition.

However, a few days passed, and nothing had happened. At this point, everyone started to be impatient with Muhammad because the two immediate families were still waiting to see the blood.

Huda's family could not leave without the proof of the purity and the innocence of their daughter. Muhammad's family was beside themselves, and from time to time, they mentioned that Muhammad was a man, a mighty man, and they did not understand what had happened and why he was unable to deflower his wife.

Because I was a stranger in their eyes, I was not a moral person in their chosen opinion, and respect was not one of my possessions. Therefore, paradoxically, I was asked to approach the problem and talk to the newlyweds. Muhammad told me that he could not perform because Huda is not responsive. Obviously, Muhammad's previous affairs with modern women stood between him and Huda.

Nevertheless, I decided to go to a pharmacy for a fast resolution. In western Jerusalem, everyone knew Ali and Muhammad, and when I came to the pharmacy with my strange request, no one asked me any questions, and to their best knowledge, proper herbs were mixed and that same night the honor of Huda was redeemed, and her family rejoiced.

Muhammad stayed hidden behind the closed doors for the next two days, suffering some irregular discomforts because I made sure that he would not understand all the instructions I had given him concerning the herbs.

I need to mention a long and remarkable journey of friendship that began shortly after I married Ali. I befriended an American woman who lived next door to my apartment. She had a beautiful redheaded daughter that I volunteered to babysit. We became very close friends, sharing secrets and personal issues that bonded us in sincere love and care for each other. Her name was Karen, and I could write a lot about the significant effects that her life brought into mine.

Our friendship gave me courage. Loving her child Kariman gave me all I could hope for. She and her husband Joe and Kariman left for the USA twenty-eight months after we met, and I was devastated. Nevertheless, our lives intertwined again, and thanks to God who led us and protected us all the way.

How strange and deceitful was my life in the complicity of my character. I do thank my Lord for humbling and clearing my soul and for leading me to the purity of compassion and care.

Huda was my sister-in-law, but I was in charge as the wife of the firstborn son and because Ali's mom said so. I must admit I was jealous of Huda because she had family she loved and she was from a well-known family; therefore, she was respected. As for me, Ali's mom was almost forcing people to respect me. She lied about my different talents and accomplishments, but no one was impressed, so she used to say to me, "Nadia, they don't care to respect you because you are beautiful like a movie star, and they are jealous!"

Yeah, sure, I thought to myself, but I loved her for her lies. At times, I was even convinced that she believed her lies, as I believed mine.

In the Arabic tradition, everyone called her Am-Ali because of her first-born son Ali, but I called her Yama which means Mom. It was the first sincere word that came out of my mouth, and it came straight from my heart.

Yama's cancer continued to spread, and she had to visit the hospital more frequently. She suffered pain and discomfort, but she never complained. Weaker and weaker, her body started to fail and I was desperate to give her some comfort. I used to wash her and pamper her, and every day I would bring her to my apartment so she would rest from all the duties forced on her, in spite of her sickness.

In those times, she was just mine and I protected her from the world and stupid traditions because I could not protect her from her illness. We used to visit people and she was so proud to tell them that I washed her and I did her hair and put conditioner on it. She did not know about modern luxuries but considering everything in her life, she possessed great wisdom like no one I had ever met before and to this day.

Chapter 16

For three years, I made sure not to get pregnant. I was still in touch with my friend Moshe, trying to help as much as I could, but the closeness to Am-Ali and her sickness forced me to make some decisions. Muhammad and Huda had been married about one year, and everyone was saying that neither of us was pregnant yet. People viciously asked Am-Ali, "What is wrong with your boys?" So I got pregnant and month later Huda got pregnant.

I called Moshe to inform him of my pregnancy, and the only string that connected me to my Jewish roots was cut off. Moshe was furious. "How could you do something like that? How can you carry an Arab baby?" he screamed into the receiver. "We are done with you if you don't get an abortion."

I was offended, as I screamed back, "Obviously, it's okay to lie and to manipulate, and even to kill, but to bring a new life to this world is wrong?"

"Yes it is," Moshe screamed back. "It was work, not a romance novel! You killed all the hopes I had for us, Yona!"

"Come on, Moshe," I said sarcastically. "We shared one hot kiss and many insignificant dreams, and that is hardly a foundation for future hopes and dreams, and Moshe…" I said, choking on tears, "my name is Nadia… Nadia Rabia."

When I hung up the receiver, I was shaking and cold, suddenly fearful for the person that had been growing inside me. I was seven months pregnant and Am-Ali was staying for longer periods in the hospital.

One day as I sat with her in the hospital, her doctor came to visit. "What is she going to have, a boy or a girl?" she asked him.

The doctor, knowing her Arab traditions, answered her on the spot, "A boy, of course!"

"No, no," she said in Arabic, "she's going to have a girl, and she's going to call her Asalia after me. She's going to carry my name, and she is going to be free."

At that time, I did not understand yet what she meant when she said free. Freedom is precious when you do not have it anymore, and I lost mine gradually and painfully. Am–Ali never had it; therefore, in her unusual intelligence, she dreamed with a vengeance, so one way or another, she won.

Ali warned me that when I was walking on the street, not to look left or right, just down to my feet, but most importantly, he said that I must never stop by any store windows. Carrying the memory of his rage, lest he would hit me, and craving to be loved, I tried to be an obedient wife, which was extreme torture against my free mind.

One day, on my way to visit Am-Ali, I walked through a long street in west Jerusalem. There were stores on both sides of the street and the temptation was unbearable. What the heck? I said to myself, there is no way he could know that I gazed into the window. I stood by the store window, admiring a dress when I heard a familiar voice: "Do you like this dress?"

Fearful, I turned too fast and landed on the sidewalk, straight down into a sitting position. Ali stood above me, three times bigger; his mouth was dangerously twisted and he resembled a smiling dog before an attack. I extended my hand to him,

"Please, help me to stand on my feet," I said humbly, "and I am sorry for disobeying you."

I knew that he could not hit me wearing the police uniform, but he whispered to my ear, "Just wait until I come home. I have a big surprise for you."

At this point, I got upset. "Fine!" I said, managing to stand on my feet. "I will bring your mom with me. She will be very proud of you!" I left him standing there, changing colors in his rage, as I walked to my destination.

As I look back on my perplexed personality, I do see many different elements in me, but none was complete or understood, even by me. I was willing to be submissive in the name of love but not by force. I was willing to love out of my choice but not by duty or force. I was always ready to play stupid because among some people it brought the closeness I craved. People felt good explaining to me many things I supposedly did not understand, yet I would not dare to call my behavior manipulation, not then, because somehow it was out of my hand to face the truth. The games and the lies worked for me and the darkness was continually surrounding me. Did I really play stupid? Or, was I just plain stupid?

I was in my eighth month of pregnancy when Am-Ali died, and a big part of me joined her in that grave. Once again, fear became my master; I lost the only person in the world that protected me. I was very concerned for my baby as Ali already told me that he had no money to buy a bed or any important necessities.

I cried bitterly, realizing my stupid choices would affect my child forever. Yet I was too proud to call Moshe, the person I truly loved and trusted.

The labor was painful and long, but the pain and guilt I carried overtook those labor pains. Aussy (Am-Ali's name) was born Saturday at nine o'clock in the morning; she was bruised all over from the pressure of the long labor, but her brown eyes were the most beautiful I had ever seen! She stared at me with such serious intensity that I almost believed she was able to see.

Two days later, Ali came to take me from the hospital, and as I marched behind him, I discovered that I gained courage and power in conceiving my child and I knew that I would do anything to protect her.

As Ali drove us home, I tried to convince him to buy a bed for his daughter. "She has your mom's name," I said, to soften the fact that I did not give him a son. "You don't want her to sleep in our bed; she could roll from the bed and hurt herself," I said trying to convince him.

But Ali got irritated. "If you don't want to be hurt," he said, "you make sure that she doesn't roll from the bed!"

I said nothing, letting the silence take over. As I walked carefully with my baby up the stairs, I could not stop the stream of tears that overwhelmed me. I cried for my child, the God-given miracle, and I hated myself like never before.

When I arrived at the top of the stairs, I could not believe what I beheld! Before my eyes stood a beautiful red bed, with all the necessities for it! Furthermore, inside the bed and almost to the top was full of baby clothes.

No, I did not suspect even for a moment that it was from Ali. It was from my American friend Karen; she asked one of her friends in Israel to do that for me when the time came.

"God loves you," Ali said, and then he added, "because you are a Muslim."

"Am I a Muslim, Ali?" I asked him in confrontation.

"You are what I tell you to be," he said with an obvious threat. "You are my property," he added, "and you will do whatever I tell you to do!"

I did not care what he said as I had heard all this before. I did not care what he was thinking either, because for me, he was all I hated about myself. Ali was a reflection of all my lies and all the dark corners in my heart, all the secrets and all the fears; therefore, his darkness exposed mine. Besides all this, the future of my daughter was the only concern on my mind.

I realized that my chance to escape did not exist anymore; I had no one to turn to, no one.

"I can kill you!" Ali used to tell me with a twisted smirk, as his fists landed on my battered body. "I can kill you and no one will ask where you are!"

You are killing me every day, I thought to myself, but Ali was right. No one will ask, and no one will know if he kills me. It was almost like I did not exist.

"My friend Karen will ask about me," I said to him.

"Forget Karen," he said. "She wants to marry me, and she wants me bad enough not to ask about you!"

"So why won't you marry her?" I asked him at this rare opportunity.

"Don't you worry, Nadia," he said. "I am thinking about it, I am sure thinking about it."

I remembered my brother Shimon. *I should call him, I thought, and just for one second, I was hopeful and excited. Yes! I thought. He will come for a visit and Ali will see that I am not all alone in this world. Then for sure, Ali will think twice before he will dare to hurt me again.*

However, Ali was sharp in collecting information for his private ammunition, and he would easily see that my brother did not care about me, which gave him more power to torment me.

Engulfed in despair, shame, and regrets, I was falling deeper and deeper into the poisoned traps that Ali so cleverly set for me. There was not a day that Ali was nice to me. I had to beg for everything concerning the home and our child. He came home less and less, and I suspected that he was playing around and that brought some relief to my aching body. He was gambling and drinking on daily basis, and when he lost his money or his dignity,

I was the one to pay for it. He used to beat me with a fierce anger, no matter how good or submissive I had been.

Often I would visit Am-Ali's grave just to relieve my pain and to cry. At other times, vindictive thoughts would wash me with gruesome plans of retaliation, but I always dismissed these thoughts as soon as they entered my mind because, in spite of everything, he was my child's father, and I couldn't ignore my love and respect for his mother.

Each time that Ali hit me, the excuses would vanish and vengeance would surface, embracing me with painful realization, as I stepped into Ali's dark dominion, to be lost in the shadows of his anger.

Indeed those were horrible times in which I conceived another daughter and then a son. I could write a whole book just about the unspeakable abuse from Ali's hands, but I will just touch on it lightly. Struggle for food was my highest concern. As an Arab's wife, I was forbidden to work, so at times I took a chance that I would find some money in Ali's pockets when he was drunk and sleeping.

I had a set of tarot carts that I used to read to the Arab women and I did it in very broken Arabic, so as not to intimidate anyone. "You are my friends," I used to tell them when they insisted on paying. I led them to understand that baby food or fruits would be more appropriate.

In the Arabic culture, it is acceptable, when visiting someone, to greet them with fruit or chocolate or anything. However, at the end of Ramadan, which is their holiday and month of fasting, they visit families and greet the kids and women with money. I was deeply ashamed to take money or anything at all, but mostly, I was ashamed of myself because I was completely powerless, a stranger among enemies, showered in the venom of hate. I was a mere shadow of my existence, as I felt I was falling gradually into the pit of a blazing fire.

The fact that I could read the cards spread like wildfire; more and more women came to me for my prediction of the future. In the beginning, when I started to read the cards, I was just plain lying, but after so many lies and so many stories, fear was choking me, as many women came back to tell me that the things I told them happened exactly as I told them!

I did not understand what was happening, and I was drowning gradually into deep desperation, as strange feelings started to control me. Death became my ultimate escape, and I am ashamed to say that to leave this world was an attractive thought, but then I would think about the children. What would happen to them?

My daughters, in all probability, would be sold to some old man, and my son would beat his wife as his father beat me. When I conceived my second daughter Miriam, named after my mom, Ali had been so angry that he did not come to the hospital. I thank God for the easy labor, because otherwise I was too weak emotionally to deal with anything at that time.

Ali's father was angry as well because I dared to conceive another daughter, and he refused to talk to me, but I was too concerned about my newborn to entertain their stupidity. Nevertheless, I had just come home from the hospital, and one of Ali's sisters from Jordan came to visit with all her children. I think there were seven or more, but in my condition, it was like a hundred little thunders running around and demanding to be served.

They demanded tea, coffee, and other foods for me to prepare and serve; nothing was enough! "Give me this or that!" I just ran from one room to another, serving them. Eventually, when I thought they were not going to demand anymore, I served them tea.

Ali's sister stood up, and in an angry manner, said: "Why is my glass not the same size as hers?" She pointed to her oldest daughter.

At that point, I just lost it and I screamed back, "Because I am not your servant!"

"Your whole nation came from servants!"

"Remember," I said proudly, "I belong to the Chosen People, and I do not know to whom you belong with your stinking attitude!" And in the spirit of my belligerent behavior, I took my older daughter's hand, and I went to change and to nurse my baby. I was so very tired.

A few minutes later, Ali came home, and the moment he entered, his sister started to tell him what had taken place and what I said.

"She couldn't," Ali said. "She barely knows how to say a few words in Arabic and I speak with her in Hebrew, so how would she know how to say all that in Arabic?"

"Oh, but she did! She did!" his sister insisted. "Ask my daughters."

"Yes, she did," the daughters said in harmony, confirming the allegations.

I was nursing the baby when Ali came to the room. "Did you hear what my sister said?"

"No," I lied, so he repeated to me all his sister said to him.

"Did you say all these things?" he asked again.

"Don't be ridiculous," I said. "How could I say such horrible things?!"

"I believe you," he said surprisingly, but to his sister, he said that he would deal with me later.

A few months later, I was watching an Arabic movie on the TV, and I was very involved in the story when Ali came home.

"I am hungry! What have you cooked?" he asked me in Arabic. I answered and he continued to speak with me in Arabic and I was answering in Arabic. Suddenly the sound of a broken glass brought me back to reality, and with that, the children woke up, crying with fear as it was a familiar noise to these poor little souls.

"My sister was right!" Ali screamed into my face. "You did tell her all those horrible things!" And before I could cover my face, his fists landed everywhere, and thank God, I passed out. When I woke up, my children were out of breath from crying. I opened my arms to comfort them and to protect them, but I could not stop my own stream of tears. *I promise you I said in my heart, that I will do everything to free you from this monster.*

It is torturous for me to describe all the abuse. It is painful to describe it and to relive it, but especially in the English language with its own difficulties.

Nevertheless, all the violence and the constant fear conceived mental problems in me. I had overload sensitivity. As a result of it, a single thought overtook my daily life. I will have a son with Ali, I promised myself, and his own son will kill him someday.

This horrible thought comforted me somehow, but only until the moment I discovered my pregnancy, and thank God, the news cleared my mind and woke up my senses. I was deeply ashamed of my vindictive thoughts. I just wanted to be free from Ali's evil darkness that consumed all that was good and decent. I knew that I had to escape and save the children, and I needed to do it as soon as possible. However, without a plan and a good back up, I could never leave and now, above all things, I was pregnant. I had no one to turn to; nevertheless, a plan was forming in my mind.

Ali was smart and strong but he also was a narcissist, so I decided to nurture this side of him, until my plan could be effected. I was fragile and at the breaking point, but I started to move forth with my plan. First, I needed freedom to calculate and to check all the possibilities for the escape. Otherwise, I was completely paralyzed because Ali knew every move I made. I planned to have documentation for the future, to prove Ali's sick mentality and abuse, and if something should happen to me, my children had to be transferred to the Jewish side, as I never chose to be a Muslim.

In the kitchen, we had a gas oven and I waited until the gas container was empty. I put the girls to bed, closed the door, and on a big paper I printed: DO NOT LIGHT A MATCH. THE GAS IS LEAKING.

I put it on the door outside, so it would be the first thing that Ali would see. After my daughters fell asleep, I took a very strong sleeping pill that would affect me in the twenty minutes following. I went down to my neighbor's to make a phone call to the police department.

"Hello," I said. "This is Nadia Rabia. May I speak with the officer in charge?"

"I know who you are," the voice on the other side answered.

I said calmly, "May I have your name?"

"This is officer J, and I already told you many times before that we are not interfering in a family dispute!"

"Yes, I know that," I said, "But I also know that this law has been applied just for me."

"Think what you will," the officer reacted angrily.

"You see, I lied. In case something is conveniently wrong with the police recorder, I took it upon myself to record our conversation."

"So what do you want from me?" Officer J said reluctantly.

"For you to do your job," I said calmly. "Otherwise, this tape is going to be all over the news media."

"You are the one who married an Arab," the officer said viciously, "And now you are complaining to us?"

The sleeping pill started to affect me, so I told him that Ali was on his way to kill me. I knew that Ali would come home any minute, so I turned on all of the oven's buttons, hoping that Ali would fall into the trap, and the police would come in time.

I lay down on the kitchen floor, drowsy from the sleeping pills, when Ali burst into the house with a cloth protecting his face. It was theatrical, but it was also very sad because he did not run to check on the children. He ran directly to me, screaming hateful remarks about my family and about the rest of the Jews.

And just before he struck me, the police stopped him, and I went to sleep, waking up in the hospital to the pleasant face of a social worker. Thank God, it worked!

"Did you try to kill yourself?" she asked me.

"No," I said. "I am trying to save my children."

"How is that?" she asked.

So, for the next hour or so, I told her almost everything, including my plan to escape. I also told her that Ali's neurotic behavior must be documented in the police records for the future. "If something happens to me, I don't want him or his family to raise the children." I told her how I forced the police officer to do his job, but I also learned that there is always a way to beat corruption, we just need to find it.

I was transferred to the psychiatric section of the hospital, and assured that my children were safe and well cared for. In the hospital, I stayed about a month, and during this time, I was free to come and go.

My doctor was very sympathetic to my situation. She suggested to me an abortion, and for this discussion, she invited Ali.

"Out of the question," Ali screamed, pounding with a fist on the doctor's desk. "No one will kill my son!" he said.

"Please sit down," the doctor said calmly. "In her situation, Nadia cannot carry the baby to term; furthermore, can you guarantee her safety? Her weight is forty kilograms. She is bruised all over her body, and she is exhausted physically and emotionally. Frankly," the doctor said, "you don't know if she is pregnant with a son or another daughter; therefore, I highly suggest an abortion."

"She is my wife, and by law, she belongs to me," Ali said, pointing a long finger at the doctor.

"It is not up to you anymore," the doctor said. "It is up to Nadia, and if you are talking about the law, I am the law now." It was priceless to watch the unmasked rage in Ali's face.

The doctor stood up to indicate the end of the discussion. Ali took me to the cafeteria of the hospital, and he tried to bribe me not to go through with the abortion.

"I will give you forty thousand dollars, if you keep this child," he said.

"How is it that you have so much money and we have no food at home?" I asked him. He said nothing, and I decided to let him sweat. I never thought to abort my baby, but I did not let him know that.

Eventually I came back home, and six months later, I gave birth to a son. Everyone rejoiced but me. I was afraid that he would be like his father: selfish, self-centered, and abusive. *I have to go with the plan, I thought, and I have to hurry.*

When my son was about one year old and my daughters, two and a half and four years old, I attempted to escape with them. I was caught by Ali. A friend that supposedly was helping me reported to Ali every step I had made. That was the last time that I would trust anyone.

After we came home, Ali beat me so severely that he broke most of my teeth. I could not move and I barely could breathe. Nevertheless, I remember how painful it was to see my children shaking and crying. I tried to get to them, but I couldn't stand up. Blood was everywhere, and in my attempts to rise, I just slipped into the blood.

My children were crying and their frightening cries were as a thousand knives slashing my soul because I could not do anything, nothing at all.

"Look what you have done!" Ali screamed. "See all this blood? You think that I am going to clean it up?"

I just thank God that he did not hit the children, but I knew one day he would, and I could not stand the thought of that.

"Stop him!" I cried to God. "Please save my children." I prayed to the God that I did not know. In my mind, I prayed to the Giant of Justice that could do anything, and when He did nothing, it was because I did not deserve better, but my children did!

Not able to move from the floor I was listening to my children breathing. It was not a peaceful sleep; their breathing stopped occasionally, like to relieve pain ... again ... and again. Just listening to their painful sleep broke my heart. After hours on the floor, I managed to stand up. The pain was severe, but what I was about to do was insane.

I did not think clearly, I just wanted to end the pain. I covered myself completely like a traditional Muslim woman. I took the money that I had saved for the escape, a bottle of water, and in my pocket I put all the sleeping pills I found among the medications. I also took a razor.

Not far from the house was a taxi station, I sat in the back and told the driver to go to Tel-Aviv, to the seashore. Just before we arrived at my destination, I decided to take the sleeping pills, but it was almost impossible. I was so swollen that the pills did not go to the right place. It was like my mouth moved in all different directions, but eventually I swallowed all the pills. When I arrived at the seashore, I paid the driver and I started to walk toward the ocean.

"Hey!" the driver called, "It is too dark to go there."

"It is okay," I said, with great difficulty, "I know the way."

I sat by the seashore, watching the waves that once brought me so much comfort and peace. The moon was very bright and I could see its reflection in the waters. I felt empty like never before; the pains of my body were distant now. It was like I did not belong to myself, and I did not.

I took the razor and I started to cut my veins, but I was falling asleep, so I picked myself up and I walked to the sea and that was it. *Goodbye, Life.*

I was so sure that I would die with the triple action of suicide, but I woke up in the hospital and the first thing that I saw was Ali.

"If you want to die," he whispered to my face like a snake, "I promise you I will kill you, and this time, it will be slowly, very slowly."

At that point, security removed him from the room. Apparently, he had managed to come to my room in spite of the security.

"I am her husband," he protested.

"And that is why you are forbidden to visit her," the security man told him.

I was very confused and almost in a panic, but a nurse told me that I had been drifting in and out of consciousness for three months.

"Why? What did you give me?" I asked.

"Just blood and food," the nurse said, smiling, "and the reason you are alive, is two lovers decided to stay overnight on the beach, and they saw you collapsing into the sea. They pulled you out and took you to the local hospital."

After I stabilized, I was transferred to a hospital in Jerusalem, and a nurse told me that someone pulled serious strings for me, so I could get the best care possible. She said that most of my teeth were broken, and I had small fractures all over my body, plus my jaw moved in a different direction.

"But we were most concerned about your head," she said, "which apparently encountered strong blows."

Yes, I remembered these blows. Ali was very strong; he was a professional boxer before he became a police officer. I must be very strong as I survived, I thought to myself... I was angry and very ashamed of my selfish act of desperation. Thousands of questions ran through my head, but one bothered me the most: When did I begin to be so weak and afraid that I allowed my children to pay the price?

Six months later, I was well and fixed. I had new teeth that brought a new confidence as I faced my reflection in the mirror.

"You look well and beautiful," my doctor told me. "Wipe the sadness from your heart and use your intelligence," she said, "and with your new strength and determination, you will be able to fight for your children, and Yona," she added, "never hesitate to ask for help."

Before I left the hospital, I called my friend Moshe. "I am glad you called," he said, when visiting with me. I had almost forgotten how tall and strong he was, and so desirable with his fiery red hair and his piercing eyes that missed no detail, but now he gazed at me with familiar care, mixed with admiration. I would almost have felt at home if I hadn't been so confused.

"I wish you had called me before all that happened," I heard him saying.

"What happened, Moshe?" I asked in defensive confrontation.

"I know everything," Moshe said calmly, "and I knew it from the moment you arrived at the emergency room in Tel-Aviv," he said. In a flash, I understood, connecting all the pieces.

"Thank you, Moshe, for everything," I said, realizing this important moment when the pride of my heart died and appreciation took its place.

"You are not alone, Yona, not anymore," Moshe said.

"Don't be ridiculous," I said in frustration. "I am alone because of what I have done and that is a bitter taste to my soul!"

"What do you mean by that?" Moshe asked.

"Nothing really," I said sarcastically. "I just want to remind you that some knowledge can save us, while other knowledge can kill us. I learned bitterly about the price pinned on it. However, in order to restore the broken hearts of my children, I am willing to pay!"

"As for you, Moshe, you cannot do anything for me without approval from your superiors, but please tell them that I do appreciate all they have done for me, and I will gladly accept any help, any help at all."

Moshe gazed at me sadly, "Listen, Cloudy," he said, "we cannot do anything further; the rest is up to you."

Coming back home and seeing my children broke my heart into a million pieces. I hated myself for what I had done, and I knew that my act would be a guilty reminder for the rest of my life.

Again and again, I asked myself, How could I leave my little children to that primitive monster? How did I become so

*weak and so frightened? I was a fighter and a survivor, so what
happened?*

*While all those thoughts ran through my head, I caught
glimpses of innocent eyes watching my every move. I did not have
a single word to accommodate this new situation. My little
children were so sad, and at the same time, so detached. Just being
in their presence, I felt a new power forming in me.*

When I held them in my arms, in Ali's presence, they were
as dead, not responsive and afraid to move. This was one of the
moments I wanted to kill Ali, just to erase him from the face of this
earth. I wanted him in hell, the same hell that he created for me and
the children, but I said nothing. I just stared at him with all my
frustration until he felt uncomfortable.

Furthermore, my middle daughter Miriam was just sitting
and scratching her head without ceasing, so I approached her to
check it out, and when I separated her beautiful curls, hundred of
lice were moving on her little head. "Oh, my God!" I cried. "I have
never in my life seen so many lice! Quickly, go to the pharmacy," I
said to Ali, "and buy all that is necessary to kill the lice."

The moment he left, the children ran to me, embracing me
with all their tiny strength.
"Why did you leave us, Mom?" they cried. "Why did you?" But
even my tears could not ease their pain.

Chapter 17

Ali was warned not to touch me, and if he did, he would be arrested and lose his job as a police officer. Nevertheless, I knew that Ali could not survive without hurting me, so without wasting any time, I moved with my first plan, determined that my children would never again witness the ugly picture of hate and sickness. I knew I had just a short time to move freely around the city until he woke up, and once again, I would be the subject of his control.

After a quick search, I found a beautiful girl that would fit my plan; Nadgiah was her name. She told me that she was living in a cave with her mother, and I was shocked at first that someone actually lived like that in the 20th century! However, after I visited her in the cave, I was surprised even more, as it seemed much more comfortable than most of the houses I had seen in Jerusalem. They had electricity, TV, and refrigerator, and other convenient necessities.

Being fatherless and from a poor family, Nadgiah's situation would never allow her to find a suitable husband. She could only be a second or third wife or even a fourth, to a Muslim man, as Muslim laws allow for the man to possess four wives. If she had lived among the Jewish people or in a different country, men would be competing to have her as their own, but not the Arabs!

I learned many strange things about Muslim Arabs, culturally, ritualistically, and religiously and with my extra card in the sleeve, they talked freely around me, not suspecting for a moment that I could understand them. These men were intimidated mostly by three elements: women, Jews, and the success of a stranger, even though the competition among themselves was very strong and aggressive.

They sat in coffee shops which were designated just for men, and together they explained away the problems of the world, which were based accordingly on the same three elements: women, Jews, and the success of a stranger! Spending much time together, they agreed to give a name to the subjects of their intimidation, and that is how Arab politics was born. Hateful and in deep darkness, they were and are, planning away the day that the world will be at their feet, and they will drink the blood of the Jews and the American and all the infidels!

On Fridays, they hurried to the mosque to listen to the inflamed screams of the sheikh, calling them to obey the word of Prophet Mohammad and to kill anyone who refuses to be a Muslim, and promising that anyone that gives his life for a Muslim cause will be rewarded with seventy-two everlasting virgins. I always wondered what the women will get: permission to say, "Thanks for nothing"?

They were and are abusing their own families by teaching them to hate, to destroy, and to kill! I thank my God that, in those thirteen years among them, I never learned their hate, because it was not justified, as a lie cannot be justified.

However, strangely enough and in spite of everything, I loved them, because they were the only family I experienced, and as a result of all the ugly and painful reflections, I was given divine understanding and compassion that I wouldn't have known otherwise.

Knowing Nadgiah and her natural craving for a husband and knowing Ali, I knew that my idea would be as a breath of fresh air for them both. After our friendship was established, I asked her if she would marry my husband.

"You are not serious," she laughed. "We are friends," she said, doubting me.

"I am serious," I said.

"You do not want him anymore?" she asked.

"Oh, I do want him," I said carefully, lying without blinking an eye. "I just need help with the children, and I do not want more children."

"And what about the law?" Nadgiah inquired.

"Don't worry about that," I said. "I am married to Ali by Israeli law, but you could be married to him by Sharia Muslim Law that allows four wives."

"When can I see him?" Nadgiah asked.

"As soon as I tell him," I said.

"What if he doesn't want me?" she said.

"He will," I said, smiling and satisfied from the success of the plan--well, almost a success.

When Ali came home, he was already preparing himself for the evening to go out to gamble and to drink, and who knows what else.

"Ali," I said, "Before you go, can I talk to you?"

"Fine," he said angrily, "But hurry up. I need to meet some people!"

"I found a wife for you," I said, straight to the point.

"You what!!!" He turned so fast he almost stumbled.

"I found a wife for you."

"Oh yeah?" he said suspiciously. "And why would you do such a nice thing for me?" he asked.

"I did not do it for you," I said calmly. "I did it for me and the children."

"So how is it good for me?" Ali asked.

"Oh, forget it," I said, turning my back to him and walking away.

"No, no, wait!" Ali said, encouraging me to speak.

"Well," I said, "you don't have to pay for her, and she is so beautiful that everyone will be jealous of you!"

"And what do I have to do in return?" Ali asked.

"I want one day a week to be free, Wednesday will do, and I will need some money to buy books and maybe a piece of cake on occasion."

Ali stared at me, trying to read me, but he was also thinking; I felt his excitement in the air. I knew him and I knew that he would fall into my trap but not that soon. "How old is she?" he asked.

"I do not know," I lied. "She looks young," I said, "maybe fourteen or sixteen. She has no father, so you do not need to pay," I reminded him.

"Hmm, when can I see her?" he asked.

"Tonight, if you like," I said as my heart was rising with joy.

Ali prepared some good food, and without offering any to us, he went to meet Nadgiah, and I had my first Wednesday of freedom.

Chapter 18

Each time my friend Karen visited Israel with the archeological expedition, she and her friends always brought clothes for my children, which was a tremendous help.

Karen was very angry with Ali because of the situation I was in, and together we decided to outsmart him. At that time, Karen was a single mother, and it was obvious that Ali was attracted to her. Who wouldn't be? Karen had typical American beauty, natural blond hair, and big blue eyes, and a very attractive disposition, but her character and caring for people made her beauty even much more appealing.

"Listen, Nadia," she told me. "I will help you, but first we have to convince Ali that I will marry him. He is flirting with me anyway. American citizenship would be a strong incentive to divorce you, along with a good plan for escape," she concluded.

One day as she visited me, she noticed bruises on my face. Ali was sitting by the table, all smiles, to see Karen, but she was furious. "Listen, Buster!" she told him, "if you ever again touch Nadia, I will kill you myself!"

In some strange way, Ali wanted Karen even more. Somehow her attack on him made her more attractive in his eyes.

Nevertheless, I still had my free Wednesdays, among the regular beatings, pushes, and insults. When my kids started to mimic their father, I forced myself to take a different approach, with greater urgency, to save my children from his sick influence.

Ali was getting tired of Nadgiah and I returned to be his renewed subject of attraction. "Be nice to me," he used to say, "and I will be nice to you."

"I do not want any more children," I said gently, not to aggravate any of his detached nerves and to protect my free Wednesdays.

"I want sons!" he screamed.

"It is fine with me," I said. "Nadgiah will give you beautiful and strong sons like you."

"I do not want her anymore!" he screamed. "I want you!"

"You have me, Ali," I said, "but if you like, you can have Karen as well. She told me that she is willing to marry you. Would you marry her?"

The familiar suspicion reappeared on his face. "Is it a trick question?" he asked.

"No tricks," I said, "Karen is willing to marry you and to take you to the USA."

"I knew it! I knew it!" He said, pounding his fist on the table. "You both want to trick me so you can escape!"

"Oh, really Ali," I said, "Even if I had somewhere to go to, who is going to help me with three children?"

He thought for a second. "Yeah, that is right," he said slapping his forehead, as if awakening. "You have no one! He smiled in self-satisfaction. "You know," he said, "You are as good as dead if you ever think to leave me again, and if you try to trick me, I will disable you, and you will cry for mercy for the rest of your life."

"I know Ali, I know," I said quietly.

Ali was drinking and gambling, and I was struggling to feed the children. He showed his generosity only when his sisters or relatives came from overseas or when he took food to his girlfriend Nadgiah and her mother.

I used to buy food on credit from a small store, and when Ali did not pay, the owner of the store refused to give me any more groceries. Nevertheless, I found a butcher store one day and I asked him if he would be kind enough not to throw away the feet of the chicken and the other parts of meat that he was usually throwing away.

"What do you need these for?" he asked.

"For my cats," I lied.

"How many cats do you have?"

"Three," I said, barely holding in my tears, but he figured out that I may have hungry kids, so he used to put in the bag good pieces of meat and some veggies, on occasion. He was a good man and he always tried not to embarrass me.

I remember that he was a Christian Arab and he sold pork; therefore, Muslims were not allowed to buy from him. After a while, we became friends, and I met his wife who so generously used to give me food to taste, as she put it, "Just try it," she used to say, "You'll see that the kids love it." She would also say, "There is no shame in relying on your friends."

"Yes, yes," I would reply, "you know that I will be dead if Ali finds out we are friends, and I am taking food from you."

When I look back, there is nothing to cry about. I was the one that left God and denied His existence. Nevertheless, God protected me. He fed my kids and He dressed them. He guided me as much as I was willing to accept His reproach and to give in to His Divinity. He talked to my stony heart and He cleansed my rebellious soul.

I was angry with my brother, and deep in my heart, I even blamed him for Ali's abuse. *If he just visited me, I thought, Ali would think twice before touching me.* Sometimes I called him and asked him to visit, and when he couldn't, I told some illustrated fib that would bring him for a visit eventually. He would come, bringing us honey and fruits from the kibbutz. I tried to tell him about the abuse, but he diplomatically avoided anything I tried to say, and we never had a real and caring conversation. Forty years later, my brother apologized for it, and it meant the world to me. I apologized as well.

Chapter 19

Reliving everything I experienced is almost unbearable; this is especially true when it comes to the protection I wasn't able to give my children. Although painful to recall, I'd like to describe the next steps I took to release us from our horrible reality.

Before we married, and in seeking sympathy from Ali, I shared with him the injustice of my childhood mental hospitalization. Instead of sympathy, this information provided Ali with a weapon against me, in addition to other insults and disrespect.

"If ever again you just squeak to the police that I threatened you," he used to say, "everyone will know that you are crazy and all you say will come across as a figment of your sick imagination!"

Like I really care, you heartless animal, I thought to myself.

After a little research and some help, I got two strong pills: 100 mg each of *Largektin*. These pills were used for mentally disabled people. I learned that a big man like Ali would sleep with one pill for a long time. However, Ali never took any pills even for a headache, so how was I going to administer these pills to him?

I remember countless times holding a gun to his head while he slept, but I could not pull the trigger because of his mother whom I cherished and because of my children whom I needed to protect.

Ali's behavior mirrored all the bad aspects of my own nature that I refused to confront; however, holding the gun forced me to admit that I as well enjoyed power. In resisting the act, I found an inner strength which sustained me in the days to come.

One day Ali came home early in the morning. "Here," he said, giving me 500 dinars. "If I ask you for this money don't give it to me, okay?"

"Okay," I said. However, late in the evening, he came back home, demanding the money with a familiar threat in his eyes. So immediately and without hesitation, I gave him the money, which I knew would be spent for gambling and alcohol.

The next day, he woke up in the late afternoon, suffering from a hangover. "My head is exploding," he complained.

"I can give you a pill for it," I said, with my heart pounding like a thousand drums.

"No pills," he said. "You know I don't take pills."

"Fine with me," I said. "It is your headache, not mine."

"Listen," he said, "all the units are celebrating the New Year in the hotel, so go to your friend downstairs, and borrow a dress from her for this occasion."

"Take Nadgiah instead," I said. "You would look better with her."

"No!" he said, "You are coming with me!"

I did as he said. I felt good in the Victorian-like dress I borrowed, and at that moment, I wished for a bit of happiness and for less fear. If I could just converse with Ali, none of this fear would be in my possession, but how could I communicate with evil?

At the entrance of the hotel stood Ali's superior. He greeted Ali with a handshake, and when he shook my hand, he said, "Ali, your wife looks more beautiful every time I see her."

Instead of saying *thank you*, Ali snatched his superior's collar and said, "No one will say that about my wife! Be careful!"

I was in shock when he dragged me out, shouting, "You were flirting with him! I saw it! You did it with your eyes!" He started to hit me and hit me and hit me, and I just covered my head with my hands curled into a ball. I had learned not to resist or to defend myself, so this way he might get bored and stop beating me.

The beautiful Victorian dress I had borrowed was stained and ruined. I remember that, in tears and shame, I tried to remove all the blood from it. *Was I sorry for myself? Maybe, I really did not know because, in that stage of horror, I could not distinguish anger from sorrow or weakness from desperation.*

I was still waiting for the right time to give Ali the pills, but my patience was ending, and pills in his coffee became an appealing resolution. Blessedly, Ali suffered again from a hangover, but this time he asked me for a pill.

"I do not know if it will work for you," I said, stalling. "You are a big person."

"How many do you take?" he asked.

"Two," I said.

"So give me four," he replied.

"I only have two left," I said.

"Okay, okay, just give them to me!" he said impatiently, so I did, but not before I asked him when he was scheduled to work. "This afternoon," he said.

"Okay," I said, "If you fall asleep, I will wake you up."

"You'd better," he warned me. After a while, when he reached a deep sleep, I took his gun and I shot two shots into the wall. Then I ran to the neighbor's to make a phone call to the police.

"Ali just tried to kill me," I said to the superior.

"Where is he now?" the commander asked.

"He collapsed on the bed after he shot at me, and I think he is on some kind of drug," I said.

"Where is the gun?" the commander asked.

"I took it from him after he collapsed," I said.

"Is he still sleeping?"

"Yes, he is," I said, "and I am afraid he will wake up."

"Do not worry," he said. "We are on the way with an ambulance."

I did not know what was going to happen. I was fearful and excited at the same time. My new courage washed me with new strength. The children arrived home from the school at the same time as the police. One of the officers stayed with the kids, as I went upstairs with the others.

Ali was snoring loudly.

"Did he take any medications?" the officer asked.

"He is a heavy drinker," I said, "but I've never seen him take any medications."

"How long ago did all that take place?" the officer asked.

"I do not recall," I said. "I lost track of the time."

"You know that we warned him not to touch you," the commander said.

"Yes, I know," I said sarcastically. "Your warnings were so serious that he dared to spit them right in your face. Nevertheless, I do hope that this time you will do your job."

"I am sorry," the commander reacted. "You are the one that chose to marry an Arab!"

"I heard that before," I said. "Apparently you, sir, never made any mistakes."

"Oh, yeah, I did, and plenty of them, but even the worst of my mistakes never came remotely close to yours! However, Miss Nadia," he said, "I promise that he will not hurt you any more, and we will certainly encourage his resignation."

I was dumbfounded! "Why won't you just fire him?" I asked.

"Because we do not have enough reasons to do so," the commander concluded.

"Really?" I said. "The fact that he beat me so severely that I needed hospitalization and the fact that he broke my teeth, leaving me to swim in my own blood, is not reason enough? So what is?"

"You did not bring charges against him," the commander said.

"I thought it was your job to charge him!" I said, infuriated. "I was in a coma after he almost killed me!"

"He was drunk, and he did not remember what he had done," the commander explained.

"I tell you what," I said, "if he hurts us just one more time, I will bring charges against the police department because my children aren't going to witness any more violence or any more bloodshed. And when you deal with him," I said, "don't think about my children. Think about yours, because I promise you, if my children do not get justice, you will see your picture on the front page of every newspaper, and the ugly truth will stare back at you through every woman's eyes that will identify with me!

"I promise you that every mother and grandmother will beg their husbands for support, demanding the return of justice to its rightful place! Furthermore, and regardless of my mistake of marrying an Arab, wrong is wrong, even with justifications and the reasons attached to it!" I was out of breath, saying all these things, as well as gambling that my threat would work.

"We are taking him to a mental hospital for observation," the commander said, "and we will see later how we can help you," and before he left, he turned back. "I don't take threats lightly," he said.

"Good," I said, "Because I don't take abuse lightly, not anymore."

A few days later, Ali's psychiatrist invited me for a session with Ali. The moment Ali saw me, he exploded with fury, calling me names in Arabic.

"Speak Hebrew," the doctor instructed Ali.

"This is her fault I am in here," he said with a long finger pointed against me."

I said nothing; I just smiled, hoping to infuriate him even more and it worked. My cheerful silence brought the beast out of him!

In preparation for my next step, I learned that the doctor's presumption would be probably an obvious case of paranoia, and if Ali indeed was diagnosed as such, he would remain in the mental institute for some time.

The same day, as I was leaving, Ali stopped me, "If my mom was alive," he said, "you wouldn't do this to me."

His words touched my heart with sorrow, but knowing his game, I replied, "If your mother was alive, you wouldn't do to me and the children all you have done."

After a month or so, Ali returned home, tamed and relaxed. Knowing him, though, I knew that he would seek revenge and the abuse was just around the corner. He still worked as a police officer, but only on the surface, filing paperwork, which put him down in his own eyes. After a few months, he resigned, but not before he got a visa to the USA.

With Ali's dignity and pride compromised, I was the one to pay for his past sins. He beat me mercilessly with calculated strikes, totally inflamed with fury and hate. When I cried out, begging him to stop, his satisfaction grew, so I learned to be silent to cut short the beating and his satisfaction.

Nevertheless, one day in the midst of one of these episodes, the cries of my children pierced my heart and I woke up! Kicking him with all my strength, I managed to jump up and embrace them. My poor little children were out of breath, scared and crying, but Ali demanded his satisfaction. He was approaching me again with a familiar threat.

"Stay put," I said to the kids. "Please, please, do not move!"

"Okay, Mom," they nodded their heads.

I barely escaped Ali's clutch, and I ran to the kitchen as fast as I could. I grabbed a knife and I waved it in Ali's face: "How dare you scare the kids this way! How long do they have to suffer?"

I screamed, but it did not scare him. He just grabbed my two hands and easily released the knife from my grasp. Before I realized it, there was a knife stuck in the right side of my chest. I was stabbed! I pulled the knife out and blood gushed out, but I did not feel any pain.

Thankfully, the knife was not big and not sharp enough to cause serious injury, so I just sanitized the wound and stuck some clean cloth on it and that was it.

Ali was long gone by then; he did not stay to find out the outcome of his despicable actions. He left for his usual parties to gamble and to drink. I knew that Ali was right when he said that no one would ask about me if I ever vanished. I also knew that Ali could have stabbed me deeper, but it was just a warning of what he could have done. I already concluded his brain disabilities; after all, how hard is it to recognize stupidity! A genuine man would never solve his problems by abusing others.

I knew where he kept his gun, so I took it, intending to use it. I shut the door and I moved a heavy object against it, ready to fight for my children and even for myself! The door of the apartment was very thick, but I did not want to take any chances. After all, Ali was big and strong, and being empty of soul, added to his strength which was conceived from an irrational and burning hate.

It was still daytime when he returned, banging on the door, and screaming at me to open it.

"Get away from the door!" I screamed, "or I will shoot!"

Ali was obviously confused for a moment, and then he tried to break down the door. All that noise scared the children, and they started to cry.

I was very weak; I weighed only 85 pounds, so I held the gun with both hands, and when I shot at the door, I fell flat on my back! For a moment, there was complete silence and my heart stopped. Did I kill him?

Then I heard footsteps on the stairs someone running, so I ran to the window. There he was, running like the devil himself was chasing him. Wow, it was indeed a sight to my soul!

"Do not come back, you coward!" I screamed. "Do not come back if you cherish your life!"

In an odd way I gained Ali's respect, but shortly after this ordeal, he left for the USA, leaving us with 100 dinars, which supported us barely for two weeks.

The apartment we lived in did not have any warming devices. My kids' lips and fingers were blue from the severe cold, and in order to warm up, I burned charcoal and paper in an aluminum basin and we sat around it. Our unity warmed us and supported us, as we watched the dancing flames that gradually died as we fell asleep.

God was merciful to me even in my progressive blindness. My eyes were fine, but my spiritual vision was blurred and foggy. Nevertheless, my Father in Heaven knew me, and He was my spine that held me up and held me high, showing me the responsibilities of my conscience.

Everything in our lives continued to tumble. I had no means to pay the rent, so soon the owners of the apartment served us with an eviction order. When I turned to Ali's family for help, they ignored me completely. However, help came from a surprising source.

Representatives from a Muslim organization visited me and told me, if I would veil myself properly and put my kids in their highly religious school, they would help me. Being ignorant of their intent, I agreed. Covering myself helped a lot and I got new respect from everybody, even Ali's family. They visited with food and good cheers. People were kind and almost loving, and most of all, Arab men that had bothered me before were tame now and very polite.

The Muslims showed me their unlimited power, but I began to realize the false security that indulged me with a lie, and I forgot with whom I was dealing, until my children brought to my attention the teachings of the school.

It is senseless to repeat the ugliness of the hateful teachings against all nations, but specifically against the Jewish people. The facts were brutally twisted and the lies celebrated. I was empty of ammunition against such absurdity.

I did not know how to explain to my children that their mother was not an evil monster and what they were being told was merely a harmful conspiracy. I did not know how to explain to a child the serious dilemma of a hateful intent. Nevertheless, confrontation was in order. I took my children to a nearby neighborhood in which all the houses were donated by a Jewish person to disadvantaged Arabic families. Divorced and widowed women that, after the Six Day War, used to linger on the streets of Jerusalem, begging for a handout, now found rest, joy and respect. I encouraged my children to listen to their stories of gratitude, and I suggested confronting the teachers with the truth.

My children at that time were ten, eight, and six. They told me that they were afraid of such a confrontation because this school did not allow them any kind of self-expression, and if they disobeyed, they would be physically punished. I was furious! What do they want? To create a little Hitlers out of my children?

So, soon after, I took them out of this devilish environment and transferred them back to the school across the street from our apartment. Immediately, the things became worse. The power of the Muslim fanatics escalated beyond words and with colorful threats! But I was a fighter and after Ali, anything was possible!

I got a job as a waitress at the Hilton International. That was a miracle in itself. With my first check, I got an electric warmer, so my children would never again be cold. In a short time, I was in charge of the Parliament members who used to meet in the hotel for lunch twice a week.

They heard me speaking in Arabic, and they were mesmerized. "What is your name?" they asked me.

"Nadia," I said.

"Are you an Arab?"

"Yes," I lied.

"It cannot be," they said. "You look so European, and you speak Hebrew so well."

I said nothing; I just smiled. I did not tell them the truth because I wanted them to be more curious and more talkative, hoping to build some kind of bridge that would warm the stage for my request.

I loved working at the Hilton and meeting so many famous people. There was Rock Hudson, Robert Mitchum, and Eddie Murphy, and I even exchanged words with them in my very broken English.

Nevertheless, I learned fast enough that the members of the Parliament were not the bridge for my desperate request; their life was senseless to understand someone like me. Some of them even flirted with foreign women, passing notes like teenage boys, using the wait staff to do so. Being disgusted by this behavior, and having the authority, I transferred them to the back of the lunch area, so they would be separated from the rest of the guests, but mostly away from the sharp eye of the media. It bothered me that they never paid for anything, and they never left any gratuity for the waiters.

I confronted the issue with the manager of the hotel who informed me that it was great for the hotel to have the members of Parliament staying in the Hilton and not other hotels. However, after I told him what was going on and how they used the waiters to pass notes and to serve them continually, the manager gave me a free hand to do what I thought was right.

That was the day that I happily transferred them to the back room of the lunch area. I put out a beautiful arrangement of fruits and pastries. On the warmers, I put coffee, cocoa, and tea. I set out cold drinks, orange juice, apple juice, and water also, with a sign that said, "Compliments of the hotel. Please help yourself."

As you can guess, they were very unhappy! "Who is responsible for all of this?" they complained.

"It would be me," I said.

"We were quite happy before," they said.

"I know you were," I smiled pleasantly, "but no one else was. You were interrupting the waitresses for no reason at all, you passed notes to the foreign women, you never left a gratuity, and above all, you needed to be noticed for who you are! Believe me," I said, "all of that brings a bad name to the hotel, and in my private opinion, to Israel as well. If all that were to be leaked to the media, no one would be happy!"

"Does the manager of the hotel know about this new arrangement?"

"No," I said, "but he gave me a free hand in the lunch, and you are free to inform him, if you are not happy."

"No, no," one of them said, "it is unnecessary. Obviously, you are a smart girl, and we are trusting you. And please," he added, "do not hesitate to ask any of us if you need anything, anything at all."

Yes, I thought to myself, perhaps a new government.

The walls of east Jerusalem were closing on us; no one wanted to sit with the children when I worked. The constant harassments from neighbors and the Muslim authorities almost brought me down to my own unsettled nature, and somehow I started to act at their level, planning unconventional steps of revenge.

One day, as I worked, I received a phone call from my oldest daughter. She was ten years old at that time, and she was a great help to me in taking care of her sister and brother. "Mom," she said, "What is a zona?" [*prostitute* in Hebrew]

"Where did you hear that word?" I asked.

"From a neighbor downstairs," she said. "Mom, he told me that you are not working in the Hilton because you are a zona."

"Okay," I said, "I am coming home!"

The manager of the Hilton was very gracious to let me go. I took a taxi, and I felt like I would gladly kill all my neighbors! When I arrived, I rang the bell of the neighbor's door, and when he opened it, I came in.

This neighbor was about thirty years old, and he lived with his parents. As I came in, I found out that they were entertaining guests. I was so frustrated and bitter that I did not care. I took a glass from the table, and I dropped it on the tile floor.

"Oops," I said, as the glass reached the breaking point. Then I picked up another glass and another glass, furiously dropping them to the floor!

"Are you crazy?" they screamed. "Why are you doing that?"

"I will tell you why," I said, "because if my dignity is your property, then all you possess is mine! Furthermore," I said, "you can replace all these broken glasses, but how can I replace the trash you have put in my children's mind?"

I was so inflamed with anger and bitterness that I barely noticed a small white puppy jumping on me, wiggling his little tail, so, as I opened the door, I just picked up the puppy and I left for my apartment.

"My baby, my baby," I heard cries behind my back. "We will call your brother-in-law!" they screamed.

"Do it," I said, "and I promise you that, by the time he comes, your dog will be dead!" Nevertheless, they did call him.

Basem was like my own son, and he was also the only one who would come to our aid in time of need. Still, he was very young, about eighteen at that time. "Nadia, open the door!" he called, banging on it.

"Tell them that the dog is dead, and I killed him!" I screamed back through the door.

"Come on, Nadia, open the door," he said. "You could not kill a fly. Give back the dog before the woman has a heart attack!"

"I killed the dog!" I screamed louder, so the listening neighbors would receive the bloody news.

"Oh, my God! Oh, my God!" I heard the woman cry.

"Nadia, give me the dog right now!" my brother-in-law demanded, so after another long minute, the deep cries of the woman softened my heart. I returned the puppy, and yes, he was alive!

It was close to impossible to live as we did. My older daughter took care of her younger sister and brother, who were quite mischievous at all times, and she herself was so young. I felt so guilty because my mistakes robbed my children of a normal childhood. I was in constant fear that someone would hurt them. I told them to close the door when they came from school and not to go anywhere until I came home.

Knowing that no one would help me, I wrote a letter to the wife of the Israeli president, Mrs. Hertzog. I did not think that she would reply, but I took a chance anyway. I poured out my heart in this letter, which was sincere with sorrow and regrets, as I pleaded for my kids' future. Nevertheless, to my great surprise, I got a reply with an invitation to visit, which was beyond any honor I had ever experienced.

We had a painfully honest conversation, in which she informed me that legally there is no way for a resolution because of a signed agreement between the Israeli government and all the religious parties in Israel that indicates freedom to keep all religious traditions.

"Therefore, by law," she said, "you belong to your husband, regardless of whether or not you became a Muslim."

"Are you sure you cannot help me?" I begged. "Could you at least find a way to save my children?"

"I am so sorry," she said, wiping invisible tears.

Deeply disappointed, I thanked her for seeing me, and as I said goodbye, she stopped me.

"Wait," she said, "there is someone that I think would help you. Have you heard about Rabbi Cahana?"

"Of course," I replied, "everyone knows who he is."

"Before you go to see him," she said, "I want you to promise me that, under any circumstances, you will not say you heard his name from me, as I myself refuse to believe in all he is doing."

"You have my word," I said. "As long as you are the first lady, my lips are sealed."

Chapter 20

Like everyone in Israel, I had heard about the rabbi; Arabs hated him and some Jews hated him. He was notorious for his actions, and he worked furiously against the Jewish cabinet. If there was a terrorist attack somewhere in Israel, Rabbi Cahana was always the first on the scene. He also participated in retaliatory actions, but no one could ever prove his direct involvement. Israel was left to blame and to answer to the United Nations.

Nevertheless, since Rabbi Cahana took charge against the terror, Arabs feared him, and there were fewer terrorist activities and much fewer casualties. Still Israel accumulated all the heat for his actions, refusing to acknowledge the truth, as there was always violence attached to his name.

I personally admired his strategies because he spoke the terrorists' language. When they barked, he barked back; he did not try to reason with them verbally, politically, or even psychologically because terrorism was indeed the only language that they understood.

When I found Rabbi Cahana's offices, my heart was pounding with uncertainty, and the truth, as he may see it, hit me straight in the face. *What am I going to tell him, I thought in desperation? I did not have an excuse or explanation for my actions, and I was scared.*

"Can I help you?" one of the men in the office asked me.

"I'd like to see Rabbi Cahana," I said.

"What about?" he asked.

"It is a private matter," I said.

"The rabbi is not here right now, but we need to search you for weapons before you see him."

After an hour or so, Rabbi Cahana stood before me and invited me into his office. "What I can do for you?" he asked.

"Not for me, for my children," I said, leading him to focus on the children and not me.

"Okay," he said, "Go on."

"I married to an Arab, and when I realized my mistake, it was too late."

There was complete silence in the room. As I fearfully anticipated his reaction, he stood on his feet, and without warning, he screamed into my face, "How could you desecrate our race like that! Where are your parents?"

"Dead," I said.

He gazed at me for a second and then he began to walk back and forth with his hands locked behind his back. "You are from Europe," he said, "right?"

"Yes," I said softly.

"Speak up! Speak up!" he said impatiently. "How many children do you have?"

"Three," I said.

"Boys? Do you have boys?"

"One boy," I said, "and two girls."

"So, what do you want me to do?" he asked.

"Could you save them?" I said reluctantly.

"And why should I do that?" he burst into unexpected rage.

"Because they are Jewish!" I screamed back with increased confidence.

"You said it! You said it!" he said, pointing at me with a big fist. I was puzzled and afraid at the same time, and I did not know what to expect from his peculiar behavior.

This is just a small scene from our hour-long session of blaming and screaming and I took it, because in my small world, the rabbi was my only chance to freedom. Eventually, the rabbi relaxed and pointed out a few reasons why he was going to help me. He liked the fact that I was from Europe, and most importantly, he endorsed my heritage, which was from the Levi tribe.

"Moses in the Bible was Levi," the rabbi said.

Who cares? I thought with a rebellious spirit, as I refused to accumulate more information about my race. However, I was happy that the rabbi had his justifications for helping me.

I received precise instructions about how to manipulate Ali into divorce and giving up his children, so we could come back legally to Judaism.

By the time Ali came back for a visit, I was well-equipped and prepared for him. Rabbi Cahana had offices in many locations in the United States, and through his contacts, we received constant

162

information about Ali's life. At that time, Ali was involved with an American girl who was pregnant with his child, and I hoped that this information would work for my benefit.

When Ali returned for a visit and found out that I was working at the Hilton, he was furious! "No wife of mine will work outside the house!" he screamed in front of his family. "What people will say?" he continued, "that I am not a man?!"

You are not a man, Ali, I thought to myself.

Instead I said calmly, "I will leave the work at the Hilton, if you give me two thousand dollars a month."

"What!!!" he shouted. "What do you need so much money for!?"

"Listen, Ali," I said, as the rabbi instructed, "if I work or not, the Israeli government will take care of us. They will give me $500 for each child and another $500 for rental, and that is only the minimum.

"You are not going to ask for their assistance!!" Ali said, threateningly.

"Yes I am because what I am earning at Hilton is not enough to pay for rent, food, clothing, books, and other necessities," I said.

"You cannot do that to me!" he screamed like crazy. "I know the law; they will force me to pay them back, and if I refuse, I will go to prison!"

"Well," I said, "It may be another solution."

"Like what?" he screamed.

"Divorce me and give up all the rights to the children," I said.

All eyes in the room froze on Ali, as he put his hand on my neck. "You will be dead before I do that!" he said, through his clenched teeth.

"You are jumping too fast to the wrong conclusion," I said, clearing my throat, as my heart was pounding with all its might.

"How wrong could I be?" he said in sarcasm.

"Completely wrong," I said with strength and confidence.

"I would still be married to you," I said, "by Muslim law, if you divorce me just once. Then you can marry my friend Karen or any other American girl, so you can get American citizenship, and then you can bring us to America."

Ali said nothing, but I watched him calculating everything.

"Okay," he said after a few long minutes, "we will go to the court tomorrow, and I will divorce you just once!"

"Do not forget to bring a lawyer with you," I said.

"What for?" he asked.

"Well," I said carefully, "so everything will be legal, and the government will not demand child support from you. After you give up your rights to the children, the responsibility will be all mine."

He stared at me for a moment and I knew that he was fighting the urge not to hit me. "You think you can play me or outsmart me," he said. "If I sign the papers, you will disappear with the kids!"

"Yeah, sure," I said confrontationally, in spite of a paralyzing fear crawling all over me. "Where would I go?" I said with a trembling voice. "I have no one, and the Jewish people would spit me like a poison after what I have done! I am alone, Ali, completely alone, and I have no one to trust or depend on but you."

"Fine, fine," he said impatiently. "I will bring a lawyer, so everything will be just as you said, but if you betray me, I promise you that you will be begging to die! Do you understand?"

"Of course," I said, not believing how smoothly it went. However, the fear that he might change his mind still lingered in my heart.

From this point on, everything went into motion. Ali was still around, but I could not wait any longer to prepare the children for the future. I needed to introduce them to a new and different culture, and I was hesitant and afraid.

The divorce was final, and only by the hand of God, I was the only custodian of my children. I was just waiting for the legal papers. People that I worked with invited us to their homes frequently, and my children began to understand that the Jewish people were not so bad after all.

In one of the visits at a Jewish friend's home, my oldest daughter whispered into my ear. "Mom," she said, "their houses are not like the Arabic houses."

"What do you mean?" I asked.

"They have many books, Mom, and they have them in every house we visited."

"We have books," I said.

"Yes, Mom," she whispered, "we have books, but they have ninety-nine libraries!"

"Sweetheart," I said, holding her little hand. "Remember one thing always: the Jewish people are also called the People of the Book."

"What does that mean?" my daughter asked.

"Well," I was thinking frantically what to answer, as I did not remember a thing beyond the remark I'd just made, "you see, Precious, God gave us His Book from the heavens written by His hand for us to follow."

"I do not understand," my daughter said, "to follow what?"

"To follow God's instructions," I said.

"Do you follow, Mom?"

"No, Sweetheart, I do not follow because I do not understand the writings in the Book."

"How is that, Mom? You do know Hebrew, don't you?"

"Yes, I do," I said.

"So why don't you understand?" my daughter insisted.

"I do not know why, Sweetie. It may be because it is written in God's own Hebrew, and not the Hebrew that I know."

Yes indeed, God has His own language. I remembered many chapters from the Old Testament, but the heart of it all was a puzzle to me. However, in my sincere submission, I began to understand because, only in my willingness to sacrifice my will, was I able to break through the thick fog that surrounded me. As I dared to hope, I dared to believe, and as I grew closer to my Savior, I knew why I needed to be born again and what that meant.

On October 4, 1982, I held the divorce papers and the legal document wherein Ali gave up all the rights to the children. Before Ali returned to the United States, he took us to the zoological center that is in a small city called Ramat-Gan near Tel-Aviv.

On the way back to Jerusalem, I remembered that my childhood friend Pnina lived in Ramat-Gan. I told Ali where to turn and there we were. It was quite a few years since I had seen her last. Ali stayed in the car with the children, as I ran upstairs to find out if my friend still lived there.

Pnina opened the door and when she saw me, she screamed, "Yonush!" (We always called each other "Pninush" and "Yonush" to sound like Polish.) "Come in, come in," Pnina invited me.

"I can't. My family is in the car," I said.

"So, bring them along," Pnina said.

"I can't right now," I said, "but I promise you, I will keep in touch."

"Where have you been all these years?" Pnina asked.

"I married an Arab," I said, hoping that this information would not make a big difference.

"So that is why you stopped the contact with me?" Pnina said.

"There are more reasons, Pninush," I said, "and one day I will tell you the whole story."

Pnina introduced herself to Ali and the children, and Ali made an extra effort to impress her. I felt so ashamed, and not because he was an Arab, but because of what he really was.

"He is so handsome," Pnina said when we were saying goodbye.

"Is he really?" I said, puzzled. I gave her my address and I told her where I was working, and we departed.

One day when I came home, I found Pnina with my children.

"How could you leave your children all by themselves?" she said with an accusatory manner.

"You have no idea," I said, telling her all the machinations I created and the regrettable results of it all. "However, the victory is at hand," I said, "because in a few days, Rabbi Cahana will take us to safety."

"I am so happy for you," Pnina said, emotionally, "and I promise you, we will celebrate your freedom."

"Let's hope so," I said. "Rabbi Cahana said we will have to hide for a while, but I promise you, Pninush, you will be always informed."

"Do you remember, Yonush, a few years back when I came to visit you in the house on the seashore?"

"Yes, I do," I said.

"You were practicing trapeze, remember?"

"Yes, I remember. I was performing with Tommy in different nightclubs at that time."

"Yes, I know," Pnina said, "but you told me also that you were in the service. You told me that they did not take you into the army; instead, you were learning the Arabic language to be a part of some kind of unconventional service."

"Pninush," I said, "I was lying to you."

"No, you were not!" Pnina burst out, offended. "I know you too well to believe that! How could you do this to me?" Pnina said. "I searched for you everywhere; I wanted you to meet my son, but I could not find you."

Then I saw a beautiful boy playing with my children. "He is a copy of you," I said.

"Yes, I know," she said sadly. "He was born with disabilities, and he has developmental problems," and as she said that, she burst into a painful cry. "Oh, Yonush," she cried, "why is God doing this to us? Why, why?! They told me that he would never develop beyond the capacity of eight years of age."

I was stunned and empty of emotions. Thoughts ran through my head like thunder and lightning. I felt her pain and my heart cried with hers, as I hugged her with all my might.

"I am fine," Pnina said, pushing me gently away. "Let us talk about you," she said, "and what you have done in all these years!"

"I already told you," I said defensively. "I was performing in different nightclubs."

"Yeah, yeah," Pnina remarked, "I just want to hear about the unconventional service you told me about, remember?"

"Oh that," I said, taking a deep breath. "I am sorry, Pninush, but I lied to you."

"Very well, then," Pnina said, "but know just one thing, Yonush: I am not stupid because here in Israel no one studies the Arabic language without good reason!"

"I had a good reason," I said smiling. "I wanted to be friendly with our cousins the Arabs."

Pnina looked at me intensively, squinting her eyes, and waving a finger at my nose. "I know this smile," she said victoriously. "This is your smile when you try to deceive. This is your manipulative smile!"

"What do you really want from me?" I asked seriously.

"The truth," she said, "and nothing but the truth!"

"If I told you I was a terrorist, would you believe me?" I asked her.

"It depends," Pnina said.

"Depends on what?" I asked.

"Well," Pnina hesitated, "if you give me the names of the Jews that you killed..."

"Jews?!" I burst out laughing, "You think that I killed Jews?!"

"You said that you were a terrorist," Pnina said defensively, "and there is only one kind of terrorist that I know: the Arab terrorists!"

"Pninush," I said, "I did not tell you that I was a terrorist. I just said, 'WHAT IF I WAS?' but nevertheless, I lied to you because that is the only thing I do well. I lie and I pretend that I am someone else and that's what gives me self worth."

"Fine!" Pnina said angrily. "You said that you lied, so lie to me. Tell me all the lies you lived by, and I will encourage your self worth or whatever it may be!"

Eventually, I gave in to her pressure. "Fine," I said, "If you insist..."

"Once upon a time," I started.

"Yeah, yeah, yeah," Pnina cut me off, "just get into it!"

"There were many reasons for the establishment of the organization, but the main one was to prevent terrorist activities in Israel. The person who established the organization believed that we would stop terrorism only by terrorism; therefore, our duties were to eliminate the power and the influence as much as we could.

"There are many terrorists groups active from many continents; unfortunately, most of the Arab countries give them shelter, weapons, ammunition, and constant financial support. The United Nations manages always to ignore the simplest justice for Israel, and the Arab propaganda against the Jewish people has prevailed!

"Our organization was completely private and without obvious connection to the Israeli government. If we had been

168

caught in any illegal activities, Israel would never acknowledge us."

"Who was the head of the organization?" Pnina asked.

"He called himself the "Partisan"; he was very resourceful and highly intelligent. His connections spanned the world, and many powerful people were supporting him."

"Did the Israeli government know about him and the organization?" Pnina asked.

"Maybe..." I said.

"So, what were your duties besides performing on the stage?" Pnina asked.

"Part of our duty was to confuse the terrorists by providing them with false information which effectively created great chaos and suspicion among them, suspending the terror in Israel for a while."

"How did you do that?" Pnina asked with curiosity.

"Simply and effectively," I said, and my answer inflamed Pnina with anger.

"At times, we did take drastic steps," I said.

"To kill, to kill?!" Pnina suggested, all excited and wrapped up in her bloody scenario.

"We did not kill, Pninush," I said. "We didn't have to; they always killed their own. We just pushed them a little when we released information that created suspicion, and they did the killings."

"How did you release information?" Pnina asked.

"By a sophisticated communication system," I said.

"I don't understand," Pnina said. "Could you explain?"

"They listened to false information through their own communication systems installed by our expert. They thought they were spying on Israeli intelligence units when we played them."

"Wow," Pnina sighed, "How unbelievable!"

"I told you," I said, "I can lie!"

"I don't think you are lying," Pnina said. "Nevertheless, lie some more. What else did you do, Yonush?"

"We traveled all over Europe and the Middle East. We preformed in villas and palaces, the riches and the beauty of which were beyond any imaginary description. We as Jewish Israeli could have been killed easily if found out, but none of us looked like a

Jew; therefore, no one suspected us, because we also had exceptionally clean documentation."

"I don't understand," Pnina said. "You are beautiful, Yonush, but you never knew how to be attractive, so how did you do it?"

"Do what, Pninush?" I asked.

"You know, be a spy and all."

"First, I wouldn't call it a spy; that makes it sound too glamorous. Let's just say that I was a good manipulative source, and I could gather information very effectively because no one ever suspected me. I looked more like a twelve-year-old, and it was a very attractive age for many Arabs who wanted to purchase me."

"What?" Pnina said. "They wanted to buy you for money?"

"Only a few times," I said, "and there were times that we barely escaped with our lives, because in spite of everything, I was not for sale. We just led them to believe otherwise!"

"Who is *we*?" Pnina asked. "How many of you were there?"

"I never knew how many were in the organization. I just knew the people I worked with in different settings, but we didn't need more than three or four to accomplish each task," I said.

Pnina look at me sharply and said, "I don't believe that you did not kill."

"Well, Pninush, I am sorry to disappoint you, but I did not kill, not even for self-defense! That's it, Pninush," I said. "I am done telling you stories until the next chapter is complete."

Chapter 21

Rabbi Cahana instructed me to be ready with the children the next morning; he said that his men would come to help us with things we needed to take, and to give us protection, if needed. He did not tell me where we were going. I was very anxious and scared that someone would see we were moving and notify Ali's family. I also feared someone would notify the religious Muslims, and I would be dead in a flash, leaving my children orphaned.

About seven o'clock the next morning, we were ready and waiting; we did not take much, just a few clothes. As I was waiting by the window, a white truck stopped, and six men with guns jumped out.

They were wearing T-shirts with a logo of a big fist inside the star of David and underneath was written in Hebrew, KAH, which is translated "This is the way," or, as the picture described, "Power in Control."

They positioned themselves in a way that no one could come into or get out of the area. One of them came up to escort us, and my son happily locked his little hand in the hand of the stranger. The tough expression on the man's face softened immediately when he picked up my son into his arms. "Are you a redheaded troublemaker?" he asked my son.

"He doesn't know Hebrew," I said. "I was forbidden to teach them."

"What beautiful children," the man said, smiling.

"And I can say that they are truly Jewish," I said, "although they look more like their father."

"Perhaps externally," the man said, "but the light in their eyes is God's light!"

Great! I said in my heart, another religious fanatic! I just hoped it would not be another side of the same coin.

After a few more minutes, we were on the way, and anticipation overtook the fearful feelings I had experienced in the past few weeks. We all sat in the back of the truck; my daughter Miriam was struggling with her terrified cat and we were trying to help her, when the men in the front screamed, "Put your belts on. We have company!"

Shaking with fear, I fastened my children's belts, barely able to hold in all the stress. Suddenly the truck spun around and stopped across the road, blocking the little car that was following us.

I heard the sound of shots being fired, or maybe it was just the sound of stones aimed at us. Whichever it was, it was enough for Rabbi Cahana's men to jump immediately from both sides of the truck with their automatic weapons in hand. They blew out all four tires of the little car.

They jumped back in like nothing had happened, and I sensed that the truck was picking up speed and going very fast through the streets of old Jerusalem. "We should have finished them off," one of the men said.

"Yeah, and give them more ammunition against us," the other man answered, realizing at the same time that we witnessed the entire scene.

"Don't you worry," one of the men said to us. "They probably were after us and not you, and in a little while, you will be safe."

The truck entered a very narrow street and stopped.

"Quickly," one of the men said, "follow me." Miriam was upset again about her cat that was hiding under the seat, and after a few complimentary scratches, I managed to grab the cat and take it out. We ran after the man until we reached a different truck.

"Hop in," the man said. "You are safe now." It was a bigger truck with a lot of communication equipment, as well as a police radio. They gave us drinks and food and even some goodies.

"You'd better go to the bathroom," one of the men said. "It will be a while until we stop again." So we did, and after we came back, all the men were wearing different clothes, probably so they wouldn't be recognized by Cahana's famous symbol.

It would have been a good movie, I thought to myself, if we were not involved in it. Nevertheless, I started to feel much more secure; even the children felt more secure as they discovered the generosity and kindness of these puzzling men.

All the way to our destination, we were listening to the police radio and the regular radio. The reports claimed that "three Muslim children were kidnapped by their unstable mother, and that they are probably in Jewish territory among Rabbi Cahana's people who are helping them." Furthermore, the police warned anyone that would dare to help us. It seemed very strange that, in such a short time, the media was involved.

We arrived at a place called Kiriat Arba, which is above Arab-populated Hebron and about an hour from Jerusalem. We were pleasantly surprised at the beautiful, spacious apartment provided for us. The people who welcomed us were pleasant but careful. We were at that place for a few days, and I was happy to see my children playing outside with other children and catching on to the Hebrew language very quickly. As we visited different people's homes, our hosts were often fascinated by the story of my (stupidly) marrying an Arab and my life among the Arabs.

One day, as we came back from such a visit, our apartment was crowded with people. Rabbi Cahana handed me a newspaper; on the front page, there was a picture of me and the children, next to a picture of Ali, sobbing. What a joke, I thought to myself; it read: "Devastated father flies from USA to Israel… to save his children after his brother notifies him that his wife Nadia took the children and fled with Cahana's people."

"He was in my office," Rabbi Cahana said, "but we kicked him out. However, the justice department and the police are helping him, so I arranged a meeting with a news reporter to explain our side of the matter, and of course, to gain some sympathy."

Until we met the reporter, we did unbelievable maneuvers, dragging the poor reporter from one destination to another, until we were sure he was alone.

From that point on, and for a long time, we were on the first pages of the newspapers. Palestinians and Israelis were intrigued by the escape. The Arabs and Jews bet on who would win and who was going to get the children, and the newspapers sold like never before.

We weren't in any one place for long. We constantly moved from one generous family to the other, always fearful; sometimes we were forced to leave in the middle of the night, and other times, we gave interviews to the media in the middle of the night including the British TV, BBC. At this point, the children were so afraid that I decide to put an end to this travesty and when we came back to Kiriat Arba to the apartment designated for us, I called Ali.

"Listen, Ali," I said, "let us put an end to the insanity. Let us meet somewhere and talk."

"Are you coming alone?" he asked.

"Yes," I said. We met in a small café in Jerusalem. Ali was alone, but he sat by the wall just in case. He was afraid, but in his strange way, he was happy to see me.

"Are you alone?" he asked.

"Yes, Ali, I am alone, and if Rabbi Cahana finds out that I met with you, I will be in deep trouble. I am thinking of the children," I said. "They are tired and scared, so tell me what you want, Ali."

"I want two hours with the children to restore my dignity. I will take them to the Arabic newspapers, so they see I am the one who has the children, and after that I will return them to you. On the weekend, I'd like to spend time with the children in the hotel in Tel-Aviv."

"Fine," I said.

The next day, without telling anyone, I took the children to Jerusalem. Ali was already waiting.

"I will bring them back in two hours," he said. It was the longest two hours of my life, but he brought the children back and he himself drove us to Kiriat Arba. I took him inside the apartment to show him that our life is much better than the life that he had for us. Before he left, he handed to me two hundred dollars.

"No, thank you," I said proudly. "We have everything we need." Then I took the money anyway.

"Why did you trust me with the children?" Ali asked me.

"I didn't," I said, "but I knew about your woman in the USA, and I gambled on that and on your selfishness."

As we said goodbye, I knew that the children and I could breathe freely at last.

It was also near election time, and Rabbi Cahana was one of the candidates for the senate. I suggested to him to rescue other women who were married to Arabs.

"Out of the question!" the rabbi screamed. "I helped you because you are European, and there was no one to mourn for you when you married the Arab." (There is a custom, in the Jewish

174

tradition that, if a woman marries a non-Jew, she will be as good as dead, and her parents and family will sit on the floor for seven days to mourn her.)

He was adamant, but I did not give up because I knew the pain and the turmoil that these women encountered from the hands of their husbands. "Rabbi," I said, "if you open a shelter for these women, I will take care of the rest. I am sure that you will get more votes in the election because it will show your humanitarian side."

The rabbi thought for a minute, scratching his beard, "You just may be right," he mumbled. "You just may be right!" And the shelter was born.

From this point on, everything went crazy. I will mention only a part of it; otherwise, I will need to write another book concerning just this subject.

Knowing the Arabic language, I was able to find out about other Jewish women and their locations. We went to the Arab villages and took the women and children; sometimes a child was left behind, and we would come back to take him home. It was more and more dangerous as deep threatening sounds were heard from the Arab population.

Because of the media's constant reports, Jewish parents called us and begged us to bring their daughters back home. Some of the women were married to Arabs; others were street workers with an Arab pimp.

The strategy of Rabbi Cahana was simple: If the pimp did not let the girl go after a calm first time warning, he would experience a small accident that would encourage him to rethink his decision. If he still did not let the girl go, the next accident would be much more painful, and if that did not work, the pimp would be cornered, and acid would be forced down his pants.

I will never forget the horrific screams that crushed the still of the night, but I was detached. My soul was blank and not responsive because the screams of my heart blended with the screams of the pimp. I had just started to realize that, in spite of my heart's desire to be a better person, I was incredibly detached. Maybe I just agreed with Rabbi Cahana's actions ... yes, I did and I did! It was like a healing justice to my disturbed soul.

Nevertheless, by the time the rabbi called for help, (which he always did) the poor pimp had already lost his productive organs. Many young girls returned to the arms of their families, saved.

Sadly, some parents did not want their daughter back. "She is dead to us," they used to say. "Please do not call us again." But I did not stop calling because I knew that their hearts would soften, as I know the Jewish heart. We can make a lot of noise with anger and fury, but in the end the forgiveness comes easy—joyful and teary—but easy.

I was happy with every reunion. Everyone cried and every soul cheered. A few families stayed in the shelter, and we managed fine with the allowance. I would go to Hebron's Arabic market and buy fruits and veggies. I always bought the kosher meat and chicken because we were under the spying eyes of the religious fanatics; obeying their rules was our goal.

All this serenity came to an end when the rabbi was elected to the Senate. The allowance for the shelter stopped, and I couldn't reach him, so for the time being, I took more work cleaning houses just to provide food for the women and children in the shelter.

I was exhausted from cleaning all day, but at night, I crocheted hats for the religious women. My oldest girl Aussy would sell them and she was very good at it, as she was good at anything she took upon herself. Miriam, my middle daughter, is just all heart; she always managed to find injured animal's or injured people. She loved babies and she had a heavenly touch; when a baby cried or screamed, her touch always brought silence and smiles.

My son Ahmad was all energy, fast and happy and always up to no good! He is my youngest and he knew how to manipulate me. He was very polite to the older people but not to young girls; he used to pull their hair and push them and bother them. Almost daily, I was forced to face angry parents.

When I asked my son for an explanation, he moved his shoulders up and down, and when I was ready to punish him, he always managed to escape. Living among religious people, I used to wear long, modest dresses, and when my son started to run, I picked up the dress with two hands, running to catch him, my goal being to slap his behind. I never could catch him; nevertheless, I provided free entertainment for the people who watched, clapping and cheering.

My son would reappear an hour later, peeking through the window and asking in hesitation: "Mo-o-o-om, are you still mad at me?" While I never had the satisfaction of slapping his behind, in order for him to understand and to stop his behavior, I asked my daughters to push him and bother him like he did to the young girls.

Shortly after, he came to me running and squeezing invisible tears. "Aussy and Miriam pushed me for no reason!" he cried. I just moved my shoulders up and down. And as smart as he was, he got the message, and I never again heard a bad thing about him... well almost never!

My children and I had our own apartment but we mostly spent our time in the shelter apartment. One night, as I came to the shelter, I was notified that a woman and her two children had left and gone back to her Arab husband. "Why did they leave?" I asked. The remaining women looked down, refusing to meet my eyes.

"You all know what will happen to her," I said. "She is as good as dead!"

"What do you care?" one of them said. "You are part of them!"

"Who is 'them'?" I asked, a little confused. "Part of Rabbi Cahana's people," the woman said.

"Listen," I said, "You need to tell me what is going on because I do feel responsible for you, and if I was a part of them as you say, I wouldn't work so hard to provide for all of us!"

"What about the money you get from them?" one of the women asked.

"Since Rabbi Cahana was elected," I said, "I have not gotten any money; I just took more cleaning jobs to provide for all of us." For a moment, everyone in the room was silent, and then all of them began to talk.

I found out that some of Cahana's men were asking for sexual favors, threatening to take the women back to their abusive husbands or to take their children away. I was beside myself! I could not understand how a man that had children and was highly religious could do such a despicable thing.

"I need your testimony on paper," I said, "because this will be your protection." But no one volunteered.

"What about you?" I asked one girl named Aliza.

"They have my son," she said, "and I will do anything they ask me to do."

"Oh no!" I said. "Not while I am alive! How dare they do such an ugly thing! Listen, Aliza," I said, "I promise you that I myself will bring your son back, but you need to write all that they have done."

I gave her paper, and I told her how to write so it would be sufficient in a court of law. She hesitated for a moment, but she wrote everything. "If they come to take you," I said, "and you feel that you are in danger, you tell them that you wrote everything and that your testimony is with me."

"Just remember," she said, "they have all the power."

"Not anymore," I dismissed her concern. "Now that I have all the papers for me and the children, I do not need to depend on them anymore, but I do feel a responsibility for you, as I feel for my own children."

I gave the paper to my oldest daughter, and I said, "Take it and hide it and remember where it is, but do not hide it in our apartment."

At three o'clock in the morning, I heard banging on the door. "Who is it?" I asked.

"Open the door," the familiar voice ordered. So I did; it was Cahana's friend or secretary or whatever his title was. He obviously knew about the shameful acts, but did nothing.

"You woke up my kids," I said.

"Give me the letter," he said, ignoring my complaint.

"I do not have it anymore," I said.

"And who has it?" he insisted.

"A lawyer," I lied. "I was concerned, so I added my testimony as well, and if anything should happen to me, or the children, or any residents in the shelter, you and your friends will get vacations in prison!"

"Well," he said angrily, "is that how you repay us for what we have done for you?"

I eyed him with disrespect. "I never forget a favor," I said. "The moment Rabbi Cahana was elected to the government, I repaid you, and when I myself provided for the shelter, I repaid you."

Powerless for the first time, he stared at me with rage. "Tomorrow," he said, "I want you out of this apartment!"

"I will do just that," I said, "after I speak personally with Rabbi Cahana, and if Aliza does not get her son back, I will release her testimony to the press!"

His rage was obvious; even my children sensed it, as they hurried to hide behind me. "Remember whom you are dealing with," he said. "Accidents happen every day."

"Yes, I know," I said. "That is why I took precautions," I lied. "I have recordings of your criminal activities."

"You are bluffing," he said.

"Fine," I said, "Believe what you will. If something happens to me or to the women in the shelter, you will find out soon enough how much I was bluffing. So go ahead," I challenged him.

"Why you are doing all this?" he said. "We were good to you! The women in the shelter are not your concern." He added in a softer tone, "Think about yourself, and your kids, and what is beneficial for you."

"How can I?" I said. "There is no difference between me and them. You betrayed us all!"

Nevertheless, I need to admit that my admiration for Rabbi Cahana grew each time that I witnessed women and their children reunited with their families. I considered him a hero and he was a hero indeed, proclaiming the Word of God through the scripture. He stood always firm in his convictions.

Thirty years later, his predictions revealed in the exact order as he said. Rabbi Cahana was not silent, and he did not play politics. He raised his voice in a fist of the truth, which the rest of us denied, and for that Israel is paying a heavy price. As Rabbi Cahana predicted, even Europe is choking by the laws of Islam.

I tried to show power and confidence as I spoke to Cahana's secretary (if he was his secretary). "You taught me a very valuable lesson of power and deceit," I said. "You also taught me how to fight without fear and how to justify any wrongdoings! It is always convenient," I said, "but not acceptable; therefore, the truth is my weapon this time and no one can fight against it, not even you!"

"Nevertheless," he said, repeating his last words. "Do not forget who you are dealing with. You have been warned."

After he left, I just collapsed into the chair. I knew that I could stay longer in the apartment, but emotionally I wanted to evacuate as soon as possible. I told the kids to go back to bed and I remained in the living room, planning our future. In the morning, I called my brother-in-law Basem, and when I told him that I was leaving Cahana's shelter, he rejoiced.

"Could you call Ali in the USA and ask him to send us some money?"

"Sure, sure," he said, "How much do you need?"

"Five hundred dollars will be enough," I said.

"But why are you staying there?" he asked me.

"Because I am waiting for important papers that will arrive in here," I lied. I already had the papers proving that we legally came back to Judaism.

What a joke, I thought to myself, remembering all the rituals we had gone through. First, they poked my son until they drew blood, to seal his circumcision. We heard him scream, and my daughters began to cry.

"You see what you have done," they accused me.

Then my son came out, walking funny, as he announced proudly: "I am Jewish! I am Jewish!" and our tears turned to laughter, but not for long, because my son wanted to share this news with everybody, pulling his pants down and showing where he was poked.

After that, we had to go to Micva, a pool of water for purification. We took a bath first, and a woman explained to us why we needed to go under the water thirty-six times. She gave us long white robes to put on for this ceremony. In the next room we heard a rabbi talking to my son: "Your father is Moses," he said.

"Oh, no," my son replied, "my father is Ali."

"No, no!" the rabbi said irritated. "Your father is Moses and no other!"

"Do I know him?" my son asked, as my daughters and I listened, breathlessly holding in our laughter at this comedy.

"You will meet him after you die," the rabbi said.

My son started to scream, "I don't want to die. I want my mom-m-m! I want my mom-m-m!" And we couldn't stop laughing.

Because my son is a male, he went under the water just once, and that was it, and of course, he was in a different pool. My daughters and I were positioned in the middle of the pool. Four rabbis were reading from a book, when they told us to go under. We went under and the pure white robes floated upwards, revealing our nakedness!

I'll be dammed if I will allow these sick rabbis to witness our shame, I thought angrily, jumping from one conclusion to another. "Don't hold your nose under the water. Hold your robe instead," I said to my daughters in Arabic, so the rabbis would not understand.

Indeed, this was a task: to go under the water so many times holding the robe, but we got the necessary papers to survive in Israel. *I knew I was Jewish, I felt it on my flesh and in my soul and these four hypocritical rabbis just earned my disrespect, but at the same moment, I realized an urge to study my heritage because, after all, I did have one! And it was mine and not theirs and not anybody else's in this whole world!*

In the next few days, I received the money and an apartment. I made sure that the apartment would be on the fourth floor, so the religious police women would have a hard time checking on us! It was incredible how they checked every step we took. They made sure that we had two sets of dishes, one for dairy and one for meat, and for the Passover we needed another set of dishes. They checked to see if we kept Shabbat according to their rules!

They checked if everything was kosher because they knew that I was buying fruits and veggies from the Arabic market. They checked whether the lights were on or off. They checked and checked, as if we were the only people on this earth. However, it was very hard for them to climb four stories, so they were finally gracious enough to tell me that I was trustworthy.

I was still the main caregiver in the shelter, and I was very tired from all the work I did. On top of that, a young pregnant prostitute was added to the shelter, and the only language she spoke was so colorful, it would make anyone blush.

The three families in the shelter did not want her among their children so I took her in. My kids picked up her slang very fast, and I needed to do some explaining to her and to my kids. She was a kid herself, and I was very sorry for her and all she experienced in her short life. Her mom was a prostitute, so she had become one as well. Now pregnant, she wanted to give her child a different life.

Kiryat Arba was populated mostly with different Jewish religious people that I did not care for. However, I liked Hasidey Chabad; they were different, they were genuine in everything they did and never forceful or judgmental, so I decided to speak with their rabbi about the pregnant girl.

"Hmmm, very sad," the Rabbi said. "We need to help her."

"I know," I said. "I have three families in the shelter and also my kids, and as you know, Rabbi Cahana isn't helping us much. He's just paying the shelter fee. You see, Rabbi," I said, "Rabbi Cahana sent this girl, knowing that I would take care of her when no one else would."

"Don't worry. I will find a good and strong family for her," the rabbi said, and I believed him.

I was very angry with Rabbi Cahana, so I called and I left him a strong message about his character and the character of his men. It was senseless to remind him of his promised obligations. I thanked him for helping us, and added sarcastically I was not happy anymore for having a part in his election to the Parliament.

I told him that I had no choice but to turn to the media with the truth because it was an impossible task to take all the work upon myself. By the end of the same day, I had a reply by one of his men.

"Go ahead," he said, "bad press is always good news for us." I suspected that Rabbi Cahana may never have received my messages, and being so busy with the government, he left everything to his deceitful friends.

"Okay," I said, "I will do just that." He left, believing that I was bluffing. The next day I called the newspaper *Yediot Aharonot.* They knew who I was because they covered my escape with the kids.

"I am on my way," the reporter said, all excited. "It will be the cover of the weekend edition."

I had just hung up the receiver, and the phone rang again. It was Pnina, my best friend and only friend.

"Do not do it," she said.

"Do not do what?" I said, puzzled.

"Don't talk to the press."

"Who told you about it?" I asked, little irritated.

"Shemu" [a false name], she said. "He has children; think about his children."

"He did not think about them when he abused the women in the shelter and kept them in fear," I said. But then I realized that something strange was happening, and knowing Rabbi Cahana and his people, I asked Pnina, "Is he sitting with you?" I asked her in Polish, just in case.

"He is," she replied.

"Tell him that it is too late; the reporter is on his way."

Pnina almost cried, "Don't do it!" she said. "You know how dangerous it could be for you and the kids."

"Pnina, relax," I told her, "nothing is going to happen to us because I have information about each of them and each piece of information is attached to proof that I have!" I lied.

"Ask her why she gathered all the information," I heard Shemu whispering to Pnina.

"Because I trust no one," I whispered back. "Pnina, tell 'Shemu' to leave your premises, or I will call the police right now!" Later that afternoon she told me that eventually he left.

In the weekend edition, the newspaper designated four long pages to Rabbi Cahana and his organization KAH. I asked the reporter to release a few clues as to the information I had in case they were planning to hurt us.

My actions were cold and calculated, and I felt like a hypocrite because, in the depth of my heart, I agreed with most of the methods Rabbi Cahana used. His scare tactics and his retaliations worked, and the terrorists always considered the outcome from Cahana's organization.

It was devastating for me to call the families of the women in the shelter. They did not want to hear about their daughter or their grandchildren. They just said, "Our daughter died long ago." Therefore, I decided to take a different approach; I called the same reporter who wrote the article about Cahana. I asked him if he could bring a professional photographer with him, and after the women in the shelter agreed, we all decided to share our stories with the media.

I knew that dramatization of any event sells news, and we did not have to dramatize ours, as the bitter flavor of our lives was associated with the worst of human error. The stories of the women in the shelter were to be revealed for the first time, as Israel acknowledged new threats that came out of the terrorist organizations. First, they planned to destroy the Israeli army by smuggling drugs to the solders, and the second plan was to marry Jewish girls in order to pollute the origin of the Jewish race.

However, they did not understand that according to Jewish law (the Mishnah) a person's birth ancestry is always based on the mother's lineage and not the father's. I implored the reporter to put emphasis on that because some of the Jewish people might have forgotten that as well.

In the shelter, the photographer took pictures of the women and their children. Their heartbreaking stories were all over the pages of the magazine, for all of Israel to know, and for young girls to learn. The next day, when I came to the shelter, the women were admiring the pictures of their kids in the magazine.

One of them said in tears, "If my mom sees them, she would love them to death, but my dad would never change his mind." The other women agreed, as they were in the same situation.

"Stop worrying," I said. "Everything will be fine one way or another." I did not tell them that the rabbi from Hasidey Chabad was helping me with the pregnant girl, and he was helping them as well. He also, thank God, contacted the three synagogues where the fathers of these women attended. He had long talks with the rabbis who agreed to talk to the parents and now, at any moment, the parents of these women would enter the room, and I was so excited for them that I began to weep.

Many years had passed since these women had seen their parents, convinced that their parents would never forgive them. Occasionally, they visited their neighborhoods for just one glimpse of their father or mother or a sibling. "I was hiding like a thief," they told me. While I knew their hearts' yearnings, I understood the pride that reflected the resistance of their own parents. The rabbi from Hasidey Chabad told me that it was an easy task convincing the parents to take their daughters back, and they could not wait to pamper their grandchildren.

Where did I go wrong? I thought to myself. I remembered hundred of times calling these parents, and each time with a different approach. They always said the same thing: "Our daughter passed away long ago," or in an even worse scenario, they said, "We are still mourning her." But the worst was when they told me, "We never had a daughter by this name."

The doorbell rang and I stood up to open the door. The rabbi from Hasidey Chabad entered, accompanied by the parents. Time stood still, and no one moved. Even the children in the room froze, sensing that incredible event.

"Greet your parents," I said choking on my tears. There was some hesitation, but seconds later they fell in each other's arms, sobbing and thanking God.

The pregnant girl was adopted, and by the time she gave birth to a beautiful boy, her language was proper and polite. I could not believe that it was the same girl.

Alone with my children and free from the responsibilities of the shelter, I was going to move on, but I wasn't quite ready. I had suddenly acknowledged the fear that lingered in me. I was convinced that I by myself could not provide for my children.

I met a nonreligious married woman who confided in me about her lovers, and I shamelessly started an affair with her husband who helped me to move from Kiryat Arba to Jerusalem. We never had intimate relations because I lied to him that I would give myself to him only in marriage.

I knew that it would be close to impossible for him to get a divorce, because they had had a religious wedding and I knew the religious laws. When I was married to Ali, and he was with his girlfriend, every Wednesday I used to go to the court and listen to different cases and lawyers' manipulations, and indeed, I learned much more than I would have from books.

I remember specifically a couple that for three years tried to get divorced, every time the rabbi sent them back home to fix their broken marriage. There is only one reason to get a divorce in the religious court; that is, if a woman is not faithful. Her claim must be backed up by serious evidence.

Finally one day, the couple, plus the lover, entered the room, just as I did. The rabbi gazed at the papers and touched his beard to emphasize the heavy load before him, and then he looked at the couple. "Hmm, hmm," he said, as he moved his head in disbelief. "So you have a lover, huh?" he said to the woman.

"Yes, Rabbi," the woman replied.

"Where is he?" The rabbi looked around the room above his thick glasses that were barely hanging on his nose.

"Here I am," the lover responded.

"What is your whole name?"

The lover gave the rabbi his whole name.

"You can sit now," the rabbi said, as he addressed the woman.

"How do I know that this is your lover? You could be lying just to get a divorce."

"I am pregnant," the woman said, handing the rabbi proof of her pregnancy.

"So be it," the rabbi concluded. Then he addressed the woman, saying, "You are forbidden to your husband and to your lover. The baby you have conceived will be pronounced a bastard. This is the law of God, so be it!" This law forced the Jewish people to be married elsewhere.

In Jerusalem, we stayed for a while in some vacant offices. The married man found work for me in a security company, and I put part of the money I earned in my closed account from the days when I worked in the Hilton.

The guilt I felt was unbearable, so I rented an apartment in Jerusalem just to escape the guilt and the married man, but he found us, and he refused to leave.

"I lied to you," I said to him. "I used you to escape from Kiryat Arba, I am sorry for all of that, so please, leave us alone."

He refused, so I decided to escape again. I found an apartment near Tel-Aviv. I called the owner and he was waiting to meet us. It was already evening when we arrived at the apartment. I paid the trucker who brought us to our destination and helped us with our furniture. Then the owner of the apartment demanded deposit.

"I do not have it with me," I said, "but I will pay you with interest, I promise."

"I am sorry," he said. "If you don't pay, the deal is off."

"I will write you a check," I said.

He gazed at me suspiciously: "How do I know that the check is good?"

"You don't," I said, "but I am a daughter of Shevah Wais" (a well-known Parliament member), I lied, "so I couldn't cheat you."

I did have money in that closed account, but if I took it out before a designated time, there would be penalties and I would lose a lot of it, so I gambled that maybe the bank would give him money against my closed account. When he heard the name of that well-known Parliament member, however, he left confidently with the check. Once again, I was convinced that lying is my best of talents, if I can call it that.

I bought pizza for the kids, and a few candles, because the apartment had no electricity yet. Thank God, my kids did not fear the night and they enjoyed the candles. I left my oldest in charge; she was nine years old at that time. As I look back, I know that only God sustained and cared for my children, as He did for me.

I took some cosmetics with me and I went to search for a job as a waitress. The center of the town was close by, and there were many restaurants and coffee shops all around.

I chose a coffee shop that was almost empty but unique. I went to the lavatory to straighten myself up and to put makeup on, in order to be more attractive. I was noticed immediately as I sat by the table to observe the surroundings and the work of the server.

"Just coffee," I said to the waiter, and with a quick glance, I met the eyes of the owner who stood behind the espresso machine, assessing my appeal. I drank the coffee, and I enjoyed a cigarette while reading the menu and purposely ignoring the intense stares of the owner.

"New in town?" I heard him asking.

"Yes," I said shortly.

"From where?"

"From Jerusalem," I said.

"What brings you in here?"

"A big truck," I said.

"Do you have a job?"

"Not yet," I said, "but I am going to apply in one of the hotels on the seashore."

"Why don't you work in here?" he said.

"How much will you pay me?"

"Nothing, you would work for tips."

"Sorry," I said, "I cannot. I was a supervisor in the Hilton and I need to have a secure income."

"Five dollars an hour," he said and I almost fell out of my chair. It was 1984, and no one in Israel paid wages to the waitresses except in hotels in which gratuities were included; nevertheless, I acted like I deserved it.

In a very short time, the coffee place flourished with more and more people, and my boss was forced to open another two rooms. I was not happy working at night because it took me away from my children; therefore, I decided to learn the art of massage therapy, and surprisingly, my boss insisted on paying for my studies.

"Out of the question," I said, "You have given me so much already!"

"I just want your friendship," he said.

"I am your friend," I said and I meant it. I knew that he and his buddies were well-known criminals who possessed many businesses, and against all odds, I felt very secure with their friendship.

My boss stupidly believed that I was some kind of a lucky charm, and every time that one of his buddies opened a new business, he asked me if I would be willing to step into it for their success.

"It is stupid," I used to tell him. "If I was indeed some kind of a lucky charm, don't you think I would be blessed first?"

"No, No! You don't understand," he explained. "This is from God. He gave you this gift so you can bless others!"

"I did not know you are religious," I said sarcastically. "Are you?"

"Not really," he said, "but I know that you have blessed me, and you blessed others, so what proof do you need?"

None, I guess, I thought to myself, because somehow I liked all the attention of being a lucky charm.

For about a year, I studied different methods of therapeutic massage from a Japanese shiatsu who taught me Swedish and Russian massage. I found a job very fast and the hard work began.

A few months later, I got enough clientele, but this took most of my time. Most of the working days I did thirteen massages at 45 minutes each. My whole body ached, but I couldn't refuse anyone because they asked for me by name.

I began to be very tired, physically and emotionally, especially because the world of massage started to change, and some men took the liberty of suggesting inappropriate acts. However, I learned quickly to maneuver things to my advantage by asking them about their mothers or sisters. About 90 percent of the time, they recognized their shameful suggestions. That worked good for my behalf.

One day, as I entered my massage room, there was an unfamiliar man sitting on the massage table.

"My name is Yona," I said, "and I will be your masseuse today."

"I am Gregory, and I know all about you," the man said.

"What do you know?" I asked, puzzled.

"I know you are trustworthy," he said, "and I have a proposition for you."

"Sorry," I said, irritated, "I don't accept any propositions!"

Immediately I hurried out of the room when he stopped me. "Victor sent me," he said.

"Why didn't you say so?!" I said.

"I just did," he said smiling.

"Anything for Victor," I said.

"I just got out from prison after eight years of incarceration," he said. "I purchased a three story building, in the center of Tel-Aviv across from a movie theater. After what I have heard about you, I would like you to transform two of the stories into a health spa which will include the best exercising machines, saunas, Jacuzzis, hospitality room, and massage rooms. I will pay for these, and for the rest, I will give you $50,000 to make the place presentable and appealing. I will pay you $150 daily, in cash. So what do you think about all that?" he asked.

"It is too good to be true," I said.

"So it is," he said, "but it is your project if you accept."
And I did.

The building was about two hundred years old, and the architecture was European Classic with fireplaces and beautiful curved walls. The floor was one of a kind, a beautiful glossy orange and all of that just embraced me with excitement and new inspiration.

I ordered three aquariums—ten, seven, and four feet long--which I transferred to tables. I attached colorful florescent lights to them and I put in salt water, a variety of glass pebbles, and big gold and silver carp that reflected beautifully, as in a mirror into the glossy floor. I closed the two fireplaces with glass, and inside I put naturally curving woods, stone, and lights. In addition, I put in small colorful live snakes to arouse a sense of guilt in men with wrong ideas.

I purchased comfortable, soft-colored furniture, framed with curved wood that complemented the beauty of the floor and the character of the hospitality room. I closed off part of the room with glass sliding doors and created a masculine office. A black desk and leather chairs with black accessories were exactly what I had in mind.

From Italy, I ordered a machine that provided a variety of coffees, cappuccino, and cocoa, and with the help of a well-known carpenter, we created seven massage rooms with attached showers. The focal point of each room was a wall aquarium with exotic fish.

I ordered two saunas, one wet and one dry, and the Jacuzzi was big enough for twelve people. In every door, I placed an eye to see through, in order to monitor the work.

Along with Gregory, I looked through many magazines to find good exercise machines, and we decided to order from the Universal Company in England.

When everything was complete and done to our satisfaction, Gregory offered me a partnership.

"Absolutely not!" I said.

"Why not?" Gregory asked.

"I cannot be responsible for all the girls. If just one of the girls is tempted to do something she's not supposed to do, I will carry the responsibility, and I have three children that look up to me."

Nevertheless, we went to a lawyer, and Gregory became a silent owner, and I became his employee. The lawyer wrote a contract for every employee to sign. In addition, employees had to present a certificate or diploma for their practice. My salary was set at four thousand dollars a month, tax-free.

In addition, if I did a massage for my personal clientele, the money would be all mine. I was numb for a while, as this was a miracle of provision I never would have expected.

Indeed, the Lord built a fence of feathers between me and the prince of darkness.

The first day of work, I came dressed professionally with a nice suit and an empty "James Bond" brief case. The big leather chair swallowed me completely, and my feet hung mercilessly far above the floor.

The big desk was too much for a little me, and I needed some accommodations in order to feel confident as a boss. Besides that, everything was in order. There were twenty employees who worked with me and no one knew about the arrangement between Gregory and me.

In the fitness room were two trainers who advised about health and how to use the exercise equipment.

I put four people in charge of cleaning and serving the customers with complimentary coffees and desserts. The first time customers were served, they signed a contract, including their medical history. Also, they were asked to sign an agreement to not touch any of the employees at the time of treatment, and to not suggest things that were not a part of the massage.

The year 1984 was a time of health awareness in Israel; therefore, many people opened health spas and vitamin stores. The competition was fierce, and I was forced to stay above any competition. No one ever sensed my fear or lack of confidence because I knew the game of survival well enough.

I hired homebound women and their phone numbers to answer and to lead customers to our location. I put a few ads in the newspapers with all the women's phone numbers, and the customers did not cease to come. I must mention that, at that time, not every resident in Israel had a telephone. It had to be a big industry to have more than one phone, and I challenged myself to build such an industry by hiring all these women.

Gregory was awestruck with all I had done, and I barely hid my stupid pride.

I feared everything in life. I especially feared for my children. I had lived among the Arabs almost thirteen years, and in my sick mind, I learned to love them and to care for them, knowing that they didn't give a damn about me. Sadly enough, I did the same, as I hated myself with all the passion that still was left in me, refusing to face the reasons. I was always the last in line but first in unpleasant situations.

In the Arabic culture, they always consider one's family tree, and I hid mine in a cave of my subconscious and among terrifying memories. Yet I understood that I had no right to take my children from their family, as I had known the painful absence of family in my life. So one day, I called my brother-in-law Basem to take my children for a visit. When they came back they were all excited with stories, talking all together at the same time.

My son told me that it was late at night when they arrived in Jerusalem. Early the next morning, they ran to surprise their grandfather who was working in the garden.

"How are you?" the grandfather rejoiced, hugging the children.

"We are fine," my oldest said,

"And how is everything else?" he asked.

"Everything is fine," my oldest said, as she was always in charge.

"Are you going to ask about my mom?" my son asked his grandfather.

"Cursed would be her name and her father's name and whoever brought her to this world!" he said it and collapsed unconscious to the ground. He had had a stroke, and cursing me were the last words he said, as the stroke took his ability to talk. I was sad that he choose to hate me with such intensity that affected his health.

As for me, I was still battling my demons and somehow I continued to stumble all over myself until, late one night when I got a call from my semi-lost brother.

"Hello? Who is it?" I asked.

"It is your brother Shimon." The confidant answer embraced me with a surprise.

"Why are you calling so late? Did something happen in the kibbutz?" I asked, trying to recover from this unbelievable call.

"I am calling you from America," he said, "and I would like to share good news with you." There was a short pause as he took a deep breath, "I found Jesus," he said, "And for this reason I called you."

The familiar name of Jesus brought immediate warmth and comfort into my soul, but I did not act upon it; instead, I commented sarcastically, "He must be a good guy to encourage you to call me."

My brother was gracious enough to ignore my sarcasm as I, once again rejected the truth, crawling back into the darkness of my false reality. Nevertheless, my brother did not stop calling me and the walls of my resentment started to crumble.

To work as a masseuse taught me a great lesson about the true character of men. Thailand brought a bad name to the world of massage because of the services given there, and morality was not a part of it. Therefore, some men did not have respect for the masseuse and they showered me with all their secret dreams and desires, leaving me speechless and confused. At first, I was offended and angry, but then I tried to understand the world of a man, reading books that were written by men and about men, and the more I understood the way they think, the less disturbed they seemed in my eyes.

A woman's power is acknowledged with respect by a man's perspective. His world is built around physical performances and achievements that we as women so often disregard. Women's insecurities and vulnerabilities can disarm any strong-willed man but only for a season. Furthermore, a manipulative woman knows how to use intimate and informative tools that eventually will consume the man with painful guilt and shame, so that what is meant to be natural becomes perverted by judgment. After never-ending separation from the judgment of their mothers that holds "guilt pointers for eternity," a man falls again into the same trap with his wife that enforces his self-condemnation in harsh ridicule for expressing absurdities!

Unfortunately, guilt has never been a friend to anyone, but still, it is an excellent tool for insecure women. Everyone has dreams and fantasies, and everyone suffers from a guilt complex;

*however, we never heal if we don't examine our own souls
because, as we learn to forgive ourselves, we learn to forgive
others and anyone who is guilt-free can fly!*

*Connect with your wife, I used to advise anyone that
listened. Share your heart and your dreams with her and
encourage her to talk about hers. Secrets are very dangerous in
relationships, and so is judgment that can easily conceive
animosity between a wife and a husband. Sharing the most
intimate thoughts will always bring an incredible closeness, as
long as it is not used as a weapon against each other in a
disrespectable fashion.*

*Sadly, I have learned that many women are still putting
themselves above men. With games, manipulation, and
negotiations, and mostly in the midst of intimate times, they bribe
their husbands by taking charge and control. They may win the
games, but surely, they take the chance of losing their husbands.*

*If a woman will put her guard and her pride down and
allow herself to see her man as the head of the household, her
protector, and her lover, he would be as she sees him. The more
she will love him, the more love she learns, and the more love she
will accumulate. Think about it: your husband is not a disabled
child to order around, and he is not your emotional servant. He is
first a precious gift that God has honored you with; therefore,
learn about him and learn about his heart and about his soul and
he will do for you much, much more.... You may change your man
for a season and he may allow you to do so, but this will end.*

*Therefore, the resolution should be to change your own
attitude, as your tools for such a project are more functional in
your willingness than his. Your reward will be to be filled with
deep appreciation of the pleasantness of your relations.*

*God created us differently, physically and emotionally, so
we would search for each other and complete each other, but not
compete with each other. However, we choose to see the
differences with animosity and ignorance: Why can't he be like
me? Why can't she see things my way? Moreover, to accomplish
that, we need to search the differences, and in discovery and
acceptance, we will become one, exactly as God in His wisdom
created us to be.*

My dear friend Pnina has been married 41 years, and all this time, she has had disagreements with her husband. Their arguments are always of the same nature. Right now, she is very sick, diagnosed with multiple sclerosis, and because of the frequent arguments, the disease has accelerated.

When we talk, she painfully describes to me their dysfunctional interactions. "Leave the house immediately when the argument starts!" I have told her a thousand times.

"And where would I go?" she'll say.

"Anywhere!" I scream impatiently into the receiver. "You have been with him for 41 years," I tell her, "and all that time he is screaming at you the same allegations, and you are screaming back the same words that both of you have already heard a few thousand times. I suspect that both of you get some kind of satisfaction from it or maybe it's your only line of communication; otherwise, why would you do it?"

"I do not know," she says. "I guess I feel like I have to."

It is so easy to be angry with Pnina and to take credit for my better understanding, but in reality, it is not so, because Pnina's behavior and her low self-image expose my own insecurities. For this reason, I was forced to understand myself first, before giving her any advice.

"Pninush," I said, "I need to be honest with you. I myself have always felt that I needed to defend myself, and even if nothing happened, I still endured the urgent sense that something would happen, and whatever it would be, it would not be good.

"I said to myself countless times that these feelings are part of life and I could overcome them, but I was wrong. I was very wrong until He found me… and there was hope. So I beg you, Pninush, listen to me. I am your kindred sister and I would never lie to you. Please open your heart and let the Lord step in. I don't promise you it is going to be better, but it is going to be understood because, when you understand His way, like the fractions in mathematics, you have solved the problem.

"However, and most importantly, Pninush, you will never be lonely again, because the Lord will carry your burdens, and the light that He will give you will shine on many. Through His wisdom, Pninush, and your faith, you will realize that nothing in this world is worth living for, except salvation."

"I cannot betray God the way you did," she said. "I am Jewish!"

"So am I, Pninush; nothing changed except the truth," I said, almost in tears.

"We believe in one God," she said, "and you, Yonush, believe in Three, which is One!"

I interrupted her, "And you can find in the Old Testament that God referred to Himself as Us and We."

Sometimes we converse on the phone up to three hours. Mostly, we are addressing our insecurities, and we are learning not to blame life and other elements in life for our pains and fears. We are trying to rebuild our ways of thinking, but mostly, we are learning that holding onto the past is not a security blanket but the devil's den.

I know well enough that even faith in God does not come easy, not for us. We learned to mistrust our parents and we were too young to pity them. Therefore, to trust God's demands as our Father was out of our realm of thinking because innocence was not a part of our lives; to the contrary, our goal was to manipulate life.

Today I know how God is working on my soul, and I am changing every day. He is helping me to see Him through His Word, and I am free in His embrace, learning to understand love....His Love.

Most of us do not take the time to rethink our own behavior; somehow, it is always more interesting to criticize others because that makes us feel so much smarter in our own eyes. I have learned that the more compassion I possess, the less critical I am. As I look into my actions, I can resolve the complexity of my confusion. Yes indeed, my God and my Lord privileged me with courage to gaze into my actions and to seek resolution at His altar.

At first, it felt good to be responsible for the business; I set certain rules with which every employee must comply. I worked with a store that sold orthopedic shoes that all my employees wore, in addition to modest and comfortable uniforms for the girls, and for the guys, almost the same. I ordered the uniforms in a variety of colors to ease formality, and with the okay from Gregory, on each uniform was embroidered "Yona's Institute of Health."

Every morning before the work began, we had a meeting to address problems and share new ideas. Everyone participated. I made sure that the girls specifically did not lead the customer into private conversations.

"People come here to relax," I used to tell them, "and not to listen to your problems. Even when a customer tells you personal things, you never react with your own problems; you must react with compassion and understanding. However, when the customer asks directly for your opinion, you always turn the conversation back on him as you say, 'You tell me first.' The more you encourage the customer to talk, the more he will talk until the treatment time is over."

"Why can't we participate in a regular conversation?" the girls asked, and I shared some of my experiences with them.

"I have learned man's hunger for respect and appreciation," I said. "Therefore I ask for your best, using your common sense but nothing else, and this is what I do: I listen! And I listen sincerely. That is the most important rule. However, if the customer insists on involving me in his private life, or his problems with his wife, I maneuver the issue back to him, asking, 'What do you think should be done?' Most of the time, they have the best answers. I also would encourage a man to tell me something good about his wife and to focus on that.

"However, be careful with a woman customer, as 90 percent are in complete chaos, and they need to be handled with kid gloves. Do not agree or disagree with a woman; just let her talk. Her husband who was once her friend and her lover now is her number one enemy in a fierce competition. It is needless to ask her for some good qualities in him because they vanished after the wedding celebration. It is very sad that today so many women seek careers, instead of motherhood and the companionship of a loving husband; the worst element in their life is dissatisfaction driven by a desire for power, a worldly desire.

"Nevertheless, in the massage world, there are times that it is necessary to put a muzzle on our tongues in order not to add to the inherent intimacy of this profession. Be genuinely sympathetic and a good listener. This is the bottom line."

I did not worry about money at that time, as I had more than I could handle. I bought a piano for the children, and each of them chose to play a different instrument. Aussy chose to play piano, Miriam chose violin, and my son trumpet. I used to buy their clothes wholesale, and what they'd outgrown I always managed to sell to a store or to neighbors; therefore, in the end I spent nothing at all for children's necessities.

I had money everywhere, in shoes, in books, in pockets, everywhere, just in case.

I had good cleaning people in the business, but I really trusted no one; therefore, on Saturdays I would take my children with me, and I would personally check and clean everything. After I cleaned the Jacuzzi, I would let the children play and swim in it and they had a good time.

What I thought of as an accomplishment, along with my pride, robbed me from the last bit of respect that still lingered in me. After I caught two girls not complying with the rules, Gregory asked me to close my eyes to what was happening in the massage rooms, and I am ashamed to say that, for a while, I did just that.

When Gregory offered me hashish, I did not refuse, lying to myself that it would erase the guilt I carried, but hashish was a deceitful tool, and as I gazed at my actions, I became detached to my surroundings and a complete stranger to myself.

One day, after the children left for school, I was smoking a second hashish cigarette. My daughter Aussy came home because she forgot something. "Mom, what is that strange smell?" she asked.

"What smell are you talking about?" I said.

"Mom, look at the dogs and cats; what has happened to them?"

When I looked, I saw the animals losing their balance, dragging themselves around and falling. Immediately, I threw the cigarette away from me, and there was not a strong enough word to describe the shame I felt when I recognized the dark dominion that was choking me.

My judgment was impaired, my hearing selective, and my feelings definitely dead. I sold myself low, and I was not the mother I wanted to be. How could I think that food and clothes, along with a roof over my children's heads, would be enough? Indeed, it was one more lie added to the collection of all my lies. My God, I thought to myself, what have I done? What have I done!?

"I am leaving," I said to Gregory the next day, and he let me go without any problems.

"I understand," he said, "and if you need anything, you know where to find me."

I was wounded and fearful without a reason; therefore, after I got enough courage I went to a psychiatrist for a consultation. After long description of all my disabilities, the psychiatrist gave me a prescription for all my burdens.

Once again, I chose the easy way to escape my battles. I took the medications and my past came to life once more. Drugged heavily, I lost all common sense in everything, and sadly enough, this time I took drugs freely and not by force.

One day, a journalist called me for an update. "Are you still working as a massage therapist?" she asked.

"Oh no!" I said, "Never again!"

"Can we meet, so I can ask you few questions?" she asked.

"Sure," I said.

Drugged with medications when we met, I described without restraint all the dirt I had witnessed. Thankfully, I did not name anyone specifically. She took a few pictures for which she helped me to stand and pose. A few days later, I stared at a big headline that said: "I have never sold my body, just my hands" and semi-attractive pictures that implied otherwise.

It is impossible to say how much it hurt my children. I hate you! I hate you! I hate you! I screamed at myself, taking more of the medications to calm down the pain. But it was not about me; it was about my children!

First, they suffered in the Arab population because their mother is a Jew. Later, they suffered in the Jewish population because their father is an Arab. Now, heavy judgment engulfed them because their mother was weak and stupid! How could I hurt them so much? How could I??

Ali came back from America to demand the children back. I just hoped, for the children's sake, that his action was sincere and because he cared for them. But I knew better, as I knew him. He came back for the spotlight and also, in having the children in America, he would get a good tax break. He could not have them legally or any other way, and there was nothing he could pin on me, in spite of the article in the newspapers. After a weekend with their father, my children came to me and asked to go to America with him.

"You don't know him," I tried to discourage them, but they were persuaded well, and I knew that the only way to win them back was to let them go.

They were the only family I had ever had, and they were the only reason for my life, yet I was not the mother they needed. Therefore, with guilt, regrets, and certainly against my better judgment, I let them go, and that day, I died inside.

I was like a zombie; I took more and more medications to erase the pounding pain, but nothing helped. Sometimes at three or four in the early morning, I would walk the streets in desperation. Other times, I would call my kids, just to hear their voices, and to hear if they were okay.

"We are fine," they used to tell me. "We are fine, Mom. We are fine."

Every time I just collapsed, crying, I felt that everything was wrong, but I could not trust my feelings, because subconsciously, I hoped they would need me, and I hoped they would desire to return to me. One day, three months after they left, I got a letter from them. "Mom, come help us. He is killing us!" The letter saved my life, even though I knew that their description was extreme. Nevertheless, the fighter in me woke up and in all its strength. I cleansed myself from all the medications, and I was ready to plan for the future.

However, until the time I would arrive in the USA, I was worried that Ali might physically hurt the children, so I called him. "How are you, Ali?" I asked.

"Good, good, and you?"

"Good as well," I said. "I hope you are not hurting the children," I said, straight to the point.

"Why?" he responded. "Did they tell you something?"

"No, not at all," I said. "I'm just concerned, and knowing you, I know you could hurt them."

"And if I do," he said viciously, "you cannot do anything about it!"

"On the contrary," I lied, "in America, I have more power through Rabbi Cahana, and just one whisper from me, and you are history!"

"You are bluffing," Ali said.

"So try me," I challenged him. "You know, Ali," I said, "I may have been weak and defenseless against a coward like you, but if I hadn't had ammunition against you, I would never let the children go with you."

At that point, Ali started to lose his confidence, but his retaliatory nature jumped into action. "You need a visa to come to the US," he said, "and you are not getting one!"

"Fine," I said, "but if I get a visa, what will happen then?"

"You will stay with the family, Nadia; after all, you are one of us!" I was not confused from his sudden change of mind. I knew him better than I knew myself. He was vicious and twisted, but to flatter myself, he did have a fair amount of intelligence; otherwise, I wouldn't have fallen into his trap.

From this point on, things started to change for the better. My good friend Moshe gave me keys to an apartment. "It is yours," he said, "paid in full and you have earned it."

"From the government?" I said cautiously.

"Call it what you wish," he said, "but it is yours."

"Listen, Moshe," I said, "I need you to do something for me."

"Anything for you, Cloudy."

"I need a visa to the USA," I said.

"You got it!" Moshe said. "Pick it up anytime in the embassy."

Two days later, one of Ali's brothers came for visit. He was a newlywed, and he needed a visa for his wife.

"Great," I said, "Let us go together. I need to pick up my visa as well."

"You don't pick up a visa. You apply for it," he said.

"You may apply for your visa, but my visa is ready to go," I said proudly.

"Come on, Nadia. You know better; no one gets a visa so easy the first time."

Nevertheless, he got a six-month visa for his wife. He himself already had a green card, thanks to my friends who took him in and helped him get established in the US. I was still waiting in line, hearing refusal after refusal. The man in front of me was asked why he was going to the US. He answered that he was going for a religious celebration of the Rabbi of Lubavich.

"Are you a believer?" the consul asked him.

"Yes, I am," the man said.

"So, could you kindly tell me what the fifth commandment in the Bible refers to? The man did not know, and he did not get a visa.

"And why you want to go to the US?" the consul asked me.

"To see my children," I said. He took my passport, went to the other room, and in a few seconds, he returned, giving me the passport back.

"Next, please," he said, without telling me if I got the visa or not.

When I got out, my brother-in-law was waiting for me. "Did you get it?" he asked me.

"Sure," I said, trusting only what my good friend Moshe promised.

"Let me see, let me see," my brother in law insisted.

When he opened the passport, he could not believe what he saw. Just one word was stamped on it: "**Indefinitely**."

"What did you tell him to get this visa?"

"Nothing," I said in irony, "Just my own name, Yona Levi."

I could just see him going back home and the first thing he would do is to call Ali: "Nadia got a visa; she is coming. Talk to you later."

I called Ali the same day as well, to inform him that I was coming, and in that, I exhibited my renewed power.

Chapter 22

United States, 1990

My first trip to the United States was with my ex-brother-in-law and his new wife. We all stayed at the house of another brother named Ebrahim. Ebrahim was married to an American girl who was completely submissive to him and to all Muslim traditions. She was covering herself and studying Islam. Now she was forced to live in the same house with her brother-in-law and his wife, and she hardly could hide her disappointment. Furthermore, she also had me to consider, and I brought uncertainty to all the family.

I was not a part of them, yet I was, because their mother had loved me, and because Ali divorced me just once; therefore, in Islam, I was still his wife. That was kept a secret from his new wife, even to this day. There were many other secrets that, out of respect and understanding for her, I will not reveal. After all, I am very thankful to her that she took my sufferings upon herself, even unknowingly. Everyone was present at our arrival in Denver: Ali and his wife, her children and mine, and of course, the other two families.

Just four months had passed, but my children had changed completely. They were pale and sad, and it was obvious they were afraid to express their feelings for me. I was the one that hugged them and kissed them and I recognized the fear they experienced. These four months were enough for Ali to twist the truth his way.

My children completely forgot all the good things about Israel. They forgot their freedom and the love we shared, and sadly enough, my mistakes were magnified to extreme proportions. The truth did not dignify itself. I was bad and crazy in their eyes, and I just hoped to God they would remember all I did for them and not all the lies that their father hatefully inserted in their minds.

Ali's American wife told all who were willing to listen, about the horrible wardrobe my kids brought from Israel. Even if it had been so, I thought, from now on, if my children's wardrobe was not to her liking, she would have to do better. I personally avoided any confrontation with her because I knew if she were happy, my kids would be happy. For this reason, I moved to Arizona to be with my friend Karen.

Being close by, I knew that Ali would restrain his sadism against my children, but I did not take into consideration that the attacks on his wife would intensify. She blamed me, and in her eyes, I was the only reason for Ali's violence against her. She would call me in Arizona and blame me for things that never took place, and in all honesty, I was sorry for her. Other times I suspected that my children, in seeking sympathy, may have told her some fibs. After all, they were their mother's children and I never claimed to be an angel.

The next time I visited the children, I tried to befriend Michele, not knowing that, out of their uncertainty with me, the family warned her against me. For her, it was much easier to believe their lies than to accept my hand in friendship. I invited her to a restaurant for her birthday and encouraged her to talk. Ali already boasted to me about striking her, and I knew that she needed a friend to talk with, but she misunderstood me and mistakenly thought that I wanted Ali back.

She lived in denial and I understood her shame, when she said to me that Ali never hit her, and if he did, she said, her strong brother would be capable of dealing with such a matter. She never understood the important role she had played in my life, that released me from Ali's evil clutch and led me into the divine presence of God. As I found it, she gradually lost it, forced by Ali, not to attend her own church anymore.

When I first came to the United States, I had purchased an extra ticket to visit my brother in North Carolina. I flew to see him and his family.

Our meeting was awkward, considering my poor self-worth and feelings of insignificance. After years of separation, nothing had changed in my mental state. I was nothing, but he was still everything, subjectively praised, even by me. I felt lonesome, as among strangers, and it bothered me. However, a few days later, I allowed myself to be submissive to the idea of a united family and that is how it all started.

"Do you know Jesus Christ?" my brother asked.

"Do I?" I answered in humor.

"Seriously," my brother insisted.

"I guess," I said. "We used to go to a church as kids. Remember, Shimon?"

"Yeah, kind of," my brother said.

"I used to peek behind a statue of Jesus," I said, "because I believed that He was hiding behind it. But this is the past," I said, "so, just forget it!"

"To the contrary," my brother said, "it is the future we are talking about and not the past."

"Fine," I said, "as long as Jesus is not the main subject!"

"Have you heard about salvation in order to go to heaven and not to hell?" my brother asked.

"If you think to scare me with hell," I said, "I am the wrong person. I already lived in hell, burned in hell, and still have not escaped it."

"True," my brother said calmly, "you need salvation to escape it; you need Jesus Christ!"

You need common sense, I thought, irritated, even though my resistance did not sustain me, and I couldn't escape the strong desire to know more and to keep this subject in full flame.

There was a positive familiarity in the name of Jesus, but by that time, too much had happened, and not knowing about God's nature, I was convinced that God and Jesus and all the angels held a grudge against me. Therefore, I was just retaliating against them! There was a war in my soul, and I was determined to win it! I had always known that God existed, but I was convinced that He existed for Himself because he did not give me what I wanted, and of course what I needed did not count, as I got that anyway.

"You need Jesus," I heard my brother's voice in the distance, but I did not respond.

I was suddenly angry with him. He was just talking away, and I was remembering how he was ashamed of me and how he rejected me. Yeah, all that has happened to me is because of him, I thought in unexplained anger. He thinks that he is so smart; all of his life, he was protected, never hungry or homeless, never abused but loved. He was accepted and not rejected; he has people that were proud of him. He was too sheltered to know God or even to understand pain!

I held onto the anger, so as not to listen to my brother talking about Jesus Christ. I knew about Jesus Christ, and my brother did not have the right to talk about Him, I thought...but why not, why not? I was puzzled.

"You need salvation," I heard my brother talking again, "so we will spend eternity together in heaven."

Oh yeah, I thought with deep disrespect toward him. Here on earth, you were ashamed of me, and with heaven, you are so generous? Nevertheless, I did not voice any of my belligerent thoughts because, in spite of it all, I still had a few good qualities left. I was polite, or just a plain old nasty hypocrite!

I remember the first time we all went to church together, my brother with his wife and their four extraordinary and beautiful children. I sat between my brother and his wife. When my brother started to pray in an unknown language, I wondered if it was a language at all! At first, it was acceptable for me, as I tried always to be a reasonable person, and in my small world, people can pray the way it suits them! However, this was my brother, and this scenario came across to me as ludicrous and so funny that I began to clear my throat to avoid unwanted sounds of laughter.

Speaking of prayer...well, as the mighty sound of laughter was ready to burst out of my mouth, I began to pray like never before (and never since). And right then, I acknowledged my first miracle when the service ended, and I was redeemed from embarrassment. "Latin for sure," I said confidently to my sister-in-law.

"You mean the way Shimon was praying?" she said.

"Yes," I said.

"Oh no," she corrected me, "Shimon is speaking in tongues, which is a direct communication with God, and Shimon is highly blessed in the ability to speak to God in this manner."

"Does Shimon know what he says when he is praying?" I asked.

"No," she said, "but the Spirit knows, and there are other people that will translate this kind of prayer."

"I don't understand why you complicate the issue," I said. "Why don't you just pray in English and then you don't need any translations? I thought that God knows us telepathically," I said, "and he can read our minds, so it makes more sense to me if I pray with my spirit in silence."

"It is all about blessings," she told me, and I disregarded all she said as plain stupidity, and for the purpose of appearing in the eye of one's fellow man as better and as smarter, and of course, as much more blessed than others. *That's what I thought at the time, and as long as I find fault in others, I am so much better in my own eyes.*

Today I am less judgmental and more flexible to accept things I don't understand. After the church experience, I was suspicious toward my brother's sainthood, and just to enforce it, I witnessed something that sealed the matter.

My little niece suffered from an ear infection and was crying with pain. "Give her something for pain," I suggested to my brother's wife."

"Oh no," she said, "we have better medicine." She ran to the phone and called my brother at work, and they started to pray on the phone, as the girl was screaming with pain.

They prayed and prayed, until the little girl went to sleep from exhaustion, which my brother and his wife translated as a healing miracle. This healing miracle did not last, and I was sorry for the little girl and the lack of resolution.

At the same time, I sensed a strong divinity in the midst of all the negativity I fabricated. There was something familiar I recognized, something positive, something I missed, something I wanted to embrace with all my might, something that would make me complete. Nevertheless, I dismissed it as madness in my void life.

"So what about salvation?" my brother asked me.

"What about it?" I asked in return.

"Are you going to trust Jesus Christ as your Savior and repent from all your sins?"

I don't think so! I thought amused. Repent from my sins? You must be kidding! There is no god in the whole universe that would forgive my sins! Besides, I was so deep in sin that even taking a breath I considered as sin. Yes indeed, I was at the point that the sin was hurting me physically.

"God promised to forgive anything, if you repent sincerely," I heard my brother's voice say.

"Who told you all that?" I asked him.

"God," he said simply.

"Did you have a translator for it?" I asked sarcastically.

"But, of course!" my brother said. "The Bible!"

Every time we had discussions, my brother was always two steps ahead, and I was getting very tired of all the persuasions, all the holiness, and all the monkey business. However, in reality, I was afraid to open the doors into my past. I was afraid to face my actions because I was afraid of God.

"Well?" my brother asked, "are you ready to do the right thing?"

"Am I? Okay," I said, to shut them up.

"Are you doing this for us?" my sister-in-law asked.

"Oh no, I am doing this for me," and that was the truth, because I hoped to have some quiet time without their Jesus Christ at every turn. I still remembered that, at my first dawn of desperation, I confused dreams with reality, and Jesus Christ had gradually become a fairytale in my mind.

"Yona," I heard my brother's voice again, "I don't want to wait any longer," he said. "So tomorrow we will go to Charlotte to a minister we know, and he personally will explain a few things to you."

Whatever, I thought to myself, agitated.

Chapter 23

As we drove to our destination, my sister-in-law and my brother explained to me about this great minister called Harry.

"He was in prison a long time," my brother said, "and it was there when he found Jesus and his salvation."

Great! I thought, a criminal would lead my way to the Most High? What else is my spoiled brother hiding under his sleeve? Well, I wasn't a nice person, and I did not care to be one because I believed that finally I was in the place I always wanted to be. My lies were smooth and convincing, so much so that I even believed them. I can deceive anyone I want, I thought in my dumb pride. Therefore, the darkness that engulfed me was the master I served.

This crucial journey took about two hours in which my brother and his wife talked continuously, nonstop! I did not listen in depth, but my attitude was agreeable with them. Finally we arrived at our destination. I was introduced to Harry, a tall man with a simple and warm welcoming.

Based on the information I received from my brother, I had begun to see Harry in my imagination as a Pancho Vila, a very well-known criminal from western movies who was equipped with a lot of guns and ammunition on his chest, and a big sombrero that just sealed the image!

My brother and his wife left the room and I wondered where Harry was hiding his guns. "So you decided to accept Jesus Christ into your heart?" Harry asked.

I said nothing, as I did not know what to say. "Let me put it a different way," Harry said. "If you do accept Jesus, where will you accept Him? In your head or in your heart?"

"Of course, in my head," I hurried to answer. "A heart is just a muscle full of blood."

"Is it really?" Harry remarked gently.

"Yeah," I said, in the limited edition of my poor English.

"Okay," Harry said, "let me ask you: When you are crying or rejoicing, do you feel it in your head or in your heart?"

"Everywhere," I said stubbornly.

There was a momentary silence in the room; then Harry spoke again: "Your brother told me that you used to go to church in Poland. Do you remember that?"

Do I? Flashes of memories were choking me; Jesus Christ, the priest, the orphanage, the sadness, and the hopeful joys--all of that ran through my mind. Even though I knew very little English at that time, Harry still found a way to crush the spirit of resistance in me. Yes, all the memories touched me for a second or so; nevertheless, I did not want to go back there, not again.

"I do accept Him into my heart," I said, lying boldly, and Harry put his hand upon my head and prayed.

A few days later, I was happy to leave my conscience and my brother's family, and fly to see my children in Denver, Colorado. My brother drove me to the airport and stayed with me in the terminal until my flight boarded. We were finally sitting in silence, and there was not much talk between us. After so many years without contact, we were painfully strangers.

As I stood up to walk to the airplane, my brother embraced me and said, "I love you, Sister." I said nothing because the anger was burning in me!

Oh yeah, I thought, he said that because of this…this…. Jesus Christ!

As I walked through the long corridor that led to the airplane, I was finally relieved from all pressure, but all of a sudden, something happened that stopped my heartbeat: I was hit straight in my chest and into the center of my soul! At that moment, there was not a doubt in my mind what *It* was! I felt like never before. It was as if everything was divinely joyful. I rejoiced without fear, doubt, suspicion, or anger.

For a fraction of a moment, I was clean and remarkably pure. I began to greet people I did not know, trying to tell them the good news with my restricted collection of English words. Nevertheless, until I arrived in Denver, I could not shut up, questioning the people around me about their destination and asking them if they knew Jesus Christ. I used and reused my small treasury of English to express the biggest news in the world.

Finally, when I had the opportunity to share the good news with my children, they thought that I had fallen on my head.

"We don't want to hear about it," they told me, and once again, I gazed into the mirror of my self-image.

I called my brother and told him about the experience with the Holy Spirit and he rejoiced. I asked him also if he could find a church for me for the time when I was staying with my friend Karen in Tucson, Arizona, and he did. For some reason, though, every time that the people from this appointed church came, I was working or I was someplace else. I wouldn't have known about it if I hadn't asked my friend Karen if people were looking for me. She told me that she sent them away.

"You don't need them," she said. "You have me," and I agreed.

However, I still had in my possession that special Bible from Harry: *The Good News Bible for Modern Man*. I was told that this Bible was written in very simple language. If there was a day that I managed to understand only a word or two, I could not wait to know more. In my ignorance, I believed that as long as I knew how to read in Polish, English would not be an obstacle until I saw the word *laugh* and I could not articulate it.

"What is that? How do you say it?" I ran to Karen for explanations.

"It is *laugh*," she said.

"So why don't you write it the way it sounds?" I asked Karen.

"Like what?" she would ask me.

"Like L-A-F," I would say.

"It would be pronounced differently," she used to explain.

Finally I got it, and if my brain sustained me, I thought, I would have to memorize a majority of the English words.

It was a strange journey indeed, trying to learn the English language from the Good News Bible, which I never forsook nor ceased to read. It is the only book in the world with a never-ending flame and never-ending truth that, only in my future willingness, I would be granted to see.

I am thankful for the plan of salvation, and I am even thankful for my uncompleted self because, only in God's presence, will the true completion take place. Nevertheless, the true hope I possess in my Lord is the fuel that makes me whole in all I do. I am now twenty years in the USA and all I suffered in the past is a mere shadow compared to the struggle as a child of the most High.

I love my friend Karen; she did so much for me as she did for many others. She is exceptionally blessed and very bright. However, in all her accomplishments and life's temporarily joys, her free spirit is still lacking the knowledge of the most important riddle of this life.

The second time I visited the USA, I stayed again with my friend Karen, and I did not practice my new beliefs. I felt like the light of my soul died out. I knew I must stay in America for my children, regardless of whether they wanted me or not. I was bad news for Ali and his two brothers who lived in America and especially when I visited the children. I stayed, on occasion, in their houses. They did their hosting duties, as if under duress, and never hid their dislike toward me.

"They are talking about you and against you," my children complained.

"Really?" I used to say cheerfully.

"Really!" my oldest daughter hurried to show her disregard for me.

"Worry when they stop taking about me," I used to say.

"What do you mean by that?" the children asked.

"Well…" I paused, "if I were a poor homeless person sitting on the ground when they were passing by, they would probably ignore me and forget me, but I am not this person. My name is printed all over their ignorance. They learned to fear me because they refuse to understand me."

"I am shaking their world because I showed them that women can have power and victory! Remember," I told my children, "their power comes from other people's weaknesses. So, let them talk about me, let them talk, and let's hope they never stop."

"I need to be married to stay here," I said to my friend Karen. "Otherwise, I do not know what Ali will do to my kids." So Karen helped me to put an ad in the newspaper, and the hunt for a husband began. To describe the process of all my dating would be another book of romantic adventures!

I found a husband who provided me with legal status, and I stayed in the United States. Hungry and desperate for love, I was in love with this man in no time. Oblivious to my feelings, he was generous with his love for other women, and a divorce took place after deep disappointment.

At the time I was married, I met people from a Mormon church that used to visit me at the house. "Are you Christians?" I asked them.

"Of course we are," they said. "Even our church is named after the Lord--The Church of Jesus Christ of Latter Day Saints." They gave me a Mormon book and I was baptized in their church.

It was a very destructive and painful period in my life, and I do not know how I would have survived without these generous people, especially my friend Pam. She took me to her house and slept beside me and helped me with her optimism and cheer.

To repay all the good will, I decided to study the Mormon book plus the Bible. Reading so much I began to understand, and the more I understood, the more feelings of discomfort took place. Something was not right, I thought to myself, but I did not know enough yet to confront the subject. I knew Israel, but it was not the same land mentioned in the Mormon book. When the Bible spoke about a place, I recognized it immediately, but not in the Mormon book; except for Jerusalem, nothing else was familiar.

I was silent, in spite of my conclusions, because I feared being alone, and in my troublesome nature and misunderstandings, my friend Karen chose to put an end to our friendship. I was cleaning houses at that time and every week I paid tithes to the church. I always volunteered to do anything for anybody, just to be approved. One day I got the good news that I would be allowed to go to the Temple.

Out of respect to the Mormon people and my deep gratitude toward them during a difficult time, I am not going to reveal all the ceremonial secrets but only in relevancy to my story.

After all the ceremonies were finished, a woman came to the room to tell me the name that I would have when in heaven. "Your name in heaven will be Hulda," she said, and my heart stopped, with God's confirmation.

"God would never call me Hulda," I tried to protest, but everyone ignored me. After we finished, I tried to talk to my friend Pam.

"God would never call me Hulda," I told her in deep disappointment."

"We cannot talk about it," she said. "You need to talk to the bishop about it."

So I made an appointment. I sat across from the bishop, anxious to tell him the great mistake.

"I heard that you have a problem," he said.

"Yes, yes," I hurried to confirm it.

"So, what is it?" he asked.

"It is the name I got in the temple," I said.

"What about it?" he asked.

"Well," I said with some hesitation, "I do not think that God would call me this name."

"Why not?" the bishop asked.

"I know the meaning of this word," I said, "and in Hebrew, it means rat. In WWII, the Nazis called the Jewish people rats, and this is the reason that God would not call me this name."

"You don't know that," the bishop said. "God may have given you this name so you never forget it."

"And why should I remember something as ugly as that?" I burst out in anger.

"You are argumentative," he said, "and if you must know, everyone on that day received the same name."

At this point I understood that God wanted me out of this church. I eyed the bishop up and down with disrespect and said sarcastically: "When I go to heaven and God calls me, 'Rat, Rat, come in here,' so all the rats would come???"

Final Thoughts

This is my testimony and glorification of my Father in heaven. I could have written a few books from each period of my life, without mentioning the name of our Savior. I could describe the dramatization and the games I played in my past life, without mentioning Jesus Christ. I could have written many things to share with you more lies, deceit, and even death, but my soul did not lead me further than this.

Because of issues I cannot prove and because of some people who oppose my testimony, I concealed some matters and names. However, the heart of my testimony is the truth of our Lord Jesus Christ, and hopefully, an encouragement to your life. Today, life seems to be finishing before it began. In the blink of the eye, I will be on the steps of heaven reaching for the Lord's welcoming embrace.

I have experienced much pain and rejection, with many tears and sorrow. I am tempted to think that if I could live this life again, everything would be different. I would be wiser and more sophisticated, clever and bold, the kind of a person who knows everything. Nevertheless, without all the elements that transpired and molded my life, perhaps I would never have become a child of the Most High. Therefore, in His Power, I am not a victim anymore but a victorious overcomer!

As I routinely through my life fell into the pit of temptation, the Lord was there to pull me up, even when I refused to understand, He was still there...today I see and understand and I am thankful to my Father in Heaven for molding me once again into a better person.

I do understand that to be a Christian is not about me but everyone else. Jesus Christ showed us His final love offering in His life and suffering. I know that God sees the things that we sacrifice, like listening to people that aggravate us, or buying something for someone with the money that was intended for us, or volunteering to help without any desire to do so. Those are just small sacrifices; those are the things that we need to experience in order to overcome ourselves and to represent our Savior, exhibiting His grace. We receive the blessings and learn to be closer to the divine character of our Heavenly Father.

As for me and my brother: after thirty years of separation and misunderstandings and thousands of miles of separation between the United States and Israel, our Father in heaven brought us together in the miracle of salvation. Today in God's power, we are learning to overcome the past and use it for God's glory. My brother has dedicated his life completely to the Lord, although still, in his wounded spirit, he doesn't want to know or think about our very difficult past.

I am content with my life today. I have a Christian husband who loves my children. He knows how to hold my hand when I allow myself to fall into despair. I have constant contact with my two daughters and son who are not yet saved. I pray for their trials to be quicker and less painful than mine. My husband has a daughter and a son also, and we pray diligently for their salvation as well. We have been married for sixteen years and reside in beautiful Florida.

Finally, I would like to share my heart in poetry with you:

I beheld splendor in the sun's beams
And the brightness of my soul
Just for a moment it was wonder
That belonged to my heart so much more

And the brightness of the spirit
Shone like gold string in everything
So I wept and thanked my Father
For this moment of hope in me

And beneath the moment of brightness
There is world of pain and of grief
When the struggles are momentary
And the truth is buried in greed

We forget to ask for assistance
We don't trust anyone but us
We have knowledge of God and His wisdom
But we'd rather believe in lust

So we fall crying and kicking
Blaming God for everything
Forgetting our deceptive nature
And living in circles of dreams
We are lost and perplexed much too often
It's no wonder we don't know God
We all know of God's existence
But we don't know His Holy ground

To be saved is so simple
Just accept the truth into your life
And the truth becomes a symbol
And the symbol is sacrifice

This sacrifice is Jesus
The Son of the living God
He came to the world to redeem us
To suffer for us and to die

So please tell Him that you are sorry
For all the bad things you have done
Ask Him for His forgiveness
Invite Him to live in your Heart

Then the Holy Spirit will come
To dwell and to live in your heart
And then you will see the string of splendor
And you will recognize the Light